D0871771

The Blue and the Green

The Blue and the Green

*A Cultural Ecological History of
an Arizona Ranching Community*

JACK STAUDER

UNIVERSITY OF NEVADA PRESS

Reno & Las Vegas

University of Nevada Press, Reno, Nevada 89557 USA
www.unpress.nevada.edu
Copyright © 2016 University of Nevada Press
All rights reserved
Manufactured in the United States of America
Cover Design by Rebecca Lown

Library of Congress Cataloging-in-Publication Data
Name: Stauder, Jack, author.
Title: The Blue and the green : a cultural ecological history of an Arizona
    ranching community / Jack Stauder.
Description: Reno, Nevada : University of Nevada Press, [2016] | Includes
    bibliographical references and index.
Identifiers: LCCN 2015039991| ISBN 978-0-87417-995-8 (cloth : alk. paper) |
    ISBN 978-1-943859-11-5 (ebook)
Subjects: LCSH: Ranching—Arizona—History. | Land use,
    Rural—Arizona—History. | Environmental policy—Arizona—History.
Classification: LCC SF195 .S73 2016 | DDC 636.2/0109791—dc23
LC record available at http://lccn.loc.gov/2015039991

First Printing

Contents

The Blue River and surrounding region.

The Upper Blue.

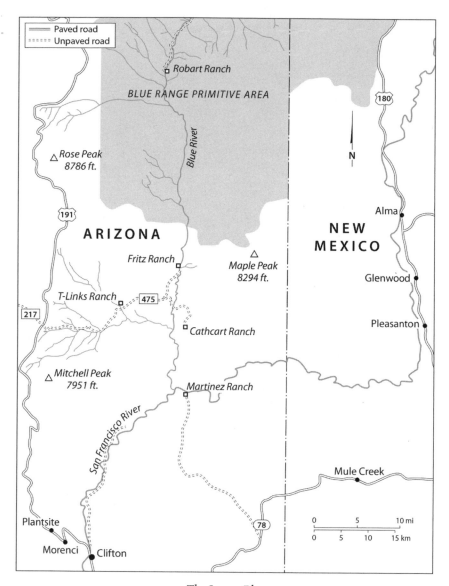

The Lower Blue.

Preface

The Blue River runs through a canyon with rugged high walls, in the eastern part of Arizona in Greenlee County, sometimes running over into Catron County, New Mexico and back into Greenlee County. . . .

Ed Richardson, former resident of the Blue, said, "Even with all the difficult times, Blue River and the Blue Range are closer to Heaven than a lot of people in this world will ever get! . . . Perhaps places like these are only little glimpses into what Heaven will be like and thus entice us in that direction."

CLEO BARBARA COSPER COOR,
Introduction to *Down on the Blue* (1987)

MOST PEOPLE WHO HAVE LIVED on the Blue would wholeheartedly agree with the sentiments above. Many have proclaimed similar feelings; this book will cite more than a few examples. The Blue River Valley, isolated and obscure, unheard of by even most Arizonans, nevertheless generates its own peculiar mystique for those who know it. I was one who came to know it.

One of my specialties as an anthropologist has been cultural ecology, and I had written previously on land use in different cultures. In the early 1990s, my attention turned to environmental controversies in our own society. I began teaching university courses on the subject. At the same time, my parents retired to live with my sister on her husband's pecan plantation near Las Cruces, New Mexico, where I had passed my high school years. I decided to spend time with them during the summers. I wanted also to use their place as a base for traveling around the West in a camper van. I could attend conferences and meet and interview people and see for myself the settings for what seemed to be a never-ending series of clashes over environmental controversies.

After a couple summers of such meandering, I decided to concentrate on a specific research topic: the conflicts that had erupted in New Mexico over grazing on federal lands. At that time the hotbed was Catron County in western New Mexico, which contains parts of the Gila National Forest.

possible → Environmental Argument
↑ / against the Ranches

There, the ranchers, the U.S. Forest Service, and activist groups such as the Santa Fe-based Forest Guardians and the Tucson-based Southwest Center for Biological Diversity, were locked in highly publicized disputes about the role and regulation of ranching on Forest Service land. I describe some of these conflicts in chapters 11 and 12 of this book.

I collected information and interviewed all the participants I could: environmentalists, Forest personnel, and ranchers who were Gila Forest "permittees" (persons with permits to run livestock on federal "public lands"). In 1997, I heard about the Blue River ranchers in Arizona, just over the state border from Catron County. Many permittees on the Gila Forest had been hit hard by the 1995 government cuts in their livestock allowances; but apparently the ranchers on the Blue had been hit harder, in fact devastated, by Forest Service mandated herd reductions. This distinction interested me. I was also intrigued by the Blue's reputation as beautiful, isolated, wild country far from any town, on a dirt road that followed a small river south for many miles until vehicles could no longer continue in the rugged terrain. The mystique of the Blue.

So I visited the Blue. I talked to the ranchers and their wives along the Blue Road (Forest Road 281). I camped out in the two small Forest Service campgrounds on the Blue. I interviewed members of the Forest Service in Alpine, Arizona. I traveled south over the "Coronado Trail" (U.S. 191) to visit and talk to people living on the lower Blue. Luckily I had a four-wheel-drive vehicle necessary to reach some of the ranches. I interviewed Forest Service personnel in the Clifton office, which manages the lower Blue. Few environmental activists live in this area, and few seem to visit it. But I found occasions in Tucson and other places to talk to representatives of the main activist organizations bringing litigation to the Blue.

Rely on himself or transportation

Eventually I reached a point known to many who plunge into research—I was accumulating too much information. I needed to limit the scope of my project, if I ever hoped to finish it. I chose to focus on the Blue for a few simple reasons. One was that it is a relatively distinct ranching community, defined by the watershed of the Blue itself. Though not a real "town," it has its own part-time post office (Blue, Arizona, 85922). Its ranchers see and refer to themselves as members of the "Blue" community. Historically, the road along the Blue linked everyone on the river until the 1940s when maintenance was ended on the lower section (see chapter 7).

The situation of the Gila Forest ranchers is different. They have organized themselves when necessary into a permittee association to confront the Forest Service but are not united by any geographical feature or common highway. Nor are those ranchers a community in any real sense, since they are dispersed over a wide area with a number of towns surrounding the large Gila National Forest.

An advantage of studying the Blue in depth was that in the 1990s it included no more than two dozen ranches in a geographically delimited area. Therefore every ranch family could be interviewed, every allotment (piece of federal land requiring a permit to use) could be studied, and I could make myself very familiar with the area. I was willing to sacrifice breadth for depth.

Another advantage of the Blue, an expression of its sense of community, lay in its possession of a wealth of oral history lovingly collected, edited, and published as a book by the ranchers' wives, *Down on the Blue* (1987). A ranch wife, Barbara Marks, also had a treasure trove of articles and information from her own research on local environmental issues that she was willing to share.

I was very much encouraged that the people I met on the Blue, like Bill and Barbara Marks (see their story in chapter 16), were so friendly and supportive when I told them about my research and explained why I wanted to hear their stories. I found a positive reception also among the Forest Service people, from the Ranger in charge, through the various staff, in both the Alpine and Clifton offices. They were invariably cooperative.

And finally, there was the mystique of the Blue. So I made my choice.

* * *

Cultural anthropologists are notorious for almost always personally identifying with the interests of the communities they research, especially if they feel "their" people need defending against the outside world. I suppose I too must plead guilty. Through many summers visiting the Blue, I did come to sympathize deeply with the people who live and ranch there. This sympathy will show in my account.

However, sympathy does not mean uncritical agreement with their opinions. Nor does it mean advocacy. This account strives to be as balanced and objective as possible. I have not written a polemic and have restrained myself from offering my own opinions on controversial questions. Instead I give the ranchers and their supporters full opportunity to voice their opinions and point of view. To do so is important, because their voice is not frequently heard, either in the media or in academia. But to present the full picture, or whole story, all pertinent viewpoints needed to be presented—those of Forest Service personnel, of environmental activists, of scientific experts of various sorts, of historians, and others who have written about the Western range. I have tried to construct my narrative to include all perspectives that need to be represented in order for the reader to gain a fair understanding of the issues covered in this book.

This history is written in the form of a scholarly monograph, and I believe it should hold an interest for experts in various fields. But it is also written for a general audience. I never presume specialized knowledge on the part of the reader. For example, a whole chapter (9) takes time away from the Blue to survey the gamut of environmental controversies surrounding ranching in late twentieth-century America: I think such background information is necessary to understand what happened on the Blue. I have been careful to translate jargon; but more importantly, I have tried to clarify issues and provide broader contexts to enable readers to comprehend unfamiliar matters. What helped me in this effort is a long experience in teaching undergraduates subject matter about which they initially know little.

Of course, some readers may come to this work with previous knowledge and even preformed views on certain of the issues covered. Fair enough, if they want to test their views against the information I present. There will be readers who already possess a developed interest in at least one of the following aspects of this book: history, especially of the Southwest; ranching, frontier and modern; the Forest Service and federal land policies; environmental issues, such as wilderness and endangered species; and the fate of rural America. I believe *The Blue and the Green* adds something of value to our knowledge of these matters.

Acknowledgments

THIS WORK BELONGS really to all those who participated in my research. Many of them are named in the narrative, especially those interviewed. I want to express gratitude to them and everyone else who helped me. I offer special recognition to a number of ranchers and other folk on the Blue for their support: Billy and Barbara Marks, Dennis and Doug Stacy, Rose Awtrey, Bill and Mona Bunnel, Otis and Judy Wolkins, Dr. Sam Luce, Chase Caldwell, Martie and Patrick Cathcart, Bill Wilson, Abelardo and Dan Martinez, Bobby Gomez, Thomas Paterson. I want to remember Tim Robart, now deceased. I also want to thank by name some New Mexico people who helped me: Hugh B. and Marge McKeen, Sewall and Lois Goodwin, Glen McCarty, Howard Hutchinson, and Caren Cowan.

I thank all the Apache-Sitgreaves National Forest Service personnel whom I consulted and interviewed; as I said earlier, they were invariably kind and helpful. Among them I owe special thanks to John Bedell, former Supervisor of the Apache-Sitgreaves National Forest; Phil Settles, former Alpine District Ranger; and Frank Hayes, former Clifton District Ranger. Various workers for the U.S. Fish and Wildlife Service and the Arizona Game and Fish Department also helped with information. Special thanks go to Jeff Dolphin.

Environmentalists of various persuasions played an important role in my research. I will mention here Courtney White of the Quivira Coalition; Kieran Suckling and Michael Robinson of the Southwest Center for Biological Diversity; and Don Hoffman of the Arizona Wilderness Coalition.

A number of scientists and experts on ranching were crucial in helping me understand the issues my research covers. I want to give credit to Nathan Sayre, University of California, Berkeley; John Fowler and his team of range experts at New Mexico State University; Jerry Holechek of the same university; Alex Thal of Western New Mexico State University; and Al Medina of the Rocky Mountain Institute.

I want to express my gratitude to persons who read early versions of my manuscript and provided encouraging comments: James Faris, Nathan Sayres, Bruce Nystrom, Bill and Denise Turner, Don and Dilli Bahr, David Remley, and Frederick F. York.

The research and writing for this work was carried out on my own time and with my own funding. However, I did receive substantial material support from two sources. During my summers of research, my brother-in-law Bill Stahmann (now deceased) and my sister Kathryn Ann, kindly gave me a home base and office space on their pecan farm near Las Cruces, New Mexico. Also, over the years I have drawn often on the resources of the University of Massachusetts Dartmouth, where I teach.

For their efforts in helping me obtain and prepare the photographs and maps for this book, I want to credit and thank Rose Awtrey, Jenny Yates, Kit Quinsler Orn, my sons Samuel Stauder and Jeffrey Stauder, and especially Allison Cywin of the College of Visual and Performing Arts of my university.

I want to express gratitude to my two editors, Matt Becker and Justin Race, and to other staff of the University of Nevada Press for their crucial support in bringing my work to fruition.

Finally, I would like to dedicate this book to my deceased father, J. Richard "Dick" Stauder. He spent a good part of his life riding the range of southern Colorado. There I grew up, learning from him the life of ranching and feeling his deep love for the land.

Introduction

With the creation of the Forest Service in 1905 . . . Secretary of Agriculture James Wilson wrote his now famous letter to Gifford Pinchot in which he laid down the dictum, ". . . and where conflicting interests must be reconciled, the question will always be decided from the standpoint of the *greatest good of the greatest number in the long run*." The [italicized] portion has not always been agreed upon by various groups or individuals outside the Forest Service."

CLEO BARBARA COSPER COOR, *Down on the Blue* 1987:87.

Ranchers also became the West's most cherished self-image: the rugged individualist who battled wild beasts and wilder country to supply a nation with beef or wool. But there was a contradiction lurking within the symbolism. Because most of their animals ranged across public lands, the freedom of the ranchers was always contingent upon the actions of the government.

THOMAS E. SHERIDAN, *Arizona: A History* 1995:306

UNTIL RECENTLY, the Blue was a ranching community with roots in the American frontier. So this historical account centers on ranching. No claim is made that the Blue was a typical ranching community of the western frontier—in various ways it differed, especially in its relatively late settlement. But the Blue is an interesting example of broader processes at work in American history: first, in its frontier experience, then in its experience with the U.S. Forest Service, and finally the changing values of a highly urbanized and regulated society at the beginning of the twenty-first century.

With the U.S. government's establishment of Forest Reserves and then the National Forests, early in the twentieth century, the U.S. Forest Service gained dominance over the rangelands of the Blue and thereby its ranch economy. Ranching on the Blue, and the destiny of the Blue community, became mingled with the actions of this federal agency. Similar developments occurred in many other ranching communities in

Tension Forest Reserves / Government and the Blue community

the American West when federal lands were brought under government regulation.

Appropriately, therefore, this book is entitled *The Blue and the Green.* "Green" can denote the Forest Service—it has been the color of most of their uniforms and vehicles (in fact, "Forest Service Green" is a recognized color among Ford pickup trucks). Green of course is the usual color of forests and trees. And, not by coincidence, green has emerged as the color symbolizing the natural environment itself, along with the environmental movement. Therefore the "Green" in the title happily appropriates these connotations, for this case study focuses on the ecological issues surrounding ranching, and especially on the consequences of governmental environmental policies and regulations applied on the Blue.

While it delights in the historical particularities of the Blue, *The Blue and the Green* presents the Blue experience as an example of larger processes, still ongoing, that over many decades have transformed rural society in the West. Accordingly, this case study in cultural ecology is an effort to contribute to an understanding of Western social, political, and environmental history by documenting the local story of the particular people who have lived and worked in the Blue River watershed over the past century and more. Especially, it attempts to give a voice to these people.

A brief summary of the book's contents, by chapter, might be helpful to the reader. Chapters 1 and 2 cover the early history of the Blue, up to the 1910s. This history has been pulled together from many sources, including oral histories found not only in *Down on the Blue* but also in state archives and other library sources. Included also is an analysis of the 1900 Census. As far as I know, *The Blue and the Green* gives the fullest account of early Blue history that exists, just as it provides the only general history of the Blue. In addition, the first two chapters go beyond simply telling the story of the Blue: they attempt to put it into the context of the larger history of the American frontier and of ranching at the time.

Chapters 3 and 4 continue the history of the Blue, focusing on crucial ecological and political developments. Overgrazing, erosion, drought, and flood occurred in the early 1900s on the Blue, coinciding with a push for government regulation of ranching by the newly created U.S. Forest Service. These chapters analyze the motives behind such developments, including the problem of the open range. They also discuss the significant role played on the Blue by the young Aldo Leopold, the early ecological visionary and wilderness advocate.

Chapter 5 describes, often through oral history, the arrival of the Forest Service on the Blue, and the relationship of the agency to the ranchers through the 1930s. It discusses government policies and the conservationist philosophy of that time. Also, it traces the end of the open range and the fencing of allotments, work often carried out by the Civilian Conservation Corps of the New Deal.

Chapter 6 covers the great changes that occurred—as elsewhere in America—in living standards on the Blue from the 1920s to the 1990s. The Blue was not isolated from technological progress. Rural home life and ranching were both transformed by modern communication and transportation, as well as new utilities, such as electricity, the telephone, and modern plumbing. The chapter analyzes the 1930 census and school records for social and demographic trends. The role of hunting in the Blue economy is described. The chapter charts the effect of World War II, the decline of the Blue population after the War, and gives a description of the social activities and institutions that have maintained community on the Blue.

Chapter 7 documents and analyzes a new and significant environmental controversy on the Blue: should it be designated "wilderness" by law? The concept of wilderness, as developed by Aldo Leopold and the Forest Service, eventuated in the Wilderness Act of 1964. But while the Forest Service, with environmental activist support, has wanted a major part of the Blue watershed to be classified as wilderness, the Blue ranching community has been united and active up to the present in opposing such a designation. The chapter documents and explains their resistance and the reasoning on both sides of the controversy.

Chapter 8 utilizes oral histories and interviews, but especially Forest Service records, to document how during the 1970s and 1980s the Forest Service succeeded in acquiring a historic ranch and other private holdings in the center of the proposed Blue wilderness and in ending cattle grazing there. This case demonstrates the role of ecological and economic factors, as well as Forest Service policies, in a struggle that played out between the ranchers and the federal agency.

Chapter 9 provides an overview of the controversy over federal or public lands ranching in the modern West—a context necessary to understand the conflict on the Blue. It presents both the environmental activist case against ranching and the defense of ranching by its supporters. Also, it looks at a third force that has recently emerged, a sort of environmentalist-rancher alliance to use grazing for ecological benefits.

Chapter 10 describes how activist environmental organizations successfully brought pressure on the Forest Service, first to limit logging, and then to limit grazing in the region. Drawing from Forest Service files and many interviews, it documents the long process of how the National Environmental Policy Act (NEPA) was applied on the Blue, and the consequences. Chapter 11 continues the story, as aggrieved ranchers appealed their case first to public opinion, then through the upper levels of the Forest Service administration, and finally in the courts (chapter 12). These three chapters are needed to cover the long struggle over what came to be called colloquially "the NEPA cuts of 1995." The ecological, economic, political, and legal issues were complex, but this critical episode marked a serious decline of cattle numbers on the Blue.

Chapter 13 is devoted to a crucial ecological issue on the Blue, and elsewhere in the Southwest. Is the grazing of cattle compatible with the wellbeing of certain species of small fish? The issue highlights the role that the Endangered Species Act, and its interpretation by federal agencies, plays in the West. Chapter 14 features two other species, the Mexican gray wolf (endangered) and the Rocky Mountain elk (abundant). In different ways the wolf and the elk have become the bane of ranchers not only on the Blue but also in the surrounding region. The two species' conflicts with cattle raising, and the response of federal and state agencies, provide two other case studies of how ecological issues play out practically on the ground, on the Blue.

Chapters 15 and 16 recount the history of the Blue from a different angle: they relate the personal histories of a selection of ranchers. The narratives are composed mostly of their own words in my interviews with them, supplemented by other sources.

The Conclusion brings events up to date as of publication, and summarizes the main trends that will shape the future of ranching on the Blue.

If there are conclusions or morals to be drawn, these should emerge from the history itself, and readers will be able to draw them. However, a recurring theme lies in what has been termed "historical irony"—when human actions have an effect contradictory to what was intended. Ecological assumptions and intentions in twentieth-century America are rich with such ironies. Various "ironies" are to be found in the pages that follow. I invite you to look for them.

The Blue and the Green

1

"God's Country"

The Blue Frontier

The beauty of that spot there in the wilderness miles from any human habitation, the river tumbling down the gorge, the towering cliffs every color of the rainbow, and the mountainsides covered with tall pines, and the lush grass up to my horse's belly, struck me like a blow from a sledge hammer square betwixt the eyes.

I says to myself, says I, "Why spend one's life behind a plow or hide one's self in a tunnel seeking gold, when there is such a spot as this in the world to build a home in—just for the takin'. This is that God's Country I used to tell the folks I would find some day." [1883]

TOLES COSPER (Cosper 1940:2)

They were riding along enjoying the scenery when Nat stopped his horse, and after one long gasping breath, exclaimed to Fred.

"This must be the Garden of Eden that the Bible tells us about."

"No," said Fred, "It is the Land O' Milk and Honey. Can't you see those wild cattle, and—unless I am mistaken—that is a bee tree right over there, and there are wagon-loads of wild grapes right up this canyon." [1884]

FRED FRITZ to his wife Katy (Fritz, 1985:iii)

THESE RECOLLECTIONS, many years after the event, reflect the mythic quality cast over their experience by the earliest pioneers into the Blue, a land of beauty and plenty, but also a frontier beset by dangers and difficulties.

The cattle were there, the bees were there, also the grapes, but all were *plenty* wild and *plenty* hard to obtain: The cattle were the sharp-horned, rusty-black Mexican, wild critters that even the wildest Apache found much trouble in getting near enough to kill one for beef; the bees were wont to sting one's eyes out when one attempted to rob their honey-store; and one had to climb a two-thousand foot cliff and hang by one hind leg to get the grapes. And the forest teemed with savage Apaches. (Fritz 1985:iv)

This last detail is hardly exaggerated. The Blue River and surrounding mountains were then a traditional hunting territory of the White River and other Apache bands (Sheridan 1995:84–5). Possibly, the famous chieftain Geronimo was born on the Blue.[1]

Other native peoples had preceded the Apache. Pots and similar relics found along the Blue, together with traces of irrigation works, indicate the Mogollon culture. This prehistoric culture prospered in settled communities in the upper Gila region of New Mexico and Arizona from 300 BC to AD 1100. Then for unclear reasons this culture disappeared. Eventually the more warlike and itinerant Apache came to rove through the Blue but left no evidence of settlement (*Down on the Blue* 7, 119, 145; USFS 1988:13).

The Spaniards arrived in Southern Arizona in the sixteenth century. Francisco Vasquez de Coronado's expedition is thought to have passed somewhere through the neighborhood of the Blue in 1540 (*Down on the Blue* 8). (Modern U.S. Highway 191 from Clifton to Alpine, winding along the high mountain country that defines the western border of the Blue River watershed, is designated "the Coronado Trail.") Coronado's journal writer described this whole region of Arizona as a huge trackless wilderness (USFS 2000a). The early Spanish explorers named the Blue River ("Rio Azul") after its sources in the Blue Range ("Sierra Azul"), which appeared bluish in the hazy distance (Barnes 1960:164).

The sparse Hispanic settlement in Arizona stayed south of the Gila. The mountainous area to the north, over the Mogollon Rim that encompassed the Blue River, was known as the *despoblado*, the uninhabited land, and was ceded to Apache control. The Apache adapted quickly to the Spanish horse, and became dangerous predators on Spanish and Pueblo Indian settlements (Pattie 1831; Pitts 1996:2; Thrapp 1967:6–8).

The first recorded penetration of the area by Anglo-Americans was in 1825, when Kentuckians Sylvester and James O. Pattie traveled down the Gila River with a small band of fur trappers. The Patties came to where the San Francisco River joins the Gila. James later wrote that the stream, we discovered, carried as much water as the Helay [Gila], heading north. We called it the river St. Francisco. After travelling up its banks about four miles, we encamped, and set all our traps, and killed a couple of fat turkeys. In the morning we examined our traps, and found in them 37 beavers! This success restored our spirits instantaneously. Exhilarating prospects now opened before us, and we pushed on with animation. The banks of this river are for the most part incapable of cultivation being in many places formed of high and rugged mountains. Upon these we saw multitudes of mountain sheep. (Pattie 1831:79)

In their journey up the San Francisco, the Pattie group must have found where the Blue enters it, not more than twenty miles above the Gila. Quite possibly the party set their traps up the Blue too. Although they found plentiful beaver, James Pattie reported no Indian contact in this area (Pattie 1831; Pitts 1996:2).

Not until after the Civil War did U.S. citizens migrate in appreciable numbers to Arizona. At first they bypassed the rugged lands above the Mogollon Rim, the White Mountains, and the Blue Range. Land more inviting for farming and ranching was along the Gila and south of it. However, reasons for avoiding the Blue country probably also had to do with the Apache who dominated these lands. In fact, in 1872 the U.S. government initially assigned all the mountainous land from central Arizona to the New Mexico Border, including the Blue, to the newly created San Carlos Apache Reservation (Debo 1976:85).

Yet the presence of rich copper deposits in the Clifton-Morenci area, among other things, led a year later to shrinking the Reservation boundary (Debo 1976:127, 172). The large strip of eastern Arizona that includes the Blue and what would become northern Greenlee County was legally opened for pioneer settlement. Clifton, about fifteen miles down the San Francisco from where the Blue enters, became the largest mining community in Arizona in the 1870s (Sheridan 1995:162; Patton 1977). During the same period, north of the Blue, Mormon colonists from Utah were moving into the lush mountain pastures around Luna, New Mexico, and what today is Alpine, Arizona (Haskett 1935:30).

Arizona was filling up, relatively speaking, with new settlers in the 1870s and early 1880s. In particular, the Arizona range was filling with cattle. The building of railways, and a Western cattle boom fueled by outside capital, led to fully stocked, if not overstocked, ranges in Arizona and the private appropriation of most permanent water sites by the mid-1880s (Haskett 1935:24–26, 31, 35; Morrisey 1950:153; Sayre 1999, 2002:30–32; Sheridan 1995:132; J.J. Wagoner 1952:119).

But the Blue Range country remained "Any Man's Country," according to Joseph Hampton Toles ("Toles") Cosper, quoted at the beginning of this chapter. Alabama-born, he was raised near Abilene, Texas, and claimed he had always wanted to be a cowman and to "find a God's Country to live in." In 1883 he was working for the Diamond M outfit near Magdalena, New Mexico, and was tracking a stolen herd over into the Blue Range country when he experienced the epiphany described at the beginning of this chapter.

> He went back to his job and promptly took up what wages he had coming to him in cattle, which totaled a herd of 39 head of breed cows, and which he branded Y Bar Y. He then wrote his father to sell all his personal belongings, including cattle and horses, and send the money to him to buy more cattle with, stating in the letter "I have found that God's Country."
>
> By the end of 1884, he had 260 head of Y Bar Y cattle running loose on the open New Mexico range, and at Christmas time he went home to Texas and got married. . . .
>
> In the fall of 1885, Toles "squatted" on his chosen spot on the Blue River, built his cabin, set up housekeeping, and then went over into New Mexico and drove his cattle over to his new range. . . . (Cosper 1940:1–3)

But Toles Cosper and wife were not the first settlers on the Blue. According to Walter Casto,

> My grandfather, John Casto and grandmother Betsy Casto first went to the Blue in about 1878. Betsy was the first white woman on the Blue.
>
> They settled at or above the forks of the Upper Blue. They stayed three years. The Indians were still bad. They had to be on constant watch for them. They killed several people. The Castos hitched up their oxen to their wagons and moved back up north. They stayed away three years and moved back to the Blue. . . . They cleared some land and raised a little hay and vegetables to live on and sold some to other people. Later on Granddad put in

a vineyard and raised grapes and made wine to sell. . . . (*Down on the Blue* 158)

By all accounts in the Blue folk memory, the Castos were the earliest settlers. And by the Casto account the Apache were a definite deterrent to early pioneers of the Blue.

Despite government attempts to confine and settle the Western Apache on reservations, bands of them rebelled and mounted raids during the late 1870s and early 1880s over southeastern Arizona, up into Blue country and across the New Mexico border, and down into Mexico, under leaders such as Victorio and Geronimo (Wagoner 1952:51). It was the last of the Indian wars in the United States. Before the railway reached Clifton in 1884, freight wagons hauling copper were often ambushed (Sheridan 1995:163; 167). In 1882, a group of a hundred warriors led by Geronimo killed more than fifty people—"prospectors, wagon train drivers, ranchers, lone travelers, everyone they encountered on their raids"— as they struck out for the Sierra Madre mountains in Mexico. As part of this bloody odyssey, a marauding party successfully plundered horses and mules up the San Francisco River (Debo 1976:144).

But if Apache raids were so common over a large area of Arizona and New Mexico, their presence cannot fully explain the delayed settlement of the Blue. Terrain also played a role. The two factors reinforced each other: the more remote, rough, and sparsely populated the land, the less protection there was from Apache raiders. Ralph Reynolds grew up as a cowboy, knowing the Blue Range firsthand. His 1991 autobiography offers an opinion of the land in a chapter entitled, "A Country This Sorry Has to Be Prime."

In our time, grazing of cattle is considered lowest among the many potential agricultural uses of land. It follows, then, that people would put to grazing only that land unsuited for other use. Carrying this thought a little further, it is easy to establish that the rough and tumble Mogollon Breaks lying on either side of the New Mexico-Arizona border is country so poor that it has to be the prime cowboy land of the earth.

Conceived in the fire and brimstone of Tertiary volcanoes, this wild, wooded cowboy country, ever mysterious, sometimes graceful to the eye and sometimes awesome, is almost useless to man. For where it is warm enough to grow his crops, it is too dry.

And where it is moist enough for crops, it is too cold. And even if we could magically change the climate of this land, to warm the heights and moisten the steppe, it is everywhere too rough and rocky except for the toughest of cowboys and the ruggedest of cows.

This land is also vastly underpopulated, thanks mainly, perhaps, to Geronimo and his ilk. Generations of pioneers were stalled from settling there, for the mountains and the valleys had long before been chosen by Apache warriors as their own. Even the Spanish kings seem to have had no enemies hated or feared enough to deserve banishment into such useless and dangerous territory. Thus, the region was never included in any of the many royal land grants that gave away much of New Mexico. (Reynolds 1991:9–10)

PIONEER SETTLERS

Despite rugged country and dangerous Apache, a few early settlers persisted in the 1880s, bringing their families: "There were no windows in our house on account of Indians, and we never had a light after dark. My sister Emma and I would go out every morning to look over the place before Dad came outside the house, because we had been told that Indians always killed the man in the family first" (Graham 1953:27). The Casto family had the first house on the Blue. As another precaution, their house "had a sort of 'port-hole' arrangement so they could look around for Indians before leaving the house" (Lee 1983:68; *Down on the Blue* 161).

The Castos, when they returned, were settled halfway down the Blue. The Johnson family with its little girls and cabin with no windows was north of them. Farther up the Blue towards Luna, Martin and Susana Noland had a "ranch" and log house where in 1885 the first child of pioneer stock was born on the Blue—William Levi Noland. (*Down on the Blue* 47–50). How many more settlers were living on the upper Blue in the mid-1880s is unclear—perhaps none but in any case few.

Miles to the south on the lower Blue only a handful of male squatters had arrived by 1886: Bob Bell, a rancher; an old man named Benton; the Luther brothers; and a Frenchman named Rasperrie or Raspberry. Hugh McKeen of Alma, New Mexico, managed a cattle camp across the state line (Fritz 1978:67).[2] Farther south Fred Fritz and his partner Nat Whittum lived in their "land of milk and honey." Finally, Toles Cosper maintained a cabin and ran cattle on the Blue, but he had not yet brought his bride Lou Ella to live there. "Toles and his family and John [his brother] tried moving to the Blue before they were successful in doing so, but the first night out found them surrounded by Indian fires so they returned to Luna to wait another year" (Coor, in *Down on the Blue* 201).

The small Blue population of the mid-1880s was tenuous and scattered down the winding canyons of a river that drained an area about twenty miles wide by forty miles long. Isolated cabins were more or less at the mercy of large Apache raiding parties, and most had been plundered from time to time. Cattle and horses were driven off; barns, corrals, haystacks, and cabins burned. Usually the best wisdom was to hide and not resist (Fritz 1985:v). According to Hugh McKeen's wife, "From the experience he and his parents encountered with the Indians in Texas, he learned to stay away from the main traveled trails, thereby avoiding being killed" (McKeen 1982:167). McKeen lived over in Alma and admitted not staying much at his "ranch" on the Blue.

Definitely come to settle was Fred Fritz, the son of immigrants to the German colony of Fredericksburg, Texas. As a young man, he found work in west Texas on ranches and as a stagecoach driver in Comanche country then drifted farther west, helping to build the Mexican Central Railroad out of El Paso. He tried other lines of work around the mining towns and forts of southern New Mexico and Arizona. Trapping beaver along the San Francisco like the Patties, he first encountered the Blue River and in 1884 returned with a partner, an old Army scout named Nat Whittum (Fritz 1978:65–66).[3]

While trapping, Fritz and Whittum hoped to establish a ranch by catching and branding the many feral "Mexican" longhorns found on the Blue, as well as wild ponies.

> The first two wild horses that Fritz & Whittum managed to rope and break to the saddle were stolen right in front of their very eyes, so to speak—just *taken* in broad daylight. Since there were about fifty or more of the Indians and only two white men— with little ammunition—they just kept quiet and let them take the horses.
>
> Along in October (1884) Fritz and Whittum had a corral full of mavericks ready for the branding iron the next morning, when just at dusk, while they were eating supper, a band of perhaps one

hundred or more Indians rode up to the corral, opened the gate
and stampeded the cattle.

All the Indians carried rifles, which was something new to
Fritz and Whittum. . . . (Fritz 1985:v)

In 1886 the Blue saw the last Apache raid in the Southwest that
caused fatalities. Providentially, Bob Bell and Toles Cosper were elsewhere when the Apaches struck, but Toles's cabin was burned and most
of his stock stolen. Fred Fritz was also absent, selling furs and laying in
supplies of food and ammunition in Clifton. There he heard that Indian
raiders were crossing the country. Hurrying back to his cabin on the Blue,

he drove up to the back door and called to Whittum; there was
no answer. He went in and found Nat Whittum in a pool of blood
on the floor near the fireplace; Nat had been in the act of making
biscuits and still had fresh dough on his hands and his body was
still warm. (Fritz 1985:ix).

Whittum had been shot in the back. Fritz rode to warn McKeen, whose
camp was off the river trail. By the time the two returned to the Fritz
place it was on fire and painted warriors were leaving.

Most of the small population on the lower Blue had been wiped out.
Benton, Raspberry, and the Luther brothers were killed. Also on the San
Francisco, near the Blue, the Pippin ranch had been attacked, with Mrs.
Pippin slain and Mr. Pippin left for dead. Fritz helped bury them all. Nat
Whittum was buried on a mound overlooking his Garden of Eden, but
Fritz went ahead with plans to establish his ranch in this now bloodied
land of milk and honey (Fritz 1985:xi).

"Somewhere in Alma, New Mexico country, the soldiers, after a
fight, captured the Indians and returned them to the reservation" (Fritz
1978:67). This raid through the Blue occurred the same year that Geronimo was forced to surrender to U.S. troops in Mexico (Debo 1976:281–
312; Thrapp 1967:350–367; Wagoner 1952:51). Whether any of the
Apache who raided the Blue were sent with him and his followers to exile
in Florida, or were punished at all, is unclear.

After 1886, there were no more fatal raids, but "even in the early
1900s people thought that the Indians were responsible for stealing many
horses on ranches. They always blamed the "Apache Kid," but no one
ever remembered seeing him" (Cleo Coor, *Down on the Blue* 7, 209; Gra-

ham 1953:27). Stories of theft and the fabled Apache Kid aside, Indians occasionally left the reservation to hunt their old grounds on the Blue.

Nowhere in the Blue pioneer accounts is any mention of them killing Apache, or even shooting at them. The settlers hid, if they were lucky, and left the Indian fighting to the U.S. Cavalry. Rustlers, however, were a different story.

> Prices to the East and West were sliding down to rock bottom due to overstocked markets, but even with the decline, Toles felt that he could have made money in the cattle business had it not been for the rustlers and raiding Apaches. Each time he managed to get a herd ready for market something happened—Indians or rustlers helped themselves—until Toles became 'fighting mad.' (Cosper 1940:4–5)

He hired some gunslingers from Texas to work for him, and joined with other ranchers on the Blue and San Francisco Rivers to deal with the threat to their livelihood.

> The soldiers were doing a very good job taking care of the Apaches, but were having their hands full at that; it was up the ranchers to take care of the rustlers with the only law they knew anything about, "Gun Law."
>
> When any new outfit, single, or in groups, were discovered on the range, they were met with a very unfriendly welcome and were watched with open hostile suspicion until they proved themselves worthy of staying there; and if they failed to measure up to the standards set by those first settlers, they either left the country or *else*—and there were many bleaching bones and unmarked graves scattered over the Blue range.
>
> Toles says, "It was not a case of overcrowded range, as some people are wont to opine, as there was plenty range for all at that time, nor was it a case of Big-I-and-Little-You, with us ranchers. Each of us realized that live men—who are men—build up a country and dead ones have to be buried. It's unsightly to run across human coyote bait when riding the range, so we usually buried 'em. We were just plumb fed up on being burned out and stolen blind." (Cosper 1940:4–5)

Fred Fritz also discovered rustlers messing with his brand: his 3—X (Three Bar X) was altered to 8—X (Eight Bar X). Cosper's Y—Y (Y Bar Y) could be carved into the same rustlers' brand, unknown locally. After spying on a rustler camp on Pipestem Mountain, and discovering a party of at least six strangers, Fritz and his men gathered neighboring cattlemen to pursue the outlaws but failed to catch up to them before they had shipped the stolen cattle from Silver City. Afterward Fritz adopted a new brand harder to alter: XXX.

> That wholesale rustling got the "danger up" among the ranchers on Blue River and they began to mistrust their neighbors to the west of the mountain ridge, knowing full well that whoever rustled that herd *must* have known the country pretty well or they never could have made their getaway so easy—and too, all the rustled cattle in that herd seemed to have belonged to the ranchers to the south and on Blue River.
>
> Every newcomer to Blue River after that was viewed with suspicion and watched like hawks, but every precaution the ranchers took seemed to fail until most every one of them were about "cleaned" out of cattle and horses. They grew so hostile toward newcomers that it just wasn't safe for a stranger to make the least false move. (Fritz 1985:xiv–xv)

Rustling was a problem for ranchers throughout Arizona in the 1890s and into the new century (Wilson 1967–68:33–35). The Blue was not spared. It did avoid, however, the war between sheepmen and cattlemen that raged at times across the mountains in the vicinity of Magdalena, New Mexico (*Down on the Blue* 119), for the simple reason that no one tried to bring sheep onto the Blue.

Fred Fritz went back to Fredericksburg, Texas, in 1894 to marry Katy Knapp, also of German ancestry.

> The Indians had been quelled by that time, but there were still the rustlers and killers of every caliber to contend with through this section of Arizona territory. Fred refused to expose his bride to such dangers so he built her a house in Clifton where she spent two long, lonely years. (Fritz 1985:xv)

In 1896 she finally went to live on the Blue, riding the thirty-two miles side saddle and "holding her daughter in her arms, over a mountain trail no more than three feet wide, with a 700 foot drop on the canyon side" (*The Copper Era* newspaper, Feb. 8, 1957, *Down on the Blue* 220). The home where he brought her was built "as a hide-out, for this close to the Blue River the cabin could not be seen from the river" (Fritz 1978:67).

In 1895 Toles Cosper also brought his growing family onto the Blue, and in 1897 acquired the place that became the Cospers' Y Bar Y Ranch (*Down on the Blue* 197). By the 1890s, the Blue appeared relatively safe enough so that many families were settling there. They were ending the local frontier, one of the last in Arizona and the West. The national frontier as a whole would officially be proclaimed "closed" in 1890 by the Superintendent of Census, as noted three years later by the famous historian Frederick Jackson Turner (Turner 1962:1).

Despite Apaches, rustlers, rough terrain, hardship, and risk, the Blue was irresistible to those who wanted land. It was not of course the beauty of the rugged landscape that drew the pioneers, though its beauty did not escape them. What made the Blue God's Country, and a potential Land of Milk and Honey in their eyes was something simple, relatively scarce, and of utmost value in the Southwest: the water of the Blue River itself. As Fred Fritz Jr., who lived eighty years on the Blue in the secluded spot where his father brought his mother, wrote,

> when I was a boy I asked my father why he passed through some of the best range in western New Mexico and eastern Arizona with those long horned cattle...and then located in the roughest part of Arizona, the Blue River country. His answer was "water." During my lifetime on the ranch I discovered how right he was. (Fritz 1978:93)

NOTES

1. Some locals have believed so (Reynolds 1991: chapter 3). On the other hand, historians make a good case for Geronimo's birthplace on the upper Gila, north of present day Silver City, New Mexico (e.g. Roberts 1994:104, 327). Angie Debo, however, points out that while Geronimo located his birthplace at the headwaters of the Gila, he always insisted he was born in Arizona. The matter could be adroitly resolved if, in Geronimo's ethnogeography, the Blue River was seen as a headwaters of the Gila, its westernmost branch. General Crook, the later pursuer of Geronimo, apparently made the same terminological assumption that the Blue was a branch of the Gila (Thrapp 1967:99). Nomenclatures can differ, but geographically the Blue is in fact an upper branch of the Gila River system.

2. In "Hugh Bronson McKeen: His Family History" (McKeen 1982) he is said to have moved to the area in 1888. But in the same history his wife places him in the area at the time of the 1886 massacre, and both Fritz accounts (Fred Fritz 1978:67; Katy Fritz 1985:vi) agree he was present in 1886.

3. Whittum is sometimes Wittum or Widdom in different accounts, but Whittum was the name officially adopted by the early post office named after him (*Down on the Blue* 173). More importantly, some significant differences exist between the history given by Fred Fritz Sr.'s wife, Katy (Fritz 1985), and that of his son Fred Fritz Jr. (Fritz 1978). The son's account has Fritz Sr. coming onto the Blue with cattle in the fall of 1885. The wife's account has Fritz and Wittum arriving in 1884 without cattle. Such differences point to the pitfalls of relying on testimony from memory, especially decades after the fact. In this case, I choose to follow Katy, because she lived closer in time to the actual events, and also her account appears to have been written down long before her son's. The manuscript by Lathrop n.d. (see Fritz 1985) has no definitive date, but circumstantial evidence in the manuscript files of Kathlyn Lathrop points to around 1940. By the time Fritz Jr. wrote his history, his mother was dead.

2

Cowboys, Farmers, and Others
The Early Blue Community

The first white man or pioneer, looking for a home site and a place to raise cattle, must have thought [the Blue] paradise indeed! Lush feed and plenty of water. They moved in, brought their families and built cabins and schools, all without the use of roads. They probably brought their few possessions in on their backs or horseback or perhaps on burros. Who knows? Families increased, a wagon road worked out to nearby towns. The river part was easier, it just wove in and out and around rocks or any obstacle. One wagon followed the tracks of another, and tracks washed away with each flood. Very little was done to improve it at first. Maybe for the lack of funds. Supplies could then be brought in easier. A post office and a mail route were established. More settlers came in. They built homes, mostly of logs, and built fireplaces. Meals were cooked on these or on fires outside. I doubt if anyone knows when the first cook stove was brought in. They ran their cattle and horses on the forest land. They raised some crops, a garden, planted orchards, milked cows, raised chickens, canned and dried their fruit and vegetables. There was some fishing along the river and wild game was plentiful, especially deer and turkey. There were also bear and mountain lion. Some people probably trapped the fur bearing animals for ready cash.

LULA MAE BROOKS (*Down on the Blue* 9–10)

THE SETTLING OF BLUE, ARIZONA, can be viewed as a late extension of the cattle-ranching frontier into the American interior.[1] Early pioneers—Fritz, Cosper, McKeen—who came to the Blue out of Texas, had previous experience working as cowboys for large outfits. Most likely, their imaginations took inspiration from the great cattle boom that swept over the western states in the second half of the nineteenth century.

Toles Cosper, after finding God's Country on the Blue, mustered his own and his family's resources and put together "a herd of around 500 head of herefords and longhorns," which he eventually took onto the Blue (Cosper 1940:3). Fritz and Whittum started their "ranch" in a different manner,

> by building their log cabin, and strong corrals; they fashioned their own branding irons and went to work. The wild cattle and horses that roamed this rugged wilderness may belong to anyone who had the strength and courage to master them, and there was no "law" to contend with. . . .
>
> [Then] they took up the idea of establishing a cattle ranch for themselves, realizing there was little local market for beef and that the Eastern markets were flooded, prices down to practically nothing.
>
> "But," they reasoned, "by the time we have anything to sell, perhaps the market will up a little." And that set the wheel of the cattle industry in motion along the Blue River. (Fritz 1985:iv)

In addition to branding "mavericks" as his own, Fritz bought "a few cows (about 60 head)" in Silver City and moved them onto the Blue (Fritz 1978:66).

> Up until 1890, Fritz shipped and sold around three or four hundred head of beef stock at eight to twelve dollars per head, and the prices were still going down. Fritz decided it best to try to build up his herd to better beef stock and hold them for better prices.
>
> Cosper had brought in thoroughbred Herefords and Fritz proceeded to buy ten Hereford bulls from Cosper, paying $100 each for them; then he set to *really* raising cattle. (Fritz 1985:xi)

Hugh McKeen owned five or six mares, and worked for the W.S. Ranch near Alma, New Mexico. That ranch

> had a number of wild cattle which had strayed into the Blue country. Due to the Indian raids, it was difficult to get cowboys who would go into that wild county. It took a full-fledged Texan to take that chance. Hugh was offered a good price for every head of stock he could gather and return to the W.S. range, so he took

the chance. And, thereby, his livelihood was earned until he could get into a business of his own. (McKeen 1982:166–167)

In a few years, McKeen had bought some cattle and was working for himself, ranching on the Blue.

He would ride hard all day and then come in and cook his dinner, which most of the time was lunch and dinner combined. After dinner he would go out and cut trees down and build fence or do some farming until bedtime. In other words, he, like others who made their start on Blue River, made it the hard way. (McKeen 1982:168–169)

No large cattle outfits came onto the Blue: in every case, ranching was started by young men who built up their enterprises. Cooperating as neighbors, they rounded up their cattle every fall to take to market. A trail drive of ten to eleven days brought the cattle to the railhead at Magdalena, New Mexico. With their proceeds, the ranchers would buy supplies to bring back to the Blue (*Down on the Blue* 63, 145; Fritz 1978:79).

Most Blue ranchers during the early years apparently practiced what historians have called the "Texas system": cattle were left mostly to care for themselves on a free, unfenced range, with little or no supplementary feeding or protection (Jordan 1993:210). (Ranchers today speak of the "Columbus" method—you let the cattle out at the beginning of the season, and at its end you go out to "discover" where they are.) Blue herds prospered in these early years, how much by natural increase and how much by purchase is unclear, but soon the biggest "outfits" were each running cattle well into the thousands. Toles's son James Cosper later estimated that at their "peak," presumably in the 1890s, the Cosper Y Bar Y had 6,000 head; the Fritz's XXX, about 2,500; and Hugh McKeen's HU Bar and Charlie Thomas's Flying Diamond each somewhere between 4,000 to 7,000 cattle (Cosper 1982:186; Hanrahan 1972).

Mr. McKeen ran cattle from Blue River, Arizona to Mogollon, New Mexico. At one time the records show he owned 5,277 head of cattle and 40 horses. Mr. McKeen once said that after he had accumulated a little and had a good herd of cattle, he would sit and watch those big steers come in to water and just wonder what he would do with all that money. (At that time they were worth from ten to fifteen dollars per head!). (McKeen 1982:163–164)

To which his wife, May Balke McKeen, commented that, "after 1902 he was relieved of the above anxiety; he had acquired a wife. Then he was kept busy working and wondering where the money was coming from to pay his bills. Of course, I felt sorry for him, so I got out and gave him a hand on the range." (McKeen 1982:169).

Although cattle ranching was important in pioneering the Blue, it is not the whole story. The first settlers, the Castos, as noted earlier, "cleared some land and raised a little hay and vegetables to live on and sold some to other people. Later on Granddad put in a vineyard and raised grapes and made wine to sell...," which hardly sounds like "Texas system" ranching. In fact, Casto was born in Illinois. His wife, "the first white woman on the Blue," was born in Maine. And while they may have acquired cattle eventually, there is no evidence they were in the ranching business. They appear to have been farmers (*Down on the Blue* 158).

A clearer case emerges from the "life story" written by Mattie Jane Johnson Graham, "the first unmarried white girl on Blue River," in the words of Katy Fritz (1985:vi). Her parents, John and Susan Johnson, hailed from Texas, and Mattie Jane always speaks of their home as a "ranch." But cows originally played only a small part in their household economy.

In May, 1887, Dad went over on Blue River and settled on some land. He cleared the brush and trees off and put in a crop and a garden. He had only one horse, Old Joe. He was a white horse and Dad rode him and also worked him to the plow when he put in the crops. Dad built a one-room cabin and the next June he came back for his family. He borrowed a horse from a neighbor to hitch with Old Joe to the wagon, to move us down to our new ranch home....

We had a cow and calf and a heifer and a few chickens. Dad loaded us and all our belongings into the wagon and we started for Blue River....

For two years we sure had it tough, but we took pop corn, cucumbers, tomatoes, cabbage, pumpkins and all the other vegetables we could raise [to the store in Luna] to pay on our grocery bill. Some times the cowboys would buy some of our corn to feed their horses....

The cowboys in the country were very kind to us. They told my father that when he found a mother cow dead, to take her calf and raise it for ourselves. Often this way we got a very good calf and we gradually got together a few head of cattle, but we had no milk cow so we started catching wild cows, ten or more at a time. We girls roped them and got them gentle so we could milk them.

When Mr. Johnson accumulated a little money for livestock, he bought not cattle but hogs to drive back from Clifton. He grew sugar cane to make molasses to sell, and bought a gristmill he ran by water power. As Mattie Jane tells, "We ground meal for everybody on Blue River, and ground wheat to make graham flour. I was the miller but *how I hated that mill*." The Johnsons were a farming family, even though Mr. Johnson called his "outfit" the "Rattlesnake Ranch." (Fritz 1985:vi; Graham 1953: 25–30)[2]

Other oral histories also mention "farming, "farms," and "homesteading" on the Blue in the period around the turn of the century (Cosper 1940:9–10; Fritz 1978:71). Of course, people who spend most of their time farming can also raise cattle to sell, and ranchers who run cattle for a living can also farm to provide feed for their cattle and food for their families. Later, they all did. Economic records no longer exist to classify the relative occupational emphasis of each family that moved onto the Blue, but it is clear some (mainly Texans) were ranchers by modern definition, while others were not at all in the cattle business; they were trying to make a living through farming and other pursuits. The two did not form antagonistic or socially exclusive groups: Mattie Jane Johnson married into the Graham family, who appear to be ranchers (Graham 1953:31); and Hugh McKeen the rancher married Mae Balke, the daughter of a German immigrant who was the first postmaster and justice of the peace for Blue and who "also had a small farm" (Fritz 1978:71).

During the 1890s and early 1900s a national discussion occurred over the differences between ranching and farming. Many advocated farming in the West to strengthen the country's agrarian base, replace "the barbarism of cattle ranching," and supplant the open range with the "civilization" that would come with large-scale homestead farming, irrigated or dry (Merrill 2002:40–43).

In his famous *Report on the Lands of the Arid Region of the United*

States, John Wesley Powell held that twenty inches or more of rainfall is necessary for successful agriculture without irrigation. But there were experts who believed dry farming was possible by certain methods with rainfall as low as ten or twelve inches per year. Without a record of measurements, they often failed to anticipate the large annual fluctuations common in the West. But thirsting for land, many homesteaders were willing to try dry farming, and Mormons in Utah had been successful at it. (Webb 1931:353, 366–68)

During the twentieth century, measurements indicate the Blue has received an average of about twenty inches per year, just at Powell's limit, with the upper Blue getting a little more, the lower Blue a little less. The summer monsoon concentrates most rainfall from July through October.[3] The Blue River also offers many opportunities for irrigation on a small scale, as the Mogollon native people apparently practiced it there. So it is not surprising that the Blue attracted settlers who meant to make their living by farming and maybe raise cattle too. It is unlikely they saw any contradiction between the two. Cattlemen farmed too. According to Aldo Leopold, "Orchards and alfalfa fields were started at each ranch" (Leopold 1921a:270). The national debate over ranching versus farming was irrelevant to the pragmatic concerns of people on the Blue. Open range or not, "ranchers" as well as "farmers" meant to settle and build homes, own animals, and grow crops. In the end, homesteaders ranched and ranchers homesteaded.

THE 1900 CENSUS

Yet the distinction between farming and stock raising remained, and emerges in U.S. Census Data. Unfortunately, the population schedules for the 1890 Census for the Territory of Arizona are unavailable, having burned in a fire.[4] But the 1900 Census data is available and provides the earliest picture of the Blue Community not drawn from oral history (U.S. Census Bureau 1900). This invaluable information is revealing, if sometimes puzzling.

The data that includes most of the Blue is found under "Precinct No. 15, Enumeration District 19."[5] No map of this district is provided, but it probably left out any settlement near the mouth of the Blue where it enters the San Francisco, for at the time these people were served by a wagon road from Clifton, separate from the one that entered the Blue near Fred Fritz's ranch. It appears to be this latter road along which the enumerator, Charles B. Keppler, recorded the population as he proceeded northward from Clifton, August 7, 1900. The beginning of the enumeration includes 24 people who by occupation appear to be living close to Clifton and not on the Blue: 5 teamsters, two cooks, a machinist, a mill man, a washerwoman, and their families. From where the census arrives at the Fritz ranch, 245 people are counted as living up the Blue River and its tributaries.

Of these 245 people on the Blue, the great majority are children: large families were the norm. Of children over seven, most are recorded as attending school four to six months of the year. Some are not attending school, but of these some nevertheless are said to read and write. The great majority of the adults are literate.

Only 54 individuals have listed their "occupation, trade, or profession." Wives and other females working in the home and on the farms and ranches do not have their "occupation" recorded—with one exception, a widow noted as a "housekeeper," though no lodgers are listed in her household. The remaining 53 persons with occupations are male. The occupations recorded may be those volunteered by the men themselves or by others speaking for them; but based on information given him, Mr. Keppler may also have helped determine the categories assigned to people.

Interestingly, no one is recorded as a "rancher." (This term would appear in the next Census of 1910, on voting lists beginning in 1912, and come to dominate in 1920 and after.) But 17 men are listed (or list themselves) as "cowboy," "cowman," or "stockman." At this time, "cowboy" did not have the connotation it later acquired of a hired hand. On the other hand, 24 men are recorded with the occupation of "farmer," "farming," or "granger" (one person). Twelve men give other occupations. The 1900 Census thus supports the view that farming played an important role on the Blue, which at that time was more than a "ranching" community.

The Census also allows us to look at households. There are 11 heads of household identified as "cowman, "cowboy," or "stockman." Fred Fritz is a "cowboy." So is his wife's brother, Fred Knapp, who worked in conjunction with Fritz. Another younger relative, Joe Fritz, is also a "cowboy" but is listed with people on the upper Blue. His name appears next to an older woman, A. L. White, who is "married" and has three young sons and a nephew, but whose husband is absent from the census. She is counted as "head" of the household, but no occupation is listed for her.

Has her husband gone to work elsewhere? Is Joe Fritz working as a "cowboy" for her? He is also listed as a "head" of household but is single.

Similar juxtapositions occur on the Blue census, tempting one to speculate on the practical arrangements necessary when a woman, for whatever reason, needed male help with stock raising and farming or a male needed female help to run a household. For instance, Joseph Mangano, a fourteen-year-old "cowboy" is listed as a "head" of household. His name appears next to twenty-six-year-old Olive Rogers, also a "head" of household who has 5 small children, is married, but whose husband is not in the census. Another Mangano, recorded as a "teamster," and his wife are old enough to be Joseph's parents, but they apparently live at a distance. The supposition arises that Joseph is being hired to work for Mrs. Rogers.

Leaving aside these small puzzles that cannot be solved, we can consider a better-documented early ranching family found together in the census: the Jones brothers, Henry as a "cowman" and Samuel as a "stockman." They were from Texas (see chapter 16, under "Bill and Barbara Marks").

> My dad, Henry, and his younger brother worked their way across West Texas. Dad worked for cattle companies and Samuel or Sam took care of a small herd of cattle that belonged to them. . . . Henry worked for big cow outfits during the sheep and cattle wars [between Magdalena and Socorro, NM].
>
> Henry was a line rider or hired gunman. Dad told me that killing between sheep and cattlemen got so bad they moved their camp beds every night to foil anyone slipping upon them and killing them in their sleep. . . .
>
> Dad also worked for a while at a livery stable in Magdalena. His brother, Sam, as I understand, went on West into Arizona, looking for a more suitable place to settle and found the Blue River. They then moved to the Blue in 1890 and homesteaded what is now known as the Marks Ranch. (Jerry Jones, writing about his father, *Down on the Blue* 119)

Next to the Jones brothers and their families in the census is a single "cowboy" who possibly worked for them.

There are 5 other male heads of families on the Blue denoted in the census as cattlemen.

1. [Illegible] Jackson. "Cow Man." Birthplace: Texas.

2. Charles Thomas. "Cowboy." Birthplace: Texas. (He is the one mentioned by Toles Cosper as running a very large herd in these years.)

3. J.M. Jones. "Cowboy." Birthplace: Texas. (Presumably unrelated to the other Jones, as no one with his initials appears in their family history. He does not own but rents his house, so may be a hired cowboy.)

4. M. Baldwin. "Cow Man." Birthplace: Utah.

5. Charles Adair. "Cow Man." Birthplace: Utah.

What stands out is that of the 11 heads of households identified with cattle raising, eight are from Texas. Two are from Utah, and the young Mangano was born in Arizona. From family histories and where their children are recorded being born, we know many of these Texan cattlemen had range experience in New Mexico. Scholars have differed on the influence of West Texas in the early cattle industry in Arizona (Wilson 1966–67; and Jordan 1975, 1993:230), but certainly Texans predominated on the Blue. The four largest ranching outfits at the time on the Blue (cited above by Jim Cosper) were all established by men from Texas: Fritz, McKeen, Thomas and Toles Cosper.

Hugh McKeen is not in the Blue census, because his headquarters was in New Mexico, but Toles Cosper? His occupation is listed as "farmer." This is odd, since the only testimony of anyone on the Blue having an animus against farming comes from Toles.

> By this time [1909] his family had practically all grown up, married off and began building homes of their own; his sons following the cattle business and his daughters becoming the wives of cattlemen. None of Toles Cosper family seemed inclined to revert to the farming industry [Toles's father had pursued], which pleased Toles very much.
>
> He had endeavored to teach his children that "It is good to be a son of the soil—if you like it—but there is nothing in life that can be more soul-satisfying than the call of the open range." (Cosper 1940:9)

We do not know how much Toles's valuation is a product of later reflection; nor do we know if Toles told the census taker in 1900 that he was a "farmer" or whether someone else (his wife Lou Ella?) applied the term. We do know that the Y Bar Y had a big apple orchard and a variety of crops.

> Toles raised sugar cane and made his own molasses. He raised peanuts and melons on the east side of the river. There were cellars built into the side of the hill back of the house where apples and other food were kept.... Though they were cattle people they also raised chickens and hogs. Lou Ella always planted an immense garden." (*Down on the Blue* 203)

Twenty male heads of household on the Blue were recorded as "farmers" or "farming." Only 3 of these were born in Texas, though at least 3 others (including Toles) appear to have lived there. Other birth states include Tennessee (3); Alabama (2); Missouri (2); Pennsylvania (2); and North Carolina, Mississippi, Kentucky, Illinois, Utah, Idaho, Arizona, and Germany (1 each). Four other "farmers" appear to be sons working under their farmer fathers.

Two farmers had sons listed as "cowboys"—whether taking care of the family livestock or working for hire for others is unclear. And 3 "cowboys" listed as renting, not owning their homes, appear to be hired hands of the Cosper Y Bar Y.

The 13 other occupations listed in the census reveal economic diversity in the early Blue community. There is a logger born in Utah, and a "millman" (lumber or grain?) from Virginia. Men cut timber on the Blue to send down the river to the mining operations in Clifton. The census records 3 teamsters, 2 from Utah and 1 from New Mexico; the latter is the only person with a Hispanic surname in the Blue census. Also included are a merchant, C.B. Martins, born in Mississippi; a blacksmith (Texas); a carpenter (Tennessee) who lived with his son, designated a "musician"! There is a "livery man" (Ohio) who presumably kept a stable, and a "common laborer" (Texas) who may have worked for him. There is a "miner," the son of a "farmer," who since there is no history of mining on the Blue might have worked in the Clifton/Morenci mines but kept a home for his family at his father's farm. Finally, there is Mrs. Ford from California, the "housekeeper."

BLUE COMMUNITY LIFE

"Blue" was never an actual town—only a community of people scattered along the Blue River. "Blue" appears on maps of Arizona due to the post office of that name. But the original post office on the Blue, established in 1894, was named "Whittum" after the unlucky pioneer slain by the Apache. The first postmaster was Isaac Casto, and the post office was located at his home. In 1897 Max Balke, the German immigrant, became postmaster, and moved the post office to the lower Blue near Hugh McKeen's ranch, a place named "Benton," after another of the slain pioneers.

Benton showed some sign of developing into a small town around the turn of the century. It had a sawmill. It had a school. It had a small store run by Mr. Balke (identified in the 1900 Census as a "farmer") that doubled as the Post Office. Balke was also Justice of the Peace.

> He was law and order on that part of Blue River. He held court, buried and married people. He performed the wedding ceremony for his two oldest children, Mae and George. He married Mae, who was the second child, to Hugh McKeen. Both families lived on the same flat. At that time quite a few other families lived in the near vicinity and about 25 children attended the school. . . . (Freddie Fritz Jr., *Down on the Blue* 219)

George Balke married a daughter of Toles Cosper.

In 1898, the Post Office name was changed to "Blue," to reflect what everyone called the region. And in 1900, the location was moved back again to the upper Blue to the general store of Charlie Martin.

By the turn of the century, "a number of people had located in around the junction of the Blue River with the Frisco." They comprised another nascent settlement with a store, saloon, and post office, first called "Carpenter" after the owner. After some killings at the saloon, Carpenter left in 1904, and the Boyles brothers, cattle raisers, took over, closed the saloon, and renamed the post office "Boyles." There was also a school of "over 40 pupils" to serve the large families living at that end of the Blue (Fritz 1978:71–72).

As noted, the 1900 Census shows most children on the Blue attending school four to six months of the year. On the upper Blue the earliest school appeared in the 1890s. Blue residents organized the schools and chose the teachers, who were paid by the county. Home schooling also took place. "Many of the ranchers hired teachers to live on their ranches to teach their children. A few young people went out to live with relatives or friends in various towns in order to attend school." (Cleo Coor, *Down on the Blue* 99)

Fred Fritz Jr. describes his experience.

> It was 12 miles to the Boyles School and 8 to Benton. When my sister and I became of school age, my parents hired a private teacher for six months of each year and we stayed home at the ranch until we passed the exams for the eight grade. . . . I am grateful to those private teachers for what they taught me. Much of it was at night as father's health wasn't too good and he needed me [to work]. (Fritz 1978:76–79)

His father's health "wasn't too good" because he had been mauled by a grizzly bear.

Fritz also describes each of his teachers through eight grades, or years: all were young women from outside the Blue who came to live temporarily at the ranch. His last teacher had him memorizing recitations, "like Longfellow's *Barefoot Boy*, Whittier's *School Days*, Gray's *Elegy*, Lincoln's *Gettysburg Address*, and many others. Through this practice I gained confidence in myself in trying to solve the problems and challenges I faced."

After eight years of schooling, his mother took him to the Blue School thirty miles up the river where he passed the exam for grade school. He never attended high school (Fritz 1978:76–79), but his home schooling was the foundation for a later, eminent career as a public leader and state legislator.

Ben Tenney recounts another experience. He was seven when his family moved near to the Benton school.

> We went to school there that winter of 1900 and 1901. We had a school of about thirty-two students from one to eight grades. The thing that stands out in my memory then was Bob Phillips, who was about seventeen years old and he wore a .45 six shooter strapped to him all the time. As I think back now the teacher, Mr. McGinnin, was afraid of him and gave him a wide berth at all times and seemed to be very careful not to cross his path. (Ben R. Tenney, *Down on the Blue* 54)

Bob Phillips did end up killing, not his teacher, but a man who had whipped him with a rope. Mr. Balke held an inquest, but "Bob was turned loose and was back in school." The Phillips family appear as "farmers" on the census.

If schools were present from almost the beginning of the settlement of the Blue, churches were not. Cleo Cosper Coor later summarized religion on the Blue.

> There never has been a church on the Blue, but from time to time they have held Sunday School in the schoolhouse, and at other times a minister has held church services every other Sunday or once a month. . . . Some people on the Blue are very devout and feel the closeness of God through a constant contact with nature. (*Down on the Blue* 235)

A Sunday school met at times in the 1910s in the school building Toles Cosper had donated on his property (*Down on the Blue* 103). But the nearest churches were in Luna or Alpine or Clifton, places that took hours to reach by horse and wagon. People on the Blue appear to have had diverse denominational allegiances, if they had any at all. There appear to have been a few Mormons and Catholics among a larger number of Protestants. Information, however, is mostly lacking. For whatever reason—perhaps because it was seen as divisive or too personal a topic—religion is rarely mentioned in the individual Blue histories. Important as it may have been to some individuals, religion played little role in community life.

The very privation and semi-isolation of the pioneer households stimulated people to create social occasions to enjoy. Katy Fritz gives some examples.

> Despite the dangers of ranch life in a wilderness such as this, the ranchers managed to enjoy life to a certain extent. Social activities consisted of log rollings, quilting bees, apron parties, picnics and barbeques, and sometimes a dumb supper.
>
> The log rollings: When someone wished to build a new house, barn or corral, the neighbor men would gather in to help, while the womenfolks came along to prepare a feast. Then after the work was finished, fiddles were tuned, banjos and guitars strung, and the dust knocked out of harmonicas, and the dance

began. Quadrilles, square dances, polka, schottish, rye waltz, and Spanish mazurka were the most popular dances of the time.

Apron parties were a lot of fun: All the ladies would make an apron—leaving the hem unfinished—and fashion a necktie like each apron; the ties were drawn from a box by the men, blind-folded, and the tie matching the apron determined the ladies' escort for the evening; the men must hem the apron by hand. (Fritz 1985:xv–xvii)

"Dumb suppers" (in which people maintained silence) were also a way of pairing up "unmarried folks."

But *all* the old accounts of life on the Blue mentioned the big parties Toles Cosper threw as the most memorable entertainments.

The week-long dances at the Y Bars are legend. The family cooked for about a week before the party started. . . . They pit-barbecued beef. They fed the guests' horses. . . . They had two orchestras, one to play at night and one to play during the day. . . .

People for fifty miles around rode their horses to attend these annual fiestas. The Cosper ladies (and men, except Toles) would, days beforehand, begin to cook and bake in preparation for the big event. Long tables were set up in the large hallway. Here one could find meats of various kinds: beef, venison, bear, wild pig, ham, grouse, turkey, and real mountain trout. Such a display of home-baked breads, cakes, cookies, and pies I had never before witnessed. . . . But I must not neglect to mention the famous Western Cowboy Sour-Dough biscuit. Only very few could excel the quality of the biscuit built here. The pot with beans and ham-hocks could be detected by nose at all times. Sur-prisingly, high-kicking spirits played a very minor role on these occasions as men did their imbibing aside in respect to ladies. . . .

The children were allowed to stay up and dance a little while then we were all put to bed in one bedroom. There were wall to wall kids! Kids lying cross ways like cord wood, kids on the floor, kids on chairs, kids everywhere. . . .

Toles always loved to make a speech to his guests on these occasions. He called his wife to his side and said, "This is my quail." There he stood in his cowboy Levis with the under drawers turned down over the top of the Levis. . . . (various accounts, *Down on the Blue* 102, 201, 206)

There was an orchestra from Clifton—five Spaniards—and they were good, too. He'd get them up there. They would dance from sundown to sunup, sleep part of the day, and get up and eat and go rodeo or start dancing again. And of all the parties that were there, I never knew anyone to get out of line. I never knew a quarrel, even, from any of them. There would be a hundred people there, sometimes. [Toles] would feed them all and bed them down; usually find beds for at least part of the women and kids. During the daytime, men would get out in shade or sun, whichever they wanted, and stretch out and sleep. (James Cosper, Toles's son, Cosper 1982:137)

With his relative wealth in cattle, his sponsorship of one of the first schools, and his large family—six children and a raft of grandchildren who intermarried throughout the Blue and neighboring communities—Toles became a patriarch of local society, known in his later years as "Uncle Toles." Geographically as well as socially, his Y Bar Y Ranch on the "middle Blue" between what people called the "upper" and "lower" Blue, was the center of the community for many years.

According to Toles, in 1898 he sold a good number of cattle and for the first time made a large profit. "I reckon it sort of went to my head." He built a new home, and bought a status symbol typical of the era

[H]e decided that now he had money, his daughters needed a musical education, and promptly sent an order to Sears & Roebuck for a piano to be shipped to Silver City, N.M. That was the first piano to be brought into that neck o' the woods.

He had "the devil's own time" getting that music box out to his ranch. Part of the trail was so steep and narrow that even a burro pack train had difficulty getting through; the piano was hauled part of the way by wagon, part by burro-pack, and carried by hand part of the way.

Apaches on a hunting party were overcome by curiosity, and helped to carry the piano to Toles's ranch. They "were anxious to 'hear music from the big box' and Uncle Toles admits that there wasn't a person on the place who could really play the thing." But always able to improvise, Toles "did his best with what few cords he had learned on the organ, back in Texas" (Cosper 1940:7–9).

A few years later, with similar shipping problems, the Jones family kept up with the Cospers and brought a second piano onto the Blue.

NOTES

1. See Jordan 1993:7–9. "Ranching," however, can be an ambiguous term. Sayre (1999:240–244, and 2002:51–54), following Ingold (1980), distinguishes "ranching" from "pastoralism," the latter marked by common access to land and the appropriation of the natural increase of the animals, while land in "ranching" is individually allocated, and livestock production is dominated by market inputs and considerations. In this view, the early stage of Blue "ranching" is better seen as "pastoralism" in transition to "ranching."

2. To appreciate how elastic the term "ranch" can be, one should know that W.R. Hearst always called San Simeon, his art-filled villa/castle on the California coast, (without irony) his "ranch" (Travel Channel special on San Simeon, July 10, 2003). See also the discussion in Sayre 2002:106–07, 120–25.

3. According to the website of the Western Regional Climate Center, www.wrcc.dri. edu, the average annual precipitation of Blue, Arizona, from November 1903 through August 1989 was 20.73 inches with over half, 11.99 inches, falling in the four months from July through October. A more recent measurement on www.usclimatedata.com (2015) records 21.18 as Blue's yearly average.

4. Communication from Karen Compton of the Regional Office of Census in Denver, Colorado. The manuscripts perished before the time when microfilms could be made of them.

5. The 1900 Census schedule listed people by name, relationship to head of household, race, sex, date of birth and age, marital status, number of years married, number of children living and deceased, and "nativity"—state and country of birth and parents' birth—as well as citizenship. Also asked are the "Occupation, Trade or Profession of each person Ten Years of age and over;" "Education" in terms of school attendance and whether the person can read, write, and speak English; and if the person owns or rents their farm or home. Sometimes spaces are left blank, and sometimes blotches on the old microfilm obscure them.

3

Blue Country Hurt

Overgrazing, Drought, and Flood

During the severe drought which began in about 1899 and lasted until about 1903 . . . water dried up and cattle died in great numbers . . . and all ranchers took a great loss. . . . [T]here was no way to protect your range from over grazing by others, consequently there was no effort made on the part of the rancher to reduce numbers. A low estimate would be 15 cattle [then] to 1 now (1964). . . . We all had too many cattle on the range back in those days. There was no incentive to try and save forage, you couldn't, other cattle moved in on you, consequently the range, especially around permanent waters, was abused. . . .

In addition to the large number of cattle on the range at the turn of the century there were also thousands of goats and large numbers of horses and wild burros. On our particular range there were nine different goat outfits. Most of the goats were gone by 1910 but the scars they made are still here. *It was in those early years that the country was hurt* [italics in original].

FRED FRITZ JR., *Down on the Blue* 224)

IN THE LAST DECADES of the nineteenth century, a great cattle boom swept out of Texas and over the American West. It was fueled by a number of converging factors: open range with free access to grazing; the elimination of the buffalo and the Indian threat; the extension of railroads to ship cattle to market; and ample finance capital in the eastern U.S. and Great Britain, which in seeking profits allowed ranchers to vastly enlarge their herds. The speculative boom crested in the early 1880s in Texas and the mid-1880s in Arizona. Crashes ensued: overstocking combined with drought or severe winter led to depressed prices as cattlemen were forced to sell on glutted markets.

A long-term result of the cattle boom and bust was the gradual closing of the open range and the movement to a more modern form of
ranching, one that fenced pastures and provided feed for animals whose
numbers were regulated by owner or government to protect land from
overstocking. Before this transformation occurred, however, there was
significant ecological damage (Abruzzi 1995; Bahre and Shelton 1996;
Bentley 1898:5–14; Haskett 1935:25–42; Jordan 1975:238–239; Sayre
1999, 2002:28–54; Sheridan 1995:140–143; Wagoner 1952:45–55; Webb
1931:227–244).

The Blue passed through the same process of open land; cattle boom;
overstock; drought; price crashes; environmental damage; and transition
to a new, more managed form of ranching. Yet its experiences were distinctive in certain ways. The sequence of events started later on the Blue
than in most of Arizona—and would continue longer. When drought
and crash occurred on the overstocked ranges of southern Arizona, cattle
raising was just beginning on the Blue in 1885. None of the personal histories mentions drought at that time; if rainfall was down, it apparently
did not affect early ranching there.

> When the first settlers arrived, grass appeared to be abundant
> along the Blue River and the surrounding mountains. Accord-
> ing to [Aldo] Leopold, "All the old settlers agree that the bot-
> toms of the Blue River, at the time of settlement in about 1885,
> were stirrup high in gramma grass, and covered with groves of
> mixed hardwoods and pine, the banks were lined with willows
> and abundant with trout." (USDA 1983b, McDonough)

Nor is there mention of drought or depression in the 1890s when
other parts of Arizona suffered these chronic problems. Toles Cosper
made his first, large, profitable sale in 1898. And during the 1890s "many
cattle were brought into the country," perhaps in response to bad conditions in other parts of Arizona (Fritz 1978:68). Too many cattle would be
brought in. Like ranchers elsewhere in the Southwest, cattlemen on the
Blue initially did not fully comprehend the limits of the land or the problem of overstocking and overgrazing. Naturally, they wanted to prosper
in the cattle market and provide a good living for their families. But even
if they had been restrained in their goals and possessed a knowledge of
their environment that could only be learned through hard experience
over time, the early ranchers would still have had difficulty in warding

off the overstocking and destruction that occurred on the Blue as it did elsewhere.

Just as it still occurs in some situations in the world, ecological damage proceeded from a lack of property rights. This was not in cattle, where property rights were enforced with vigilante justice, but lack of property rights in land—or rather, in enough land. Men like Toles Cosper, Hugh McKeen and Fred Fritz came to what they considered wilderness and "squatted" there, as they put it, in full confidence that they had a right to the land they settled on. They were not philosophers but probably would have agreed with John Locke, who wrote in *Two Treatises of Government* in 1689 that

> every Man has a *Property* in his own *Person*. This no Body has any Right to but himself. The *Labour* of his Body, and the *Work* of his Hands, we may say, are properly his. Whatsoever then he removes out of the State that Nature hath provided, and left it in, he hath mixed his *Labour* with, and joyned to it something that is his own, and thereby makes it his *Property*." (Locke 1993:128)

The settlers who came to the Blue mixed their labor with nature, with the wild land they found, and believed they owned the product of their labor and whatever lands they had occupied and developed. This outlook already had a long history in America, and had been legally promoted and encouraged by the Homestead Act of 1862, the main federal law governing the creation of property rights out of the vast public domain of western America.

Passed by the Republicans after the secession of the southern states, the Homestead Act embodied what has been called the "Jeffersonian vision" of an agrarian America: that the country should be composed predominantly of small farms owned by the families that worked on them. This vision was opposed to large landholdings, as existed notably in the slave South, which were seen as pernicious to republican virtue and democratic government. "A nation in which each family owned a plot of land—large enough to subsist on but not so large as to give the landowner undue power or influence—would, [Jefferson] hoped, remain virtuous and free" (Hess 1992:65). Lincoln and the "free-soil" Republicans hoped the same. To implement this vision, the Homestead Act offered a quarter section of public land (160 acres) at virtually no cost to those who would settle on it and "improve" it over a five-year period.

The Homestead Act accomplished its purpose wherever rainfall or irrigation could support farming. But west of the 100th meridian of the U.S—a line running north to south approximately through the middle of the Dakotas, Nebraska, Kansas, and Texas—rainfall for farming was inadequate (except in the Pacific Northwest), and possibilities for irrigation were limited.

Generous and well intentioned, the idea behind the Homestead Act failed to correspond to the ecological reality of much of the American West. John Wesley Powell, the famed explorer of the Southwest, warned as early as 1878 in a report to the Interior Department that the methods of land distribution and agriculture prevailing in the eastern U.S. would not work in the dry West. Land in the West was generally suitable only for grazing, and quarter sections of 160 acres were not the way to parcel out the land for grazing. Holdings must be much bigger, 2,500 acres or more, to support a single ranching family. Powell's warning, however, was something the government and politicians back East were either unable to comprehend or unwilling to accept. They preferred to view the West as a fertile garden (Shabecoff 1993:62–63).

Therefore, under the Homestead Act—its restrictions as well as its opportunities—the first pioneers on the Blue established property rights to what became their homes and later their privately "patented" quarter sections—none larger. Invariably, the 160-acre section chosen was one with water, in the river bottom or along a tributary creek. Land without water was useless. They could farm on the quarter section, and did, but by itself it was too little land for serious cattle raising.

As Powell predicted, many settlers of the West turned to livestock as their best alternative for making a living, and even those farming acquired some cattle, as we have seen on the Blue. And if the settlers did not own enough land to graze their cattle, this situation, at least at first, posed no problem. After all, the public domain around them was theirs to use—for free. As land without permanent water was useless for homesteading, the abundant pastures of the uplands remained "open range." The settlers along the river had unimpeded usufruct of the unoccupied grazing lands around them, and it was theirs in the sense that the land was everybody's. In the tradition of English law, it was a "commons."

My father filed on the place that is known as the Hale Place today. The first summer we lived in tents. Dad planted a garden and planted the field in corn. . . . The field was not fenced. We kept the cattle out in the daytime and prayed they would not destroy the crop at night. In those days, there were no fences—it was all open range. I suppose the ranchers had a certain place they tried to keep their herds in, but they could roam at will. Consequently, everyone's cattle were mixed. (Katie Hale Barnes, *Down on the Blue* 145)

There was open range and nobody was fenced and everybody just let their cattle run. The cattle from all ranches ran together. Everybody worked together in the fall to gather their cattle and get them off to the railroad in Magdalena, NM. They rounded them up and sold them once a year. (Grace Johnson, *Down on the Blue* 63)

The range was open not just to the cattle of the people settled on the Blue, but also to the cattle of neighboring settlements. People who lived in Alpine and Nutrioso in Arizona, and in Luna and across the Blue Range in New Mexico, would drive their herds into the Blue country to winter them. Such sharing of the land could be seen as a virtue. An old-timer muses,

the Blue River country was a source of security for winter range for all who had a small bunch of cattle. Those people had no other way to put them through the winter. I have often thought, "What good neighbors we had in the Blue country." They had that old American spirit that we were free to use that country as well as they. That was the freedom we had in this U.S. in those days. Now you never see any such freedom. In fact, I can't see any freedom any place, it is all dictatorship on everything. If we have a milk cow we have to keep her in the corral. (Ben R. Tenney, *Down on the Blue* 55)

What Mr. Tenney does not see, or say, however, is that the practice of an open range, free to all, would eventually be untenable on the Blue as elsewhere on the public lands of the West, as experience proved. The quotation from Fred Fritz Jr. at the beginning of this chapter shows that, at least in retrospect, some ranchers did understand the predicament of "free" land. Through its policies, the U.S. government had created a situation that in the environmental literature of today is called "the tragedy of the commons" (Hardin 1968:1243–48). Common use leads to over-use and eventually environmental degradation.

The paradigm is as follows. The first settlers to homestead the federal range find plenty of grass to feed their livestock. As more settlers arrive, however, livestock numbers on the open range grow to exceed the land's carrying capacity—the amount of livestock that can graze it without damaging future capacity. This overgrazing is predictable if no system exists to regulate the use of the range. In the absence of private owner-ship of the land, there is no incentive to limit one's own stock grazing. If you do so, then someone else's stock will take the available grass, and your restraint will have been for nothing. So your incentive is to graze the land first and completely with as many livestock as possible. There is no incentive to conserve the "free" resource. If each rancher follows this incentive, the result is severe overgrazing.

On the other hand, if one *did* own the land, it would be in one's long-term interest *not* to overgraze it but to protect its value and conserve grass for future use. Government policy, however, had eliminated this incentive for the Western ranchers who depended on the public domain for pasture they were not allowed to buy or otherwise acquire as their own property. Ironically, in striving to promote the ascendency of small, family farming and ranching in the arid West, the government created conditions that would frustrate it. Ideologically blinded by the homestead myth and the Jeffersonian vision of America, the federal government in effect promoted not only overgrazing but inevitable conflict over water and forage among its citizens on the frontiers of "free" land.

Drought and Flood

By 1900, Blue country was as full of livestock and people as it would ever be. The 245 people counted in the census that year living above the Fritz ranch, plus the number living lower on the Blue, would put the popula-tion at about 300—the same estimate an old cowman later gave to Aldo Leopold (Leopold 1921a:270). More than forty ranches or farms lined the Blue valley, and homesteaders were still arriving.

No one could accurately estimate the number of livestock there at the time, but all agree the number was extravagantly high compared to later standards. The four biggest outfits had together upward of 10,000 cattle by some estimates, but many others on the Blue and from outside the

Blue also ran cattle there. A Forest Service Agent in 1905 gave an estimate of 15,000 cattle, 1,500 horses and 35,000 goats on the lower Blue alone (Hunt 1905:7)! A later Forest Supervisor would comment, "The abundance of grasses was very much over estimated as to carrying capacity. The Blue River and surrounding area was stocked heavily" (USDA, 1983b, McDonough). James Cosper, a son of Toles, concurs: "It doesn't seem reasonable, but it seems that there was as much grass in those days when it was carrying that many cattle as there is now. They just trampled it out, so many cattle, they just killed the grass out for several years" (Cosper 1982:136).

As before in the West, overstocking, when combined with drought, brought disaster. The five years 1899 through 1904 saw precipitation well below normal—"a most severe drought" (Fritz 1978:68; Bahre 1996:2). The damage done to the upland pastures by overgrazing in these conditions, while undocumented, can be imagined.

> During the late 1890s and around 1900 a drought hit the country and lasted until the feed on the winter range around Springerville and St. John's were in bad shape. Some of the cattlemen began throwing large herds of cattle into the Blue River. As the drought continued, more cattle were thrown into Blue River until it was heavily grazed. A rancher named Wall was reported to have thrown hundreds of head of cattle into Bush Creek, depleting the range until many of them died, and others had to be removed to prevent a complete loss from starvation. (*Pioneer Meeting*: n.d.)

Cattle that survived concentrated on the river bottom near the remaining water. Competition arose over this prime land and over the water itself. Cattle raisers relied more on growing feed for their stock, which could be done only on irrigated fields along the river bottom. Serious conflict often erupted over poorly defined land and water rights.

> With the coming of feed raising on Blue River, fences became a necessity, which at first, was a bone of contention for the range riders, that brought about range feuds, quarrels, and killings, over boundary lines, cut fences, and water holes, and furnished what some of them took as an excuse to "shoot out" many other disagreements. (Cosper 1940:9)

Several such killings occurred in the first decade of the twentieth century—with no one brought to justice.

In addition to cattle overgrazing there was goat overgrazing. And in addition to grazing, there was large-scale timber cutting to serve the mines downstream around Clifton. How these factors contributed to erosion are more fully discussed in the next chapter.

The climax to disaster was the floods. Heavy rains replaced drought conditions, and a series of floods occurred in December 1904 and January 1905 and again in December 1905. James ("Little Jim") Cosper, and his father Toles were in Clifton not long before Christmas 1904, delivering cattle and buying groceries and "Christmas things," when it started raining. They loaded their mules and headed towards the Blue overland, camping because the San Francisco River had flooded out the wagon road. When they reached Pigeon Creek, normally a small stream, it was an uncrossable river.

> We walked on down toward the mouth of the canyon and looked off in the Blue, and you could see lots of cottonwood trees and sycamore and all kinds of trees—great big old trees—going down end over end. There was a lot of timber on this creek then. We stayed there three days. It rained day and night. [After two more days walking and camping out] the next day we packed up and went into the [Cosper] ranch. It didn't look like the same place, at all. Out in front of the creek was a big bottom with timber on it—a pretty stream down there. There wasn't a tree left on that flat; it took them all. Dad had some big corrals there—there was no sign of a corral or nothing. . . .
>
> Q: That changed the character of Blue River forever, I guess?
>
> A: Yes, it did. It will never be the same again. It was a good road all the way down there. . . . My dad would hook up the buggy and leave the ranch up there and trot down to Clifton in forty-five minutes or an hour. The only place you slowed down was going off the bank, crossing that creek channel. (Cosper 1982:139–40)

The wagon road from Clifton up the San Francisco and Blue rivers, which connected all the Blue watershed and went as far as Alpine and Luna, was wiped out. It was rebuilt during the summer but again destroyed by the floods of December 1905. It was never subsequently rebuilt.

A report by W.W.R. Hunt, the Forest Service agent who surveyed the area right after the December 1905 flood, says that the earlier floods destroyed "75% of the little farms along the San Francisco and the Blue." They washed away the northern end of the town of Clifton, and damaged the plant of the Arizona Copper Company. But the flood of December 1905 was worse and "completed the ruin of the agricultural lands along the rivers" (Hunt: 1905:5).

Floods recurred in 1906 and 1907. Fred Fritz Jr. recounts that

> the flood of 1906 washed the barns away and came up to the door of Uncle Dick and Aunt Theresa's house. They became disgusted and father bought their interest in the ranch and they moved back to Fredericksburg with their five children. . . .
>
> After the high floods of 1905–06 and 07, many people left Blue River. Many of the small farms were washed away. The Blue River Road, north and south in Eastern Arizona between Safford and Duncan Valleys to Alpine and Springerville, was gone. The post office at Benton . . . closed. Mr. Balke was the post-master. . . . After the big floods, the Balke and McKeen families moved to Alma, New Mexico and the school at Benton ceased to exist. Also in those early days there was a post office, store, saloon and school at the mouth of the Blue. The post office was called Boyles. Today, no one lives there. (Fritz 1978:68, 71)

The next large flood hit the area in 1916, with others intermittently up to the present. Like droughts, floods would be a continuing, if sporadic, feature of life on the Blue.

In addition to erosion and flooding, another process, less dramatic and unnoticed at the time, began to alter the Blue. In fact, the development occurred widely over the Southwest. Overgrazing led to gradual displacement of grasses by piñon, juniper, and other woody species. The process was reinforced by the Forest Service's historic program of fire suppression—now understood to be badly misguided—which allowed woody species to spread unchecked at the expense of open grassland (Abruzzi 1995:88; Bahre 1991:118–120; Herbel 1986:8–9; Hirt 1989:178; Leopold 1924; Wood 1988:34).

Three consequences ensued. First, the grazing potential of the land was reduced. Second, without grassy cover to hold it back, heavy rain could erode the soil and flow more swiftly into the canyons, increasing the incidence and damage of floods. But third, the expansion of woody species also meant that rainwater that did penetrate the soil would more likely be sucked up by the trees and transpired, rather than left to percolate slowly towards the river. So, a diminishment of the normal flow of the Blue occurred over time, together with an increase in the ferocity of floods. The settlers eventually noticed these signs. Many people who grew up on the Blue remember it running more water. Grace Johnson, who moved to the Blue in 1913 when she was eighteen years old, remembered in 1986,

> there used to be a lot more water in the Blue than there is now. There was enough water that at one time the miners in Clifton floated their logs down the river to Clifton from the Blue. They cut the logs up above the Box and floated them clear to Clifton. Not only was there more water, but it wasn't so rocky. There are a lot more boulders now. There used to be lots more land. Willows grew along the banks, not so much any cottonwoods and big trees the way it is now. . . . I guess that's what happened to the water. In fact it dries up sometimes in the summer lots of places. It didn't used to ever, ever do that. We used to have plenty of water in the ditches for our cattle, for our farming, and for everything. We just took the irrigation water into the ditches out of the river. . . .
>
> There used to be lots of ranches on Blue River; good sized ranches with quite a few cattle. There used to be lots more land. Now the floods have taken all the dirt away until it's just a rocky boulder bed. There were lots of fields and lots of orchards. (*Down on the Blue* 62–63)

4

Aldo Leopold and Erosion on the Blue
"This Smiling Valley" Ruined?

To sum it all up, we the community, have "developed" Blue River by overgrazing the range, washing out half-a-million in land, taking the profits out of the livestock industry, cutting the ranch homes by two-thirds, destroying conditions necessary for keeping families in the other third, leaving the timber without an outlet to the place where it is needed, and now we are spending half-a-million to build a road around this place of desolation which we have created. And to replace this smiling valley which nature gave us free, we are spending another half-a-million to reclaim an equal acreage of desert in some place where we do not need it nearly as badly nor can use it nearly so well. This, fellow-citizens, is Nordic genius for reducing to possession the wilderness.

ALDO LEOPOLD in 1922 (Leopold 1949:627)

AT THE TIME OF THE FLOODS of 1904–06, most of Blue country fell within the boundaries of the Black Mesa Forest Reserve created in 1898. In response to the floods, the remainders of the Blue watershed were added to the Reserve. The rationale for this addition was to promote government action to mitigate the conditions causing the flooding. The U.S. National Forest System was evolving, with the U.S. Forest Service formed early in the twentieth century. These developments had great future importance for the Blue and its inhabitants. The Apache National Forest, headquartered in Springerville, Arizona, was created in 1908 out of the Black Mesa Reserve,. It included the Blue River country.

The new Forest counted Aldo Leopold among its staff. In American environmental circles Leopold today is widely recognized, indeed revered for his writings on wild nature and conservation ethics, but most especially for his early advocacy for creating wilderness areas within the National Forests. He began his career with the U.S. Forest Service in the

Southwest, where he began developing his ideas. His initial posting as a freshly graduated forester in 1909 was to the newly created Apache National Forest as a "forest assistant," and his first important assignment there was actually on the Blue, as crew chief of a reconnaissance party taking timber inventory.

The two years he was stationed on the Apache Forest gave Leopold a good opportunity to know the Blue and its people, whom he befriended. He appreciated the excellent hunting the country offered and relished the wildness there, later calling the Blue "this smiling valley" (Leopold 1946:629; Leopold 1949:133; Meine 1988:87–93).[1] Leopold's classic, *A Sand County Almanac,* speaks several times of the Blue in lyrical terms (1949:133 and passim).

When he arrived on the Blue, memories of the droughts and floods were fresh in the minds of the settlers and Forest Service personnel there. As an assistant district forester based in Albuquerque, Leopold began addressing the problem of erosion he had witnessed around the Southwest—quite possibly first on the Blue. In 1922 at a meeting of the New Mexico Association for Science he gave a paper entitled "Erosion as a Menace to the Social and Economic Future of the Southwest" (Leopold 1946). He led off by citing the Blue as what he termed "an extreme example" of the disastrous cost of erosion.

From his own knowledge of conditions in thirty different valleys in Arizona and New Mexico National Forests, Leopold found only three where there was no erosion, six where it was "slight," nine "started," eight "partly ruined," and four "ruined." The Blue River he placed in the "ruined" category. He cites his data for Blue River, reproduced in table 1.

TABLE 1. ALDO LEOPOLD: THE COST OF EROSION IN THE BLUE

	ORIGINAL [1900]	PRESENT [1922]	LOSS THROUGH EROSION
Cultivable land	4,052 acres	472 acres	3,580 acres
Est. value [per acre]	$100	$150	
	$395,200[sic]	$70,800	$324,400
No. homes	45 (1900)	21 (1920)	24
No. people	300 (1900)	95 (1920)	205

Source: Paper presented by Aldo Leopold in 1922; Leopold 1946:628.

He goes on in sad detail:

> But after all, a cash value cannot express the loss actually incurred. Not only were 34 established homes destroyed, but the land carried away was a "key" resource, necessary for the proper utilization of the range, timber and recreational values on half-a-million acres of adjacent mountains. There is no other land, generally speaking, suitable for homes, stock-ranches, mills, roads, and schools. . . .
>
> Take, for instance, the adjacent range. This lost land was where the stockmen lived and had their little alfalfa fields, grain fields, gardens, and orchards. With no fields, all feed for saddle and work horses and weak range stock must be dispensed with or packed in 60 miles from the railroad at great cost. This may make the difference between a profitable and an unprofitable stock-raising operation. . . . Moreover a stock ranch deprived of its garden patch, orchard, milk cows, and poultry is no fit place to establish a home and raise a family. Regardless of the profit of the business, it is an unsocial institution.
>
> But this is not all. The destruction of the bottomlands along Blue River destroyed the only feasible location for a road, connecting the ranches with each other, with schools and with the outside world, and enabling timber and minerals to be put on the market. . . . The U.S. Forest Service and the counties are now actually spending half-a-million dollars on a road through this country but it cannot tap remains of the Blue River community. It must clamber over the rocks and hills at huge expense. (Leopold 1946:628–629)

The highway he refers to is the twisting and turning "Coronado Trail" between Springerville and Clifton. (Originally designated part of U.S. Highway 666, it came to be known as "The Devil's Highway" until its "cursed" number was changed in 1992 in Arizona to U.S. 191). In Leopold's time, this highway was constructed along the mountain rim at the western edge of the Blue watershed. A road was needed to transport timber from the high mountains of the Apache Forest down to the towns, mills, copper mines, and railhead around Clifton and Morenci. After more devastating flooding of the Blue in 1916, authorities had ruled out a route down the Blue River valley, where the earliest road had been. As

Leopold foresaw, the decision not to build the highway along the Blue would inevitably mean the long-range isolation and decline of the community there (Meine 1988:93, 190).

After conceding the need to build this road, Leopold closed his remarks about the Blue with the angry, sarcastic words quoted at the beginning of this chapter. He then went on to ask, "What Causes Accelerated Erosion?" and had one answer: overgrazing.

> History and experience have shown...that to graze the range at all usually means to overgraze the watercourses and bottomlands. Some concentration of stock at these points is unavoidable, even under careful management. History and experience have shown that this unavoidable overgrazing of the watercourses and bottomlands causes the first flood to begin tearing them out, starting a cumulative process of destruction that ultimately results in ruin.... [I]n the long run our "improved" valley becomes a desolation of sandbars, rockpiles, and driftwood, a scar on the face of nature, a sad monument to the unintelligence and mis-spent energy of us, the pioneers. (Leopold 1946:629; see also Leopold 1979).

Stating that "nobody advocates that we cease grazing," Leopold argued in favor of "a proper system of grazing control, *supplemented by artificial erosion control works*" (italics in original; Leopold 1921a:267). He suggested fencing the bottoms and keeping them lightly grazed, restoring willows by planting cuttings along the banks of the stream, checking gullies with logs, stones, or brush, plus more research into erosion control by the Forest Service. In keeping with his later thinking about a "land ethic," he wanted landowners to share the responsibility: "While public agencies must develop and demonstrate the technical methods and perform certain actual work on rivers and reservoirs, the real control work must be done by the landowner" (Leopold 1946:631).

CATTLE, OR WOODCUTTING AND GOATS?

Anti-cattle activists at the end of the twentieth century have cited Leopold's statements on grazing and erosion on the Blue in support of their campaign to eliminate cattle from public lands—as if conditions had not changed during the century. Also, they disregard Leopold's conclusion that the Forest Service and ranchers need to be partners in caring for the land. With cattle reduction now achieved on the Blue watershed, the question is still worth asking: was cattle grazing the sole, or even the major culprit, in the erosion that has occurred on the Blue?

In general, studies of erosion in the Southwest rarely single out only one factor. Typically, many forces are simultaneously at work (Dobyns 1978). But Leopold's 1922 paper focused entirely on "overgrazing" as the source of the erosion he decries. Also, he lumps together the cattle, goat, and burro grazing that occurred on the Blue at the turn of the century. Yet Forest Service opinion at the time of the first floods was very different. Forest Agent W.W.R. Hunt surveyed the area immediately following the 1904 and 1905 floods. His report, entitled "The Clifton Addition to Black Mesa Forest Reserve of Arizona," argued for the necessity of this "Addition" in order to check erosion (Hunt 1905:5). The northern, higher, more thickly forested area of the Blue (the "upper Blue") was already part of the Reserve. The "lower Blue," however, and the San Francisco River in Arizona, were not at the time but were soon to be added on Hunt's recommendation.

In his report, Hunt primarily blames the lack of forest cover for the erosion and flooding.

> The biggest proportion of water of course comes from the upper portions of the Blue and San Francisco Rivers, within the Black Mesa and Gila Forest Reserves. The principle [sic] damage, however, is usually done by the first rush of high water, which comes from this proposed Addition. The upper portions of those rivers have a much better forest cover to hold back the water, and also much of the precipitation is snow. (Hunt 1905)

Why did the "Addition" (including the lower Blue) lack adequate forest cover? Hunt blames not cattle, but goats and woodcutting. The cutting of wood for fuel was "entirely stripping" the land convenient to the towns and there was "absolutely no reproduction."

> The industry of woodcutting to supply the adjacent mining camps with fuel, and carried on by Mexicans, is of course entirely dependent on this Addition. . . . A strong protest may be expected from the people living in the towns of Clifton, Morenci and Metcalf, if the recommendation of this Report to forbid the cutting of pinyon and juniper is adopted. This will raise the price of wood in these towns. However, there seems to be no alternative.

Hunt also recommended banning the cutting of live oak anywhere on the Reserve and of any species of tree along the watercourses.

Goats were the other main problem, according to Hunt. He estimated that in the area of the proposed Clifton Addition there were at the time "about 15,000 head of cattle, 10,000 head of goats, and 1,500 head of horses." The goats' owners usually did not live on the Blue but had their animals herded from place to place over the range.

> The goats, owned in bands of up to a thousand head, are scattered over nearly all of the proposed Addition. The great quantities of shrub live oak browse makes this excellent goat country. There are large areas on which the only cover is this live oak, and in these areas the goats are very destructive. They strip the foliage from the bushes, usually causing their death, and this is followed by a rapid drying out of the soil, making reproduction of the timber trees impossible.
>
> Goats should certainly be excluded from this area, just as they already are from the adjoining portion of the Black Mesa Reserve. To exclude them all immediately would work a hardship on the owners. It is recommended that for the first season, whatever goats are found on the Addition be permitted to remain during that year, and then a reduction of 20% of the original total be made each year, so as to give the goat man an opportunity either to sell out without loss or to seek a new location. *It is recommended that the present number of cattle and horses be permitted to remain the entire year* [my emphasis].

Hunt reported that the cattlemen in the area were "strongly in favor of the Addition," adding, "Their attitude, of course, is due primarily to hope for relief from the goats." Also, the Arizona legislature, at the request of the cattlemen, had passed a resolution asking for the creation of the Addition. Included in Hunt's report is the text of a petition from the cattlemen supporting the extension of the Forest Reserve.

A copy of this letter-form petition is found with W.W.R. Hunt's report in the files of the Clifton Ranger District. It was posted from the short-lived town of Benton on the Blue in early 1905 to the "Chief, Bureau of Forestry" in Washington, D.C., and was signed by about twenty ranchers from the San Francisco and the lower Blue, including Toles Cosper, Hugh

McKeen, and Fred Fritz and his brothers. It supported "the proposition to extend the southern boundaries of the Black Mesa Reserve." Further,

> we respectfully assure the Department that the majority of settlers here, in fact all but those who are interested in goats, are heartily in favor of such an extension of the Forest Reserves. . . .
>
> Now there are about 20 persons owning or controlling about 7,000 head of goats, value about $25,000, employed by them around 10 persons, average wages about $20 per month. . . .
>
> If the Reserve is not extended, all cattle and horses in this region who have not died or already been removed, will be crowded or starved out by the goats within two years, if the destruction of range and underbrush and the consequent drying up of the springs continues.
>
> There are about 9,000 head of cattle, value $125,000, and about 1,000 head of horses, value about $20,000, controlled and owned by about 22 persons. Value of improvements, at least $8,000. Taxes paid by them last year, about $2,500. Employed by them, about 60 men, average wages $30 per month. One half of them cultivate more or less land aggregating about 150 acres. To this may be added that many small farmers who depend mostly on those cattlemen for support, will have to leave with them; and further, that it seems only a question of four or five years, when after driving the cattlemen out, the goat raisers will, by overstocking the range, starve each other out, and will have to be removed anyhow, leaving behind them a desert.

That the Blue cattlemen asked to be included in the Forest Reserve indicates their recognition that maintaining a truly open range was no longer workable; they accepted Forest Service regulation as a necessary antidote to overgrazing. In hindsight, their descendants might regard this as a Faustian bargain.

Goats were eventually removed from the National Forest. Political and ethnic prejudices may have played a part, as the goat owners were mostly (not all) Mexicans or immigrants from northern Spain. But a longstanding bias against goats and sheep widely prevailed in the early Forest Service. Conservationist opinion held they were much more destructive of the forest than cattle. Also earning official disfavor was the nature of most goat and sheep herding as "tramp" operations that moved through different ranges, using transient camps. Cattle raising, on the other hand, seemed more compatible with homesteading and permanent settlement, which U.S. government policy promoted (Barnes 1979:213–216; Barnes 1982:198; Merrill 2002:47).

LOG DRIVES ON THE BLUE

Nearly a century after the first big floods on the Blue, the Forest Service commissioned outside experts to assess the problems on the Blue River watershed. They called on the National Riparian Service Team (NRST). This agency gives advice and technical assistance to the Forest Service, the Bureau of Land Management, and other government agencies interested in natural resources conservation. The Team made an on-site investigation in October and November of 2000 and submitted their Final Report at the end of May 2001 to the Supervisor of the Apache-Sitgreaves National Forest (NRST 2001).

The Team found that "vegetation and site characteristics, along the entire length of the Blue River, appear to have been severely altered by a number of major impacts." Although "recovery to pre-disturbance conditions will necessarily take centuries if not millennia," the NRST found that "despite the near complete de-stabilization of the Blue River, there is remarkable evidence of recovery" (NRST 2001:3).

The NRST was aware of Leopold's analysis of erosion on the Blue, and agreed that overgrazing had been a factor.

> Continuous year long grazing was the historical norm in this area, as was common throughout most of the Southwest. Continuous year long grazing would have limited recruitment of bank stabilizing vegetation and future supplies of large wood. (NRST 2001:3)
>
> Overgrazing to the point of severely reducing upland vegetative cover further aggravates this by radically altering the hydrograph. The ability of the watershed to store and slowly release precipitation which falls on it is greatly reduced. (NRST 2001:8)

The Team made some of the same recommendations that Leopold did years before. Where possible, cattle should be kept from concentrating on the river; off-stream water should be substituted; seasonal grazing strategies and different management techniques might be used. Like Leopold in the 1920s, the Team believed that cattle are not incompatible with watershed restoration.

> We understand that there has been elimination of livestock grazing in some allotments on the Blue River and significant reductions or changes in seasonal livestock use in others. Much of the current upward trends is undoubtedly due to these changes. However, there may be additional opportunities to enhance both resource conditions and livestock production. (NRST 2001:14)

The National Riparian Service Team did not agree, however, with Leopold's view that grazing was wholly responsible for the erosion on the Blue. Though explicitly refusing to rank factors by importance, the NRST pointed to a number of other historical and ongoing causes of erosion, including road construction and maintenance, as well as channelization and diking "probably associated with agricultural development." Also, the team recognized the problem that "excess browsing by big game may be inhibiting new recruitment of woody species" in meadow sites in the upper elevations of the Blue. By 2000 elk there greatly outnumbered the few cattle (NRST 2001:3, 12, 15–22).

But the most interesting aspect of the report is the "negative impact" of the cause the NRST cites first. Leopold and Hunt never mention this factor, although it was occurring on the Blue during their time there, literally before their eyes.

> Removal of large wood. Discussions on-site and early photographs (no date) confirm that the Blue River was used for log transport down river. These logs were later used as charcoal for mining operations. Undoubtedly, the Blue River channel was "cleared" for transport. The removal of anchored trees, combined with the log floats, typically destabilize banks and scour any new regeneration of vegetation. (NRST 2001:3)
>
> In the case of the Blue River, the river and its watershed have been severely altered. Much of this alteration had already occurred by the early part of the twentieth century. Aldo Leopold went so far as to describe it in 1922 as "ruined." He attributed this to overgrazing. However, the historic photograph [displaying logs floating on the Blue River] of a log drive, taken in 1909,

suggests that a substantial amount of timber harvest had also occurred in the watershed.

The fact that the Blue River was subjected to log drives is important to any discussion of watershed restoration in that streams used for log drives were typically cleared and snagged to remove obstructions. In addition to the destabilizing effect of clearing and snagging, the log drives themselves did tremendous damage to the stream channel and banks. (NRST 2001:6–7)

The practice began before Leopold arrived, especially on the lower Blue and the San Francisco River closer to Clifton. A "logger" and a "millman" were recorded as living on the Blue in the 1900 Census. The Forest Service photograph of a large log drive cited by the NRST was taken the year Leopold arrived on the Forest. Some old-timers recalled the drives. Grace Johnson, who came to the Blue in 1913, remembered, "There used to be a lot more water in the Blue than there is now. There was enough water that at one time the miners in Clifton floated their logs down the river to Clifton from the Blue. They cut the logs up above the Box and floated them clear to Clifton" (*Down on the Blue* 62). The "Box," a narrow canyon halfway down the Blue, had a sawmill just up river. So evidence exists that the log drives continued for some time.

If the NRST is correct, we encounter a striking irony. Aldo Leopold, who denounced the ruination of the Blue River valley, was himself an unintentional agent of its ruin. Recall that his first assignment on the Apache National Forest was leading a team doing timber inventory to facilitate logging the Blue. More than that, however, his biographer writes,

Three weeks into the reconnaissance, Leopold received orders to join two "expert lumbermen" on a four-day inspection of the Blue River. The Forest Service was trying to decide how to deliver the pine of the upper Blue to the towns, mills, and copper mines fifty miles downriver. It was the wildest piece of country Leopold had yet seen, and it was about to be opened up, either by driving the logs down the river or by building a new road up from Clifton. He waxed enthusiastic about moving the timber. "With 15 million a year consumption down at Clifton and the Copper Mines, there will be something doing on this forest

before long or I'm mistaken. I am lucky to be here in advance of
the big works." (Meine 1988:92–93)

Leopold and his crew "recommended strongly against construction of the
proposed road over the top and argued instead for dams, shear booms,
flumes, and other stream improvements to permit driving logs down
Blue River" (Flader 1974:41).

The Forest Service, though it had not introduced log drives to the
Blue, looked for ways to make them more efficient. An important part
of the mission of the Forest Service at that time was to promote timber
harvests from the national forests to develop the nation. We should not
be surprised to find Aldo Leopold agreeing with this purpose. Throughout his career with the Forest Service, Aldo Leopold shared much of the
utilitarian ethos championed by its founder, Gifford Pinchot. And despite
his growing appreciation of wilderness values and his suspicion of many
forms of development, Leopold never really broke with the "wise-use"
aspect of Pinchot's and Teddy Roosevelt's conservationist philosophy.

Still, it is impossible to imagine that Leopold would have been so
enthusiastic about logging the Blue and driving the logs down a cleared
and channeled river in 1909 had he understood the consequences. What
is striking, however, is that even by the early 1920s when he was agitated
by the problem of erosion, he did not see a connection in cases such as
the Blue between logging, log runs, and erosion. And perhaps this lack of
recognition reflected a larger institutional blindness.

If Aldo Leopold and the Forest Service did not understand the consequences of logging the river, they showed the same lack of prescience as
the settlers on the Blue. The motivation of these farmers and cattlemen
was to build a good life for their families. They did not foresee how the
cattle they herded and the irrigation ditches they dug might someday
help cause the destruction of their fields and homes. The Forest Service
had been established with the responsibility to protect natural resources,
but it too failed to foresee the impact of the timber harvesting and log
driving it promoted on the Blue. Leopold had remarked about the erosion
and floods, "The ranchman accepts his losses as an act of God. But foresters should not and need not so accept them" (Leopold 1921a:268). Just so;
but what Leopold failed to see is that the foresters at the time were just as
blind as the cattlemen to the consequences of their work.

Yet, if Leopold did not understand the specific irony of his work on the Blue, the larger import of his activity at the time must also have been evident. His biographer observes,

> The Apache [Forest] had changed subtly but dramatically in the short two years he had spent there. Like his father before him who sold the barbed wire that subdued the plains, Aldo Leopold was part of a historical irony, taming the very wilderness he most loved. Escudilla was still there, of course, and the White Mountain plateau, and the Mogollon Rim, and the breaks of the Blue. Their absolute wildness, however, was gone: mapped, measured, confined to reservations, shot by a set-gun, rifled from a rimrock, broken and put to bit on a dusty street in Springerville. (Meine 1988:104–105)

Notes

1. In "Thinking Like a Mountain" in *A Sand County Almanac*, Leopold recounts killing a wolf and "seeing a fierce green fire dying in her eyes" (Leopold 1949:129–30). The experience became part of his evolving ideas about predators, the balance of nature, and wilderness. Recent research (Flader 2012) indicates he killed the wolf in an area Blue ranchers use for summer pastures.

5

Settlers into Permittees

Under the U.S. Forest Service

By 1930 most cattle outfits in this part of the country had received individual allotments and much fencing was done. I definitely think the individual allotment was the answer to the range abuse problem. By this date most permittees were able to control the grazing on their respective ranges. To me the drought of 1933 and 1934 proved this. It was fully as severe as the drought of 1921, in fact water was scarcer, but the death loss wasn't but little more than we have in an average year. We were under fence and could manage and protect ourselves.

FRED FRITZ (Down on the Blue 224)

Fred, unlike some of the oldtimers in the cattle business, does not resent being dictated to by the Government; he does not resent the fences either. In fact, he can see the advantage the modern cattleman has over the oldtimers. . . .

KATY FRITZ about her son Fred (Fritz 1985:xix)

ALDO LEOPOLD had declared the Blue valley ruined. True enough, from an ecological viewpoint, the watershed and especially the riverbed had been damaged in ways that could not soon be healed (NRST 2001:9). But the Blue was scarcely ruined for the people there. The floods were a tragedy and caused some to leave— Fred Fritz's brother and family, for example. Some farming came to an end, for lack of topsoil. Yet other farming continued, and plenty of forage remained for ranching. The people who stayed went on with their lives, no doubt still loving their "smiling valley."

Leopold cited data—whether from the Census or Forest Service is unclear—in his 1922 paper stating whereas there were 45 homes and 300 people in the Blue River Valley in 1900, only 21 homes and 95 people remained in 1920. His figures for 1900 accord generally with data obtained from the 1900 Census discussed in chapter 3. The 1910 Census does not allow the identification of a discrete Blue population (U. S. Census Bureau 1910).[1] The 1920 Census (U. S. Census Bureau 1920), however, labels enumeration district 66 as "Blue Precinct" (Arizona, admitted to the Union in 1912, had started to vote).

"Blue Precinct" lists 270 people, with 50 men claiming to be owners of farms or ranches. But a portion of the district—probably along the San Francisco toward Clifton—may be excluded from the Blue on the basis of city professions cited (barber, miner, city engineer) and by surnames not among those known for settlers on the Blue. Deducting these, one arrives at 167 people definitely living in the Blue watershed in 1920, in 37 rancher or farmer family households. These numbers differ significantly from the 95 people and 21 homes given by Leopold in 1922. Where the discrepancy arises is impossible to say. Perhaps Leopold was counting only families along the river and not those living up the many small streams of the watershed. The latter would probably have suffered less from the flood.

In any case, Leopold's description of economic ruin is misleading. Though population was down from 1900, the Blue persisted as a vital ranching community. In a change from the 1900 census, 31 men in the 1920 census were identified by the new term "rancher," 7 were "cattlemen" or "cowmen," 6 "cowboys" and two "hired ranch work." Katy Fritz, her husband dead from old wounds inflicted by a grizzly bear, was listed as "cattle owner." By contrast, 5 men were identified "farmer," 3 "farmhand," and 7 "laborer—farm work." But young "cowboys" were members of farmer families, and "farm laborers" were working for ranches.

Other occupations listed on the Blue included 2 trappers, 3 teachers (1 female), the postmaster (female), and 3 "Rangers," as apparently anyone working for the Forest Service then was called.

If the floods of the early 1900s marked the end of the frontier era—rough, somewhat Edenic, often lawless—the new era would manifest very different qualities. The U.S. Forest Service became the custodian of the resources on which the Blue community depended. In 1898, the upper Blue had been declared part of the new Black Mesa Forest Reserve; the lower Blue was added in 1906. The first Forest Ranger, Bailey Hulsey, appeared on the Blue, in 1902. In 1905, we have seen, the cattle ranchers of the lower Blue petitioned the new "Chief Forester" in Washington to help them out against the "goat men." In 1907, the Arizona Cattle Growers Association passed a resolution favoring Federal regulation of the federally owned "open range" (USFS 1988:49).

The federal government was moving towards becoming an active landlord in the American West. The Jeffersonian policy of disposing of the federal estate in the West to smallholders through homesteads had run its course and revealed its inadequacy. Most of the land in the West remained public domain that would not be homesteaded. In a turn of policy fostered by the Progressive movement at the beginning of the twentieth century and energetically pursued during Theodore Roosevelt's presidency, the federal government would now retain ownership of the public domain and move towards its own "scientific management" of natural resources. Citing a need to prevent a "timber famine" (that would never materialize), conservationist interests succeeded in passing through Congress a number of acts that led to the creation of the National Forest system under Gifford Pinchot and the U.S. Forest Service (Zaslowsky and Watkins 1994:65–69; Fox 1981:110).

"Conservation" was the guiding philosophy of the new policy. To Pinchot and Roosevelt, conservation meant "wise use," another term coined by Pinchot.

> The first principle of conservation is development, the use of the natural resources now existing on this continent for the benefit of the people who live here now. . . .
>
> In the second place conservation stands for the prevention of waste. . . . The first duty of the human race is to control the earth it lives upon. . . .
>
> In addition to the principles of development and preservation of our resources there is a third principle. It is this: The natural resources must be developed and preserved for the benefit of the many, and not merely for the profit of a few. . . .
>
> The conservation idea covers a wider range than the field of natural resources alone. Conservation means the greatest good to the greatest number for the longest time. . . thus recognizing that this nation of ours must be made to endure as the best possible home for all its people. (Gifford Pinchot, 1910 [Nash 1990:76–78])

Pinchot's vision of utilitarian conservation allied with scientific management was remarkably successful at the political level. It expressed the ideals of progressivism, a sort of bourgeois cousin of socialism. As part of the turn-of-century zeitgeist that prevailed among the educated elite, the ideology flew the banners of professional expertise, planning, economy, efficiency, stability, and "good government" divorced from interest-group politics (Nelson 1995:46–51; Rowley 1985:53–54). Pinchot's vision blossomed bureaucratically with the creation of the Forest Service and the training of a cadre of foresters (including the young Leopold) to be sent out to administer the National Forests.

Although timber production and watershed protection were the main legislated purposes of the Forest Reserves that became the National Forests, these forests also included much valuable rangeland. Pinchot, the forester, saw the importance of grazing resources in the forests and favored their wise utilization. He advocated regulation to prevent overgrazing from damaging both the forest and the range. Regulation would be to the advantage of both forest and grazing interests (Rowley 1985:45).

Many ranchers using the Forest Reserves agreed. They did not like competing with "outside" (nonlocal) outfits—whether cattle, sheep or goats, big or small—that under the rules of the open range might invade the pastures near their ranches, land that through long use and proximity they regarded possessively. They wanted stability and security for their ranching interests and thought that the federal government, through the General Land Office and its successor, the Forest Service, might give them relief. Early stockmen's associations at the state and national levels lobbied the government for regulations that would help them.

For its part, the evolving Forest Service needed expertise on range issues. Pinchot brought in a former stockman from Arizona, Albert F. Potter, to direct the Grazing Section of the early Forest Service. Other stockmen were subsequently co-opted into the agency, and these links between the ranching industry and the Forest Service gave the latter political support and legitimacy in the eyes of the ranchers, just as they opened channels for the stockmen's associations to try to influence the new policies being developed (Rowley 1985:39; Merrill 2002:47–48).

The associations, however, did not get what they would have preferred, a leasing system of grazing rights, because this would have closed the range to the cattle of new homesteaders, and Congress at the turn of the century was still committed to the homestead cause. In fact the stock associations were careful to portray their ranchers in the homesteader mold—not as the "tramp" herders or cattle barons of the old open range, but homebuilders settling the country (Merrill 2002:49–54). As seen in chapter 2, this picture was true in regard to the Blue.

Instead of a leasing system, the Forest Service developed a permit system. Leasing, after the model of the private sector, would have given ranchers a good deal of independent control over how to use the land. The permit system, however, gave the agency what it wanted: to establish grazing use as a privilege, not a right, and to give the agency the ability to regulate use (Merrill 2002:60). Its eventual effect was the creation of an odd partnership: government and rancher together managing, each in their own way, a joint operation that necessarily combined both private and federal land.

The contradictions in this relationship would emerge over the century. But at the outset the permit system achieved what the stockmen's associations had wanted. Permits were necessary to graze on the National Forests. Preference would be given first to those who owned ranch property adjacent to the Forest, and secondly to those who owned ranch property in the vicinity of the Forest and had traditionally used the Forest range. Last preference, which usually meant exclusion, was given transient herders who had no local property ownership. Large cattle companies without land nearby would also be excluded. A principle of "commensurate property ownership" was a condition for a permit: the permittee should have "enough private ranch land on which to support the stock during periods when for one reason or another the National Forest was not open to grazing" (Barnes 1979:217–220; Rowley 1985:59–62). New homesteading would also be limited by the Forest Service to land it deemed had adequate agricultural potential (Merrill 2002:54, 60–61; USFS 1988:93).

> The 1905 Forest Service *Use Book* outlined Pinchot's "wise use" approach to grazing: "The Secretary of Agriculture has authority to permit, regulate, or prohibit grazing in the forest reserves." The book further stated the objects of grazing regulations to be (1) the protection and conservative use of all forest reserve land adapted for grazing; (2) the best permanent good of the livestock industry through proper care and improvement of the grazing lands; and (3) the protection of the settler and home builder

against unfair competition in the use of the range. (Rowley
1985:59)

Permits came with "allotments," specific areas where a permittee
could graze the number of stock stipulated by his permit, a "preference"
originally based on a rancher's historical use. This number, however,
could be changed when the Forest Service desired, according to range
conditions. One condition in the early years was to redistribute numbers in favor of small ranchers and new homesteaders, though the Forest
Service would determine what land was open to homesteading. Eventually permits would be given for five, then ten years at a time, and came
to have market value, as they were transferable together with the "base
property," or complementary private land that was the "commensurate
property" for the permit (Merrill 2002:84–86; Rowley 1985:90, 134).

A fee system was also imposed in 1906, to raise money to help the
Forest Service administer the forest range. The fees were calculated to be
low enough for the small stockman to afford. Nevertheless, the Western
ranchers and their associations bitterly protested, labeling the fee a "tax"
they felt they should not pay (Merrill 2002:79–82; Rowley 1985:63–65;).
This controversy, as well as the question whether sheep should be allowed
to graze the National Forests, greatly overshadowed any complaints the
ranchers might have expressed over the regulatory control the Forest
Service assumed. But in retrospect it was this control that became the
threat to future ranching by the permittees' descendants decades later.

The Forest Service Comes to the Blue

The first Forest Ranger on the Blue, Bailey Hulsey, was hired in 1902. We
have a record of his activities from his official logs, summarized by Cleo
Cosper Coor.

> Bailey kept meticulous accounts of the day, date and duties per-
> formed each day, where they were performed, and how many
> hours were occupied. He even wrote the distance he rode each
> day. Much time was spent examining claims of settlers on the
> Blue. . . . He also patrolled in search of trespass evidence. . . .
>
> He posted Forest Service signs (fire and line warnings) and
> watched for fire. If he came to a fire already burning he stayed to
> do what he could.

The Forest Service didn't always issue permits for people to homestead certain areas, even though they might have built buildings and had been living on the property for several years. It was the job of the Forest Ranger to inform the "trespassers" as well as report the trespass to the District Office. The Forest Ranger didn't make the law, but it was his duty to see that it was obeyed. (*Down on the Blue* 85)

Bailey Hulsey also served as a game warden to make sure people fished and hunted only during the proper season. Hulsey's daughter writes,

After a little more than a year, Bailey left the Forest Service to go into partnership with his brother, Rufus, who had taken over the Cross L Cattle Company, owned by Bill Lee of Luna. Bailey thought he would enjoy being a cattleman more than a Forest Ranger. (*Down on the Blue* 86).

Perhaps Hulscy did not like evicting people. Cleo Cosper Coor observes,

When people first moved into the Blue there was not a Forest Service active in that area. People let their cattle run wherever they went. People built cabins or houses and settled just anywhere. For many people it was a real trauma when the Forest Service asked them to move their houses which were on Forest Service land. (*Down on the Blue* 87)

The criteria Forest Rangers were using to evict "trespassers" from the Blue are unclear, but the fact that they did so is attested in the old accounts. Charles Adair brought his family from Luna around 1890 to settle on the upper Blue, and had children born there. In the drought of 1904 the family went back to Luna. The family history is that

they lived on what you might remember as the old Ranger Station. . . . The place that Charles, Sr. was living on belonged to the Forest Service. They never did own the property. I haven't looked it up, but when Teddy Roosevelt became president he insisted that all so called squatters move off Forest Land. (Preston Adair in *Down on the Blue* 45)

Ben Tenney, who recounted how a fellow seventeen-year-old student and son of a farmer, Bob Phillips, killed a man who had whipped him with a rope, speculates,

> There were a good many ranches up and down the Blue. As a boy I always wondered why the Forest Service didn't run them off their places, but I guess there were too many "gun" men like Bob and they were afraid to stir up the hornet's nest.
>
> Mr. Chapin was the first District Forest Ranger [actually, District Supervisor]. His district was from Flagstaff to the Blue River [200 miles—the Black Mesa Forest Reserve] and he made the trip on an average of once a month. The people who he couldn't run off their places finally got deeds from the government signed by the President of the United States. (*Down on the Blue* 54)

Perhaps some squatters had not filed homestead applications, or had arrived after the creation of the Reserve in 1898. Like other American pioneers, they would believe they had a natural right to land they had settled and sunk their labor into. Tenney continues,

> My father traded a team and wagon to Mr. Tom Hatch in 1901 for his squatter's right in Bush Valley, now known as Alpine [near the Blue]. Mr Chapin came and tried to run my mother off this place and gave her thirty days to get off, so she went over to Old Uncle Fred Hamblin and asked him what she should do and he advised her to stand pat. In thirty days Mr. Chapin was back. Uncle Fred saw him coming and was over there when he started to get off his horse. Uncle Fred said, "Now what are you going to do?"
>
> He replied, "I gave this woman thirty days to vacate this place and she is still here."
>
> Uncle Fred said, "Mr., if you want to get along with the people here who had a right before the Forest Service did, you just climb back on that horse and don't let no grass grow under your feet." Mr. Chapin knew by the tone of Uncle Fred's voice he had better get out as soon as possible. My father was away on a mission at the time, but after he came home they soon proved up on the place and got a deed to it.
>
> So that was the way of those days, you had to fight every step of the way from the Government or the Indians. I think the

Government and the Indians owe a lot to the old pioneers for killing off the snakes and overcoming so many obstacles. (*Down on the Blue* 54)

Most settlers remained, especially the well-established ones, and the Forest Service accommodated them.

1909, settlers on Blue River were granted a patent to their home-steads, 160 acres each, with the privilege of leasing what grazing land they needed at moderate prices, 50 cents to $1.00 per year per acre, in most instances. (Fritz 1985:xvii)

1909, Toles Cosper received a patent to 160 acres of home-stead land and was permitted to continue to lease the other three sections that he had been using. (Cosper 1940:11)

This was one year after creation of the Apache National Forest.

During this period the Forest Service was apparently leasing land by the quarter section along the Blue bottomland. This was watered land, open to homesteading and considered different from the "open range" where permits were issued for livestock.

From 1890 to 1906, Toles Cosper paid lease on ten sections [probably quarter sections] of land and used all the open range he wanted besides, but the homesteaders began crowding in by that time and by 1909 he had only about four [quarter] sections under lease, which included his own homestead [quarter] section.

Soon, all the homestead land that had been opened in that [area] had been taken and the homesteaders began fencing their respective plots; range land [in the valley] must either be bought outright or leased from owners, and as most of the homestead-ers were trying to raise cattle themselves there was little [valley] range to be leased in the Blue River range. (Cosper 1940:9)[2]

Unfortunately, early records of Forest Service permits and allotments are sketchy if available at all.[3] Here is one example from documents kept by the the McKeen family:

Records show Hugh McKeen held Grazing Permit No. 76 for five hundred head of cattle and thirty horses on the Black Mesa Forest Reserve from April 1, 1901 to December 1, 1901. He was a Forest Permittee from the time the Forest Service came into being in 1905. . . . Early records dated at Benton, Graham County [i.e. Benton on the Blue] show permits on the Apache and Gila National Forests. (McKeen 1982:162)

An allotment analysis of the Fritz ranch in the Clifton Ranger District files summarizes: "The beginning of this preference was started by Fred Fritz Sr., long before the creation of the National Forest. The first application of record for the 1907 season was submitted under date of Dec. 14, 1906, applying for the 1907 season." Initially, approval was given for only 55 cattle and 12 horses. But in 1912 Fritz Sr. made application for 255 cattle, 8 horses and 12 hogs, and Fred Fritz Jr. made his first application for 5 cattle. Both were approved. In 1913, the "preference" was changed to 298 cattle, 8 belonging to the son. Fred Fritz Sr., the document notes, died in 1916 (USFS 1964).

An interesting account is found in the same Clifton files, in a letter written by a young ranger June 20, 1915 to his fiancée in Michigan.

Today I left fairly early with a young cowman named Jim Cosper, and rode up the Frisco about 12 miles to his ranch among the hills. His "ranch" is probably less than you might imagine, for it is only a little pole house roofed with tin, and with mud knocked out of the widest cracks to serve as windows. There is a pole corral outside, and a dugout which is used for a chicken house. I had to go out there to get data for a report to a supervisor, as his (Cosper's) cattle are drifting onto Forest land, and Uncle Sam won't give him a permit. It is a strange mix-up and will probably end by Uncle Sam's relenting to a slight extent, so as to give him a chance. We had dinner out there, beans, bread, coffee, and stewed apricots for desert, and they tasted good too, especially after three days of Chinese cooking in this hot town [Clifton]. (Collingwood: n.d.)

Rangers might sympathize with the people on the Blue, but they represented a new governmental authority with new rules to impose on frontiersmen much used to independence and self-governance. The situation guaranteed some tension. La Veta Suite Challis, the daughter of an early ranger, recalls an incident from the 1920s:

One man on the Blue, showing off for a girl friend, 1) killed a doe, 2) at night by artificial light (car lights), 3) on a reserve, 4) out of season, 5) without a license. The poor guy had to pay $500 for the 5 illegal counts. But laws are laws and he *did* break them. The ranger was somewhat resented by ranchers as they had always grazed the leased government land anyway they chose and of course government rules and regulations were resented. It was Dad's job to enforce them, so the ranger's job was not always an easy one. (*Down on the Blue* 94)

Toles Cosper was one who resented being "dictated to by some Government agent—a young college graduate" (Cosper 1940:14). On the other hand, there was Fred Fritz Jr., who according to his mother, "unlike some of the oldtimers in the cattle business, does not resent being dictated to by the government" (Fritz 1985:xix). Fritz and Cosper both had signed the letter asking to be included in the Forest Reserve to escape the chaos of the open range but later reacted differently to the ensuing regulation.

If the settler histories and Forest Service archives reveal some discord and animosity in the early years of this new relationship, they also indicate a good deal of cooperation and friendliness at the local level, as the agency adapted to the Blue community and vice versa. Forest Rangers lived on the Blue until 1986. The 1910 Census records two, probably living at the "Baseline" camp four miles above the Fritz ranch. One is a single, thirty-seven-year old born in New York, the other is a young married man born in Texas. The Forest Service brought in trained men with college degrees but also hired local people to be "rangers," and for fire lookouts and firefighting, road repair, and numerous other jobs.

In the 1920 census, three Rangers were living on the Blue. One, Harry Boyer, had a daughter born in Kansas, and appears to be a professionally trained forester. Another, Ulysses Casto, was the son of the earliest settler on the Blue, John Casto. And the third, David Scott Marks, born in Illinois, had married Iona Jones, a daughter of the pioneer Texan ranching family on the Blue. Marks was a professional in the Service, and transferred to New Mexico. His son David recounts,

My dad, Scott Marks, worked for the Forest Service until his death in 1932. After that we moved back to the Blue. My mother took over the ranch. The cattle were rather wild. With help from my uncles we all managed to do fair. I did a lot of trapping in the winter and worked for other ranches when I got old enough. Anything to make a few dollars. (*Down on the Blue* 125)

Another son of Forest Ranger Marks went on to run the Jones ranch, which became known as "the Marks ranch" (or the "WY Bar").

Such examples of marriage and kin entanglements between Forest Service personnel and the community were not rare while rangers lived on the Blue. The Service became part of the community, especially on the social level. The young Freddy Fritz Jr., going to get his hair cut by the Ranger at the "Baseline" Ranger station four miles upriver from the Fritz XXX ranch, found a new ranger had replaced him. Visiting the new ranger's wife was her sister, "a pretty red headed 15 year old" whom Freddy was destined to court and marry (Fritz 1978:86).

Such fraternization led to suspicions higher in the bureaucracy.

> The local forest officers, from the viewpoint of Washington were sometimes on *too* good terms with the stockmen. Washington feared that the officers were not critical enough of the local community and too reluctant to carry out all the grazing regulations if it meant risking unpopularity in the community. . . .
>
> Local officials did not live independently of their community. Their children attended the local schools, families participated in social affairs, and friendships grew. If forest policies were popular the officials' acceptance in the community was easy, but if policies became unpopular their life could become strained. . . . (Rowley 1985:92)

As a remedy, the Forest Service frequently transferred professionals to other Districts.

CATTLE ON THE BLUE, 1905–1930

In the early years of the new National Forest regime, those who received permits to run cattle on the Blue apparently were granted the numbers they wanted. At least, no evidence of discontent on this score is found in the few Forest Service records or written recollections from the time. The 1905 report by Forest Agent W.W.R. Hunt from Clifton observes that

> the cattle are divided up among small owners scattered throughout the area. . . . It is doubtful if any one party owns over 500 head. The horses are the saddle stock incidental to the cattle business, there being no one actually being engaged in the

horse business. No winter feeding is done here. In case of severe snow storms which occasionally occur in the high altitudes of the northern portion, the cattle do very well for a short time on the leaves of the shrub live oak. When not over-grazed, this is an excellent grass region, and if the present over-crowding of the range is abandoned, it will probably recover very rapidly. (Hunt 1905)

(The "overcrowding," as seen in the previous chapter, he blamed mainly on the goats.)

Unfortunately, not enough data are available to tell exactly how many livestock pastured on the Blue in the initial years of the permit system. We know that gradual reduction was the policy of the agency. When a ranch or all the livestock were sold, a ten percent reduction was mandated (Rowley 1985:135. The ruinous overgrazing that occurred before the droughts at the turn of century appeared generally to have been gradually curtailed throughout the Southwest (Bahre 1991:118; USFS 1988:96). Denying access to "outsiders" and "tramp" herds in itself would lead to significant reduction.

But on the Blue? Cattlemen with allotments on the Blue no longer ran herds of thousands as some did during the boom years. For example, Fred Fritz Sr., who had run 2,500 head once, according to the estimate of Jim Cosper, was permitted for only 255 in 1912 (USFS 1964). By the time Toles Cosper received his homestead patent in 1909, "he had sold off a lot of his cattle. . .and now had only a small herd of breed stock, just about enough to furnish him a shipment of 250 head each season" (Cosper 1940:11). Other allotment data indicates numbers in the few hundreds, and not greatly higher than later allotment "preferences."

Do these numbers tell the whole story? Fred Fritz Jr. remembers,

From 1905 to 1920 there were many good wet years. Grass came back and the cattle population again built up to large numbers and many new outfits came into the cattle business. The Forest Service was established and issued permits for grazing livestock, but there was no way to protect your range from over grazing by others, consequently there was no effort made on the part of the rancher to reduce numbers. A low estimate would be 15 cattle to one now [1964]. (*Down on the Blue* 224)

Without fencing, it was impossible to keep out others' cattle—the problem of trespass. The Blue range was still "open" in practice, including to outsiders. Fritz continues:

> We built one of the first drift fences in 1917 to cut off the drift from the New Mexico side and after its completion took out over 1,000 head of cattle belonging to other people and this was on the *east side of the Blue River only!* We all had too many cattle on the range back in those days. There was no incentive to try to save forage, you couldn't, other cattle moved in on you, consequently the range, especially around permanent waters, was abused. (*Down on the Blue* 224)

Hugh McKeen was the only rancher on the Blue who owned large herds. His preferences in the Apache and Gila National Forests peaked at 2,873 cattle and horses, year long, in 1914. However, he achieved this by acquiring and consolidating other ranching outfits and their allotments, mostly in New Mexico, where his ranch was headquartered. Only a fraction of his livestock was in Arizona on the Blue, and "stocking has been continuously reduced since the first permit" (1901). On the other hand, the Forest Service often found him stocking beyond his permitted numbers (USFS 1981). Could his cattle on the Apache have drifted over from the Gila? Or was he running cattle in excess of his permits on both Forests? Perhaps no one really knew except him.

Not every year between 1905 and 1920 was good: another bad drought combined with a bad market came in 1909 (Fritz 1985:xvii). Toles Cosper remembers,

> During the drouth, cattle went down to rock bottom prices again, and the ranchers were forced to sell or shoot their cattle on the range, most of them sold at any price which might be obtained for poor, skinny steers, which was around six to eight dollars per head. (Cosper 1940:11)

The First World War brought a boom. As part of the war effort, the Forest Service encouraged livestock permittees to put more cattle and sheep on the national forests. An effort was made to utilize all the forage resource for the Allied cause. Wartime demand raised prices too, and for a few years ranchers were flush (Merrill 2002:69; Rowley 1985:113; USFS 1988:50).

The price of beef stock soared to as high as $40 per head, and continued to rise the duration of the war. Toles, along with the rest of the Blue River ranchers, sold while the selling was good. From 1916 to 1919, the Y Bar Y outfit shipped out a total of around eighteen thousand head of cattle at $40 and up per head; Toles did not raise *all* the cattle he sold during that time, he bought up small herds of feeders at what he called "a fair price" (around twelve to fifteen dollars per head), kept them a few months and fed them and then shipped them to a good profit. (Cosper 1940:11)

Toles's ability to do this probably indicates his success at growing crops for his "feeders." The Fritzes also prospered.

Fred and Katy Fritz took advantage of the opportunity to "clean up" a neat nest egg with what stock they had to sell. Shipping during the meteoric market a total of more than fifteen thousand head left them with less than two hundred breed stock on their range to start another herd with. (Fritz 1985:xviii)

Boom, however, was followed by a postwar depression in prices, made worse by drought. Many ranchers went into debt, some into bankruptcy. To help them, the Forest Service delayed cutting stock numbers. The 1920s saw some good years but also recurring drought and spells of low prices for cattle. In general, it was not a roaring decade for ranchers but hard times (Rowley 1985:116, 146; Sheridan 1995:253; Wagoner 1952:57–59; USFS 1988:50).

Young Fred Fritz Jr., returned from the army and a brush with death in camp during the 1917 influenza (the "Spanish flu"), plunged into ranching for himself and his mother on borrowed money.

In 1920, one of the worst droughts I had ever witnessed occurred and lasted until 1924. Many cattle died in those days. . . . Yearling steers that brought $45 per head in the spring of 1920 were down to $17 in the fall. . . . Grazing fees and taxes became delinquent. . . . Many of the ranchers went broke. (Fritz 1978:83–84)

From 1921 to 1923 there was another severe drought. Again many cattle died, were sold or shipped out. It was at this time that cattle numbers came down to about what the country should or could carry in normal years under then existing uncontrolled range conditions. (*Down on the Blue* 224)

Banks and stores in Clifton were threatened too when the ranchers could not pay off their bills and loans.

> The First National Bank had our notes, etc. They also had notes of our good neighbor Fred Stacy and many, many more of my good rancher friends. A large portion of them had been discounted through the Federal Reserve Bank which in turn brought foreclosure proceedings against all of us ranchers. This was late in 1923 and we had a meeting. Fred Stacy and I were delegated to meet with the El Paso Bank and try to work out a solution if possible. The agreement we worked out . . .was acceptable to most of the ranchers, but due to the heavy livestock losses of the drought, some did not have enough cattle left to pay the indebtedness. . . . Those of us who had sufficient cattle paid out, quite a few didn't. . . .
>
> I had paid off the mortgages on the XXX Ranch by the end of June 1924. Those were long hard years, but I was able to save the patented land and still had a nice bunch of XXX cattle left. (Fritz 1978:84–85)

Fred Fritz Jr., however, did have to liquidate other of his ranching ventures. But if he managed to survive, old Toles Cosper did not. Toles tells the story this way:

> Soon after the war, prices of beef stock began sliding back down the scale, and Toles decided it high time he left the cattle business up to the younger men; he sold off his stock, down to only a few for his own use, and let his leases expire; the leases were quickly taken up by other ranchers and Toles found himself with little or no range for what few cattle he did have. (Cosper 1940:11)

Fred Fritz Jr. throws a different light: apparently Toles had taken on too much debt: "The J.H.T. Cosper Y—Y Ranch was taken over by many creditors. The court appointed me receiver in early 1924. I already had a bunch of cowboys (about 10) gathering the cattle. . . . Jim [Cosper] was with the cowboys" (Fritz 1978:88).

"Little" Jim Cosper was one of Toles's sons and the "young cowman" in the primitive home that the ranger Collingwood described in his letter to his fiancée. Little Jim had the VT ranch, not too far from the XXX, and he had married Fred Fritz Jr.'s sister Katie, intertwining the two pioneer families.

If nearly all Toles's cattle and his "preferences" (leases?) were gone, he would still keep the Y Bar Y ranch for another decade. Toles recalls the next drought on the Blue, from 1928 to 1931:

> Cattlemen in Arizona had witnessed many drouths from the beginning of the industry, but the old timers on the Blue Range aver that this was by far the worst ever witnessed in this district; the spring and lakes all dried up and the streams contained only stagnant pools here and there, the country reeked with the smell of dead fish and animals. "The very bottom simply fell out of the cattle industry."
>
> Armed riders rode out before dawn and rode far into the night putting an end to the suffering of thirsty animals—the only humane thing they *could* do.
>
> With the coming of Law and Order, when the territory became a State, range riders were no longer permitted to carry their trusty .45's without special deputy commission, or permission from the Sheriff's office, but many of them continued to carry rifles on their saddles—just in case.
>
> During this drouth, every rancher on the Blue Range had himself and his riders deputized; they called themselves "The Slaughter Brigade," for they slew cattle and horses by the hundreds to get them out of their misery. (Cosper 1940:12)

The Great Depression and the End of the Open Range

The Great Depression only increased the cattlemen's burdens. The Forest Service tried to help the permittees by reducing grazing fees; continuing to grant ten-year leases; giving guarantees against arbitrary, deep reductions; and backing low-interest loans from the Farm Credit Administration (Rowley 150–154). The concern was to avoid driving cattlemen into bankruptcy. The last thing the New Deal wanted was more unemployed men.

At the same time, the Forest Service continued its policy of gradually reducing the stocking rate. Opinion in the agency still held that the range was generally overgrazed (Voigt 1976:54, 109). The developing science of range management provided the basis for analyses and studies that could be used to provide the rationale for reducing livestock numbers. The official history of the Forest Service in the Southwest states that

> range research and reconnaissance led to downward revisions in grazing capacity, both reducing the animal numbers allowed and the number of months in which the ranges of the region should be grazed. The needed reductions were not accomplished on most national forest ranges by eliminating grazing entirely, but by gradually reducing grazing intensity while at the same time using common sense and tact in building up a region-wide system of sound range management. (USFS 1988:96)

The Forest Service had learned to avoid issuing general mandates that could lead to political clashes with the stockmen's associations. The preferred approach was to adjust stock numbers downward "on a case by case basis." That this method worked, without any great uproar, can be seen in the falling numbers for all permitted animals in the Southwestern Region:

1909: 1,449,538

1919: 1,397,618

1931: 830,485 (USFS 1988:96)

If Fred Fritz is right, however, drought and difficult market conditions in the 1920s also played a part in bringing down livestock numbers.

Fewer cattle during the Depression could be rationalized as a way to maintain prices and necessary during drought in order to protect the land from overgrazing. The Forest Service, as part of a broader New Deal national agriculture policy, took the drastic step of requiring ranchers to kill a portion of their livestock. This program is not mentioned in the histories of Forest Service grazing, but it sticks in the popular memory because of the paradoxical image of waste in the middle of want. Ranchers on the Blue remember it. Fred Fritz Jr. includes it in his business-like rendering of the Depression.

> The depression of 1929 hit hard. Money was tight. The price of cattle went to the bottom. We sold heifer yearlings for $13 per head, and $16 to $18 for yearling steers. The buyers took what

they wanted. The years of 1931, '32 and '33 were extremely dry. . . . Nineteen thirty four was worse. The government purchase program was on the calves condemned and killed. . . . Under the government kill program we received $12 [a steer]. Those I shipped brought $17 [on the market]. (Fritz 1978:89–90)

Although the cattle killed were "purchased," it was not a voluntary sale. Bill Richardson, who grew up in a cowman's family on the Blue, remembers that in the mid-1930s

a government man come to the ranch and had all the stock rounded up. There'd been a drought for 2 or 3 years and the government claimed the range was overstocked and they was proceeding to kill so many cattle off of each ranch according to the permits, a certain amount of head of cattle. So we rounded the Smith cattle up and held them on a mesa over there across the river and this man shot 'em. And then after he killed all those stock, in about a month it started raining and the country got good and feed got real good. (*Down on the Blue* 224)

However, by far the biggest change in cattle ranching on the Blue in the 1930s was the fencing and individualization of allotments. Previously, all grazing had been permitted in large "community" allotments containing the cattle of multiple permittees. These allotments had been unfenced, continuing as de facto open range. As the rangeland belonged to the government, the Forest Service would have to pay to fence it, which apparently was economically unfeasible in the rough Blue country until the 1930s, just as on most other Forest Service lands. What changed the picture was the Civilian Conservation Corps (CCC), the New Deal program to employ young men on public works. Under the direction of the Forest Service, they built roads and trails, recreational facilities, range fences, stock-watering places, and worked at other range improvements. (Rowley 1985:162; Sheridan 1995:254; USFS 1988:54; Voigt 1976:66). Of the twenty-two CCC camps in Arizona during the 1930s, one was on the Blue. And among other projects, the CCC fenced the Blue range, beginning in 1931 and continuing through the decade.

In the opinion of the local Forest Service, fencing made all the difference in managing the range. A memo submitted by the Apache National Forest Supervisor in 1967 remarks that prior to that time [the mid-1930s], the Blue River Drainage area had been grazed year long by herds estimated to range in size from 20–25,000 head. The common practice was to allow these cattle to roam throughout the unfenced country at will, and sell the natural increase up to ages including three years. Herd management was not practiced in any form until the allotments were fenced in the 1930s. (USFS 1967)

Fred Fritz Jr. agreed.

By 1930 most cattle outfits in this part of the country had received individual allotments and much fencing was done. I definitely think the individual allotment was the answer to the range abuse problem. By this date most permittees were able to control the grazing on their respective ranges. To me the drought of 1933 and 1934 proved this. It was fully as severe as the drought of 1921, in fact water was scarcer, but the death loss wasn't but little more than we have in an average year. We were under fence and could manage and protect ourselves. (*Down on the Blue* 224)

Ranchers could manage their fenced cattle better, but fencing also allowed the Forest Service to exert more management over ranching operations. For example, some ranchers had long practiced transhumance on the Blue if they could, moving their cattle seasonally.

We moved our cattle and Aunt Lula's cattle from the Blue and took 'em up to what they call the Mountain: that would be up around Hannagan and Fish Creek, every summer where there was good feed and the cattle done real well. And we'd spend the summer branding and riding and looking after our cattle and just having a good time. It rained a lot and got pretty cold (9,000' elevation) and I believe to this day it's the most beautiful country in the world. (Bill Richardson, *Down on the Blue* 185)

"The Mountain" comprised the higher elevations beyond the northern and western borders of the Blue watershed. The Cosper clan would throw big parties when they arrived on the Mountain yearly. Virginia Becker, born on the Blue, and raised on a ranch there in the 1930s, recalls

almost all the people that lived on the Blue had their cattle down there [on the Blue] in the winter time then they took them up on top. They called it up on top, but it was around Fish Creek and Hannagan Meadow and that country up there in the summer time. They summered them up there where they could have better grazing. And they would save the Blue for the winter. It worked out real well for them. All the time I was there they all did that. So the cattle were still up on the mountain when they got ready to round them up and take them to shipping. (Becker 2000)

Most of the Blue watershed was best suited for winter range, compared to other parts of the Apache Forest. This quality accounted for much of the Blue's attraction to outside ranchers during the open-range period.

With fencing, the Forest Service could control transhumance on the Blue. They wanted to encourage it, because in their opinion "year-long" grazing on any pasture was damaging. Now the agency could specify the exact dates of the transfers, as well as the number of stock permitted on each of the two allotments a rancher now needed, to utilize both winter and summer pastures.

While gradual improvements continued, the decades of the 1940s and 1950s saw no dramatic changes in ranching on the Blue. Droughts came and went, cattle prices rose and fell. As Fred Fritz Jr. said, "Cattle prices and weather have always run in cycles and we had fair conditions [after the mid-1930s] through 1950" (Fritz 1978:90). The various national controversies over grazing and public and private rights to the land did not directly affect the Blue at the time, although some of the ranchers like Fritz no doubt participated in the debates through membership in their cattlemen's associations: the Greenlee County Cattle Growers, the Arizona Cattle Growers, the American National Cattlemen's Association. Some like Fritz also served on the Forest Advisory Board that was part of the Forest Service's attempt to promote cooperation between permittees and the agency.

The Forest Service still sought to reduce overgrazing, but the emphasis was less on reducing stock numbers and more on range improvements that would boost carrying capacity. Some of these efforts had begun in the 1930s, aided by the CCC, and continued as cooperative efforts, pairing the rancher's labor with the Forest Service provision of materials. Still more fences were built to provide smaller, more workable pastures that could be rested and rotated according to a plan worked out between

the permittee and the agency. Roads and corrals were built to aid in
trucking cattle, as the old cattle drives became largely a thing of the past.
New watering sites were developed—windmills, stock tanks, piping from
streams or springs to water troughs—so that stock could be spread over
wider areas. Salt blocks were used to lure animals from congregating by
the water. Efforts were made to remove harmful or useless vegetation, to
control brush, and to reseed pastures. There was progress in combating
cattle diseases. More emphasis was put on improving the quality of herds
through better breeds of cattle, which were now sold by the pound rather
than by the head (Rowley 1985:232–3; Sheridan 1995:261). Ranches on
the Blue, as often elsewhere in the mountainous West, became "cow and
calf" operations. They specialized in raising calves and yearlings to be
sold to feeding operations off the Blue (and often out of state) that would
fatten the cattle for slaughter.

In many small ways, ranching on the Blue evolved with the industry
as a whole, and in ways that benefited the ranchers. In many small ways,
too, the Forest Service gradually extended its regulation over ranching
practices, which was its goal. If the ranchers sometimes chafed in partnership with their federal landlord, there is little evidence of serious antagonism during these years. The younger ranchers like Fred Fritz Jr. had
come of age under the Forest Service regime and generally welcomed the
new order on the range. Of course, old-timers like Toles Cosper might
complain about the present and yearn for the past, after he was too bank-
rupt and too old to remain in the cattle business. In 1935, after his wife
died, Toles had to quit his "God's Country" to move into Clifton and the
care of a daughter. His granddaughter, Cleo Cosper Coor, recounts,

> Toles loved that ranch. He hated to leave. He loved the life of a
> cowman and he liked to hunt. He liked to meet the challenge of
> living in the wild untamed canyons, the lush, green mountains,
> and he loved people, especially his neighbors on the Blue. He
> just didn't believe in *paying* Forest Service allotments, so he sold
> most of the cattle in 1927 and the ranch in 1935. According to
> him the land was free when he came there and he had run cattle
> on it for about 30 years or so during which time no one told him
> where to take his herd, how many he could have, or how many
> he couldn't have and by @#&*#@ they weren't going to tell him
> now, they could just very well have the whole bunch before he
> would give in!!! (*Down on the Blue* 203)

Notes

1. The census districts were changed from 1900. Many families like the Cospers appear nowhere under "Apache National Forest Reserve" where they should belong. In any case, the Reserve would have encompassed people not on the Blue.

2. Possibly Kathlyn Lathrop, the person who was recording and sometimes summarizing Toles's memoir, missed the distinction between "range" in the valley and the open "range," as well as between a section and a quarter section. I have tried to clarify the quotation.

3. Older records are sparse in both Clifton and Alpine Ranger offices, where I went through them. Staff did not know whether a cache still exists somewhere in storage, or whether older records were thrown out. Some records at Clifton were lost to one of the floods there. When allotments are transferred from one permittee to another, older documents may disappear from the file, but details are sometimes summarized in subsequent analyses.

6

The Blue Community Evolves,
1920–1990

From the early twenties the years have been most rewarding. I've lived in the most interesting and progressive period in history and all that has transpired in my lifetime, especially in the fields of communication and transportation, is unbelievable. We now sit at home, watch TV, and see what is happening in foreign lands. It took my father and me in my early years about three weeks to deliver our cattle to Magdalena, New Mexico. Today the cattle are inspected, weighed at the ranch scales, received and paid for by the buyer, loaded on semi-trucks and we are through, in just a few hours, until the next shipping season.

FREDDY FRITZ JR. (Fritz 1978:93)

THE BLUE HAS ALWAYS BEEN a marginal area in American history, geography, and culture. One of the last frontier areas, far from large cities, off the main routes of transportation, an obscure valley with a small population, the Blue community throughout the twentieth century lived a rural existence very different from that of most Americans. Blue people are quite proud of this difference and believe their lifestyle is superior for it. They have always been conscious of the adversity that came with their remote environment and have taken pride in this too.

But remote as the Blue is, it also experienced the changes that transformed daily life in America in the past century. In their oral histories, the older residents on the Blue express deep appreciation and wonderment over the remarkable technological progress brought by twentieth century civilization. They experienced it. Their lives were bettered in significant ways by this progress. Relative hardships still remain in the form of rough roads and long distances to drive for goods and services. But to old-timers' minds, these are nothing compared to the past.

Motor vehicles did a great deal more than help with the ranching: they broke down much of the rural isolation that prevailed on the Blue as long as families relied on animal transport. Before trucks and automobiles "the trip to town was a real trip. It wasn't made often: twice a year was probably the usual. More often than that meant someone needed a doctor or it was to go to a wedding or funeral" (Coor 1984:31).

Isolation and difficult transport necessitated a high degree of self-sufficiency. Most of a family's food came from the gardens around the "home ranch," which was the domain of the rancher's wife.

> Life on the ranch wasn't easy but we didn't know that then. That was just the way folks lived. We carried water in buckets from the creek, washed clothes on a rub board, made our own soap, cooked on a wood stove, also heated our irons on it (no permanent press fabric then), burned kerosene lamps, and even made our own cheese and vinegar. Besides this, we baked all of our bread and canned or dried our fruit and vegetables. When we sat down to rest a bit, we could sit and churn the butter, darn a few socks, quilt a little, or perhaps string some beans or shell some peas. (Moore 1982: 92; also *Down on the Blue* 228)

Motor vehicles and more trips to town led gradually to the substitution of store-bought articles for homemade, following the general American pattern over the century. Lye soap and homemade cheese became things of the past.

The roads penetrating Blue country also improved, first with the help of the Forest Service and then with the Civilian Conservation Corps.

> The first good roads we had on Blue River were built by the CC's. That was a program that President F. D. Roosevelt had in the 30s. They built roads all over the country. We didn't have many roads before that and they were very bad. They (CCC) opened many places. They stayed there, I think, a couple of years. That was during the great depression and so many people didn't have anything to do for a living, so they took them out in these camps and put them to building roads and fixing the country side with dams to stop the floods from washing away the roads and ditches. It was certainly a big help and we've had pretty good roads ever since. (Grace Johnson, *Down on the Blue* 63)

A community school bus on the upper Blue could bring the lower grades to the one-room Blue School, but older students were still sent to live with relatives or friends in town in order to attend high school. A recent option on the upper Blue is to commute two hours each way to the high school in Springerville.

The first telephone lines came as early as 1920, introduced by the Forest Service, but the service was initially primitive and party lines were not replaced by a modern call system until 1966. Electric power did not arrive until 1957 (*Down on the Blue* 234). Cleo Coor comments,

> It is hard to imagine that any place was without power so far into the twentieth century, but up until then people on the Blue used kerosene lamps for night illumination, wood burning stoves for cooking and heating, as well as fireplaces for heating. . . .
>
> Now it is amazing for one who grew up in the days when there was no electricity or running water or any of the modern conveniences to find dishwashers, microwave ovens, deep freezes, washers and dryers in nearly every house on the Blue. And indoor bathrooms the number one best invention! (*Down on the Blue* 234)

She recalls the child's fear of going to the outhouse at night, when there was no way to tell if the path might hold a rattlesnake or rabid skunk. Indoor plumbing was indeed a miracle to those who had grown up using outhouses.

THE 1930 CENSUS AND VOTING RECORDS

The 1930 Census recorded a total population of 162 in "Blue Precinct" (U. S. Census Bureau 1930). As with the 1920 Census, this area seems to have included a handful of people who by occupation (2 copper miners, a prospector, a carpenter, and a woodchopper) would seem to live close to Clifton and the mines, probably outside the Blue watershed. But the Precinct did not include another handful of people who lived over the New Mexico line, which the Blue River crosses once. Oddly, the Census does not list the Fritz family, perhaps because they had a house in Clifton and might have been recorded there.

The 1930 population was only slightly down from 1920, and the number of ranch/farm households was only a few less: 30, down from 37. Fifteen were listed as ranching (13 cattle, 2 sheep), and 15 households were listed as farming, although as in earlier censuses this wobbly distinction conceals the probability that all families were engaged in both growing food and running livestock. Of the 30 ranch or farm owners, 10 bear the names of families that appeared in the 1900 Census. But some of the other owners are married to, or descended through, women from the early settler families. In other words, half or more of the ranching and farming community had ties more than a generation deep in the Blue.

Also appearing as heads of households in the 1930 Census were a Forest Ranger, a county road worker, 4 "retireds," an electrician with a "farm" on the side, and a hunter for the Biological Survey—also with a "farm" on the side. This government program employed hunters to kill predators of livestock, and the individual engaged at this time appears to be a member of the Jones ranching family.

Other glimpses into the community during this period come from the electoral rolls of 1926 (those for 1930 are unavailable). The official register of voters for Blue Precinct (Greenlee County 1926) carries 58 names, of which 34 are males whose occupations are variously identified as rancher (13), cowman (11), stockman (4), cattleman (2), farmer (3) and a "Mech." who is known in the Census as a farm/ranch owner. Nineteen women who are members of ranching families are registered to vote, as housewife (14), ranch woman (2), ranch girl (2), and postmistress. The only non-ranching voters are Forest Ranger David Marks who has married into the Jones ranching family; and a "Fire Guard" employed by the Forest Service, likely from a local ranching family. Their wives are also registered. An anomaly, a man who would subsequently disappear from the record, is an unmarried "painter."

Thirty-one of the 58 voters were born either in Texas, New Mexico, or Arizona; one in Utah. Most of the rest come from the southern United States. For this reason, it is hardly surprising to find 56 voters in 1926 registered as Democrats. The two Republicans registered were ranchers, 1 born in New York and the other in Pennsylvania.

Separate records (Greenlee County 2000) indicate that the Blue community voted heavily Democratic during the first half of the century: in 1928, 24 for Landon, 4 for Hoover. In 1932, 42 voted for Roosevelt and only 2 for Hoover, as the voting roll swelled, probably due to fuller registration of women. This pattern of voting Democrat would not erode until the 1950s. In the 1960s and afterwards, it would change to voting Republican, but at the national level only.

Depression Years and the Hunting Business

The effects of the Depression on the cattle business were described in the previous chapter. Though families on the Blue received less cash from cattle, they were not as threatened by the Depression as many other Americans. They could fall back on the food they grew in their gardens, the beef they raised, and the hunting and fishing in their mountains. A positive side existed to their relatively self-sufficient life.

In fact, old-timers tell of economic refugees from the Depression coming to live on the Blue, camping out, and trying to live off the land.

> The deer and turkey were real plentiful to have plenty of meat...and [the people from outside the Blue] raised their own gardens and people could survive down there [on the Blue] that couldn't survive other places. That was just an ideal climate, it wasn't too cold and it wasn't too hot. During the depression there was a lot of people that lived down there. (Virginia Becker, Becker 2000).

> During the Great Depression many folks who could not find work came down on the Blue and just camped out. They were very poor, lived in tents, had very little food, and of course no money. I remember when we butchered a beef, which was quite frequent, Mother would send my brother, Dave, out with a packhorse loaded with meat and give it to these people. She was always giving them flour, cornmeal, beans, coffee and other necessities. (John T. "Jack" Marks, (*Down on the Blue* 131)

Jack Marks's mother, Iona, even nursed the refugees when sickness broke out in their camp. The Civilian Conservation Corps doctor was also called in.

Some of the contributions of the CCC to the Blue have been described: the road building, the fencing, the improvements in ranching infrastructure, and other public works. But aside from economic benefits, the CCC brought novelties from the outside world; for many on the Blue it was their first encounter.

> Anyway I remember the CCC boys inviting us children and peo-ple on the river up for Sunday dinner and I'll never forget seeing the sliced bread. I'd seen a lot of baked bread, just a whole loaf, but they had a machine to cut it with and I thought that was

really something. And they also had picture shows, which were silent movies. And they'd always invite everybody up to the movies, which was big event in my life. (Bill Richardson, *Down on the Blue* 185)

Motor vehicles and CCC-improved roads not only helped residents travel in and out of the Blue but also opened their valley to outsiders, creating opportunities other than ranching for residents to make money. Outside of livestock, commercial activity on the Blue had always been very limited. Traditionally, the postmaster or postmistress operated a small general store, working from his or her home (*Down on the Blue* 145, 173). These stores supplemented their ranching income. A different business opportunity temporarily arose with Prohibition.

Busted ranchers began looking for a "way out" [of the depressed cattle market of the 1920s] and Uncle Toles Cosper, with many of the others, thought he could find it via a "little still away up in the hills," tucked away in some secret spot on his cattleless range. It didn't work. "Federal agents located it with one of them confounded flying machines just about the time I had a good batch to run off, that would have brought me in a little cash." (Cosper 1940:13)

With repeal of Prohibition, moonshine making disappeared, but the new roads into the Blue led to a more durable enterprise that found advantage in the rough, wild backcountry. The Blue has always been superior hunting country. The Apache thought so. Aldo Leopold thought so. Elk, whitetail deer, mule deer, javelina, wild turkey, grouse, quail, squirrel were abundant game species. Native Apache trout (or Gila trout?—Forest Service biologists are now unsure) were plentiful. Hunting and fishing were naturally part of Blue life, supplementing people's diets.

Predators also abounded: grizzly bears, black bears, wolves, mountain lions, coyotes, bobcats, and because they preyed on the ranchers' animals they too were hunted. Money could be made from government and private bounties for killing major predators such as bears, wolves, and mountain lions. The U.S. Biological Survey also engaged professional hunters. Some of these lived on the Blue at times, some worked through. The most famous was Ben Lilly, who hunted often on the Blue up until 1931. Originally from the Southeast, he had left home and family behind and lived with his hounds in the mountains of the Southwest. He traveled always by foot, slept outdoors even when staying with people, ate the meat of the predators he shot, and wouldn't hunt on Sundays. A gentle Christian man whom children loved, he killed large numbers of wolves, lions, and bears, including one grizzly nine feet tall weighing 900 pounds that he fought with a knife. Many Blue oral histories mention him (*Down on the Blue* 13, 43, 56; Moore 1982:95) and a book, *The Ben Lilly Legend*, has been written about him (Dobie 1981).

Another professional hunter was Clell Lee, who would eventually marry the widow of a Cosper, and settle down to be a rancher. During the 1920s and into the 1930s he and others living on the Blue began to make money by guiding hunting parties of townsfolk (*Down on the Blue* 164). As early as 1913 or 1914, a large hunting party from Willcox, Arizona, is recorded as having come to the Blue by wagon. "So interesting were the stories of the excellent hunting and beautiful area, also of the hospitable people," that more hunting parties came in succeeding years, but in autos. The Willcox group returned in a Maxwell sedan, beginning a yearly tradition that continued until the 1980s. They received permission from the Jones/Marks ranch to set up camp on their land, hired local men as guides, and the Willcox and Blue people became regular friends (*Down on the Blue* 135). The same happened with Toles Cosper.

> Every fall there would be a bunch of guys from Clifton, businessmen, doctors and whatnot, who would come out to Toles' ranch and take twelve, fourteen, or sixteen pack mules and load them and a dozen men would take off on a hunt. They would put in most of the thirty days out in camp, hunting, kill the deer and pack them in to the ranch and hang them up. (Cosper 1982:135)

From the 1920s the seasonal occupation of guiding and sometimes "outfitting" hunters with horses or camp gear or lodging became common on the Blue and is still practiced today. The first airplane known to have landed on the Blue in the 1930s carried people from Tucson who wanted to hunt (*Down on the Blue* 63). Fishing also attracted outsiders and was encouraged by the state of Arizona's introduction of Rainbow trout, which hybridized with the native trout (USFS 1968).

The Joy family stood out as especially entrepreneurial in the hunting business, as they needed to be, because they never took up ranching. John E. "Slim" Joy, born in nearby Magdalena, New Mexico, had roved around working many jobs before he and his wife moved to the Blue in 1930. They opened a hunting business "serving primarily deer, elk, and turkey hunters," running the local post office and general store as well. Slim Joy built a hunting lodge across the river from the post office "and continued to expand his hunting business, getting some hounds and hunting lion and bear. Later he opened a package liquor business and put in a gas pump" (*Down on the Blue* 114, 135, 233). This marked the apex of commercial development, before or since, on the Blue. The gas and liquor business would expire sometime after World War II. But during hunting seasons the lodge has continued to operate, and the Joys still guide hunters and other tourists. Their main income today comes from a trout farm, but they have never raised cattle.

After World War II: Depopulation and Other Trends

The World War II effort meant the government wanted the Blue's cattle numbers again increased and its young men for the military. One of them, Bill Richardson, saw action from the invasion of North Africa to the Anzio beachhead to the D-Day landing in Normandy (*Down on the Blue* 186). Two Stacy brothers were killed in 1945, one in Belgium and one in the Philippines (Moore 1982:96). But life on the Blue changed little, except through gradual trends.

After World War II population declined significantly on the Blue. Unfortunately, there is no census data available comparable to that of 1930 and previous decades. But we do know that the population of the Blue Precinct fell from around 162 in 1962, to only 57 people by 1990, 45 of them 18 years or older (Greenlee Country 2000). In the 2000 Census 52 people lived within the Blue watershed (Best 2003) plus a handful of people across the New Mexico line—a drop of more than two-thirds from the 1930 census. Also, some people living on the Blue were retired and not living from ranching.

In 1930, there were 30 Blue households involved in farming and ranching. By the late 1980s the number of households keeping livestock and holding range allotments had dropped, by my count, to 12 living on the Blue: 9 on the upper Blue, 3 on the lower Blue. People living outside the Blue carried on another 9 ranching operations on 9 Blue allotments— a development possible with improved roads and vehicles.

The decline of the ranching population on the Blue paralleled the general trend in rural America. A number of factors were at work. With pickups, tractors, and other technical advances, fewer hands were needed to raise the same number of calves; at the same time, greater capital was necessary for ranching operations. The Forest Service was limiting and sometimes reducing the number of cattle that could be run on the Blue. Market pressures from increased productivity in the livestock industry and foreign imports were constant. Therefore, ranching operations on the Blue gradually consolidated into fewer allotment holders, each ranching more acres. Also, of course, the expansion of the American economy during and after World War II drew many out of the Blue to earn better livings than possible by ranching.

Another factor was smaller families, again paralleling the general American pattern. The upper Blue school enrollments (not including high school) dropped from over twenty students a year in the 1920s and 1930s to under ten a year in the post-World War II period, and down to small handfuls in the 1990s (*Down on the Blue* 107; 111).

But ranching remained a family affair. When extra labor was needed, the tendency was to rely on neighbors, friends, and family; only occasionally were outsiders hired. With fewer sons to help work the cattle, wives and daughters—freed by technology from much onerous domestic work—participated more, though the sexual division of labor had never been rigid on the Blue. In the early part of the century, the widow Katy Fritz supervised her cowboys from horseback while her son was away in World War I (Fritz 1985:xviii). Even earlier that century, May Balke McKeen recalled in 1956 that

> for four years we rode the range together. The first year and a half I rode sidesaddle, even though I had a little trouble keeping it on a horse when climbing those mountains. After our son, Bronson, came along we didn't want to get him skinned up, so Hugh bought me a range saddle with room for a pillow in front of me to park the young cowboy on. Then, back to the range we rode. It was a wonderful life. (McKeen 1982:169)

After the middle of the twentieth century, women helping with the cattle, and even riding the range by themselves, became unexceptional. Not coincidentally, they also began wearing blue jeans and slacks as common dress, and boots, hats, and shirts similar to those of the men. This "cowgirl" style was firmly established by the 1950s. Men's dress shifted fashion too, at least when they dressed up, to cowboy "Western" clothing.

"Of course, for working wear they wore Levis, Stetson hats, and Justin boots" (*Down on the Blue* 235).

From necessity, ranching families on the Blue often found various ways to supplement their main income selling calves. Aside from guiding hunters, they found jobs working on the county roads, on Forest Service projects, or fighting forest fires. A few took in boarders or practiced taxidermy. Some left the Blue temporarily to find work in construction and mining in nearby areas. But the remoteness of the Blue from urban areas made commuting to an outside job an unlikely prospect.

A smaller population did not lead to less social activity. In fact modern communication made socializing easier, both inside and outside the valley. "There are so many things to do here at the Blue, there is not time to do everything you would like to do. We have the Blue River Cowbelles, potluck dinners and dances, and visiting with the neighbors" (Betty Gaddy, *Down on the Blue* 118). If the several-day parties of Toles Cosper no longer took place, there were still late-night dances. Like country people in general, many on the Blue could play instruments. During the 1960s and 1970s, there was a local "Barb Wire Boys Band."

The ranchers have their local Greenlee County cattlemen's association, whose get-togethers have generally involved potluck parties as well as business. The women's arm of this association, as elsewhere in the West, is termed the "Cowbelles." The Blue section of the Cowbelles is the effective agency for organizing social and civic activities on the Blue, such as keeping up the Blue School and the Blue Cemetery, or putting together a Blue float for the summer parade in Springerville. The Blue Cowbelles also collected the oral history that went into the community history *Down on the Blue* (1987).

The Blue School, on Forest Service land, is frequently used as a community center for activities on the upper Blue.

An annual rodeo occurs in nearby Luna, New Mexico, and every year the Cosper family descendants—more than a hundred of them—have a big get-together at the KP camping ground off the Coronado highway on the Blue.

While the ranching families still provide the leadership and set the tone for Blue social life, they reach out to incorporate others from the small but growing number of retired residents not involved in ranching. Some of these are related to Blue families or grew up on the Blue. Others were simply attracted to the remote beauty of the place. In one case, Bob Deyo, a postal inspector on a visit to the small post office, "fell in love" with the Blue, according to his wife. The family went from camping there annually to building a vacation home, and finally retiring there. In the process, their daughter Barbara met and married a Blue cowboy, Billy Marks (*Down on the Blue* 128; see also chapter 16 in this book).

7

Creating Wilderness
on the Blue

He loved the Blue and the Blue Range. The canyon, the river, the mountains, and all the little canyons leading from the mountains into the main Blue River were places that he explored. He rode over every part of that area, taking it all in, listening to the silence, to the wind, to the birds, to the rocks under his horse's hooves, to the creak of the saddle, and the breathing of the horse. He took in the sights, the smells, the freedom, the aloneness of the vast country called "Blue." It was his home. It permeated his very being. When he was away he made the best of it, but on the Blue and the mountains he was at one with the wilderness.

CLEO COSPER COOR, writing about her father, Toles DeWitt Cosper,
son of Toles Cosper (*Down on the Blue* 204)

ORAL HISTORIES OF THE BLUE often testify to its people's love and gratitude for the wild, natural beauty surrounding them. Ironically, however, prospects for their future life on the Blue would in time be gravely jeopardized on the basis of that same wild nature.

The natural values of the Blue region meant that twentieth-century America would begin to look upon it as something other than rangeland or cattle country. While the Blue lacked the unique features and spectacular formations that had led to the creation of national parks in places like the Grand Canyon, Yosemite, and Yellowstone, it was a remote, wild, and sparsely settled region even for the Southwest. It was the kind of landscape a new movement emerged to preserve as "wilderness." And it was Aldo Leopold, eventually celebrated as the philosopher of this movement, who first developed the concept of wilderness protection that would come to be applied to the Blue he had known. As a major irony of his legacy on the Blue, his ideas would return to affect the lives of the people there in ways he probably did not intend.

In the early 1920s, Leopold was an assistant district forester in Albuquerque, the Southwest district headquarters of the Forest Service. His love of the wild was always associated with hunting, and he was critical of the new potential of automobiles to disturb wildlife habitat and the hunter's communion with nature.

> Who wants to stalk his buck to the music of a motor? Or track his turkey on the trail of a knobby tread? Who that is called to the high hills for a real *paseo* wants to wrangle his packs along a graveled highway? There's car sign in every canyon, car dust on every bush, a parking ground at every watering hole, and Fords on a thousand hills. (Leopold in Zaslowsky and Watkins 1994:198)

Leopold therefore searched for roadless areas to keep in that condition and proposed that a large section of New Mexico's Gila National Forest north of Silver City be preserved intact as a wilderness area without future development. State game protection associations, which Leopold had helped organize, supported preservation as a way to safeguard wildlife habitat for future hunting.

What about the cattle ranches in this area? Leopold wrote,

> the entire area is grazed by cattle, but the cattle ranches would be an asset from the recreational standpoint because of the interest which attaches to cattle grazing operations under frontier conditions. The apparent disadvantage thus imposed on the cattlemen might be nearly offset by the obvious advantage of freedom from new settlers, and from the hordes of motorists who will invade this region the minute it is opened up. (Leopold 1921b:721)

Local stockmen registered little opposition to the designation, as it allowed "conservative" grazing to continue and did not at the time interfere with their operations. (Only later, as they mechanized their operations, would ranchers come to rue the restrictions on motors that came with wilderness designation.) Thus a portion of the Gila received its unique designation from the Forest Service in 1924, as America's first official "wilderness area" (Meine 1988:194–198, 200, 224–227).

The Forest Service followed up with an initiative to survey other national forests, looking for additional roadless areas to preserve. In 1929, this survey led to an administrative regulation called L-20, giving the Forest Service authority

> to do what had already been done in the Gila—to establish "primitive areas" that were to remain primeval in their "environment, transportation, habitation and subsistence."...Logging was still allowed, because it was believed that, if properly regulated, it would not be incompatible with the ultimate purpose of the reservation.... Most public land historians have viewed the L-20 regulation as merely a stalling measure to keep the most scenic lands within the national forests from being transferred to the national parks, which had often been the case. (Zaslowsky and Watkins 1994:200)

Leopold and the Forest Service might have considered the Blue area for an early wilderness area like the Gila, except for the fact that the "Coronado Trail," Highway 666, had just been constructed along the ridge at the western edge of the Blue watershed (Meine 1988:556, n.27). Nevertheless, in 1933 the whole center of Blue country east of the highway and over into a part of New Mexico was declared the "Blue Range Primitive Area," an area of about 200,000 acres. Leopold's ideas had returned to the Blue.

Leopold had envisaged roadless areas as the main criterion for wilderness, but on the Blue as in other "primitive areas," including the nearby Gila National Forest, roads *did* penetrate portions of the designated area. Therefore, boundaries simply were gerrymandered ("cherry-stemmed" in Forest Service jargon), around roads and the private "inholdings," leaving some ranch families surrounded by the official "wilderness." As elsewhere, ranchers on the Blue were allowed to continue grazing the lands they had traditionally used within the Blue Primitive Area, which incorporated at the time all or part of nineteen different allotments. There is no evidence that people on the Blue opposed the designation at the time, or that during the next few decades they felt it impinged on their lives. As on the Gila, ranching continued.

The Wilderness Act of 1964 and Blue Opposition

The Forest Service designation, however, contained latent questions about the future of the Blue that would be raised later in the century. In

1964 Congress passed, and President Johnson signed, the Wilderness Act. It embodied a concept pioneered by John Muir and Aldo Leopold, that some lands' value lay *not* in development for human use but in being preserved in their natural state for recreational or spiritual uses, with human access only on foot or horseback.

The statute contained this definition:

> A wilderness, in contrast with those areas where man and his own works dominate the landscape, is hereby recognized as an area where the earth and the community of life are untrammeled by man, where man himself is a visitor who does not remain.

Following Leopold's logic, this definition proved in practice to mean blocks of roadless areas of "at least five thousand acres of land." Official wilderness would also be an area that "retain[s] its primeval character and influence, without permanent improvements or human habitation . . . [and that] appears to have been affected primarily by the forces of nature [with] outstanding opportunities for solitude. . . ." (U.S. Congress 1964)

Following the Act's passage, tens of millions of acres would eventually be set aside as protected wilderness—including to date over six percent of the state of Arizona—or as areas to be studied for future inclusion as wilderness, a process that continues today. Most wilderness would come out of Forest Service lands. Once officially designated by Congress, wilderness areas are off limits to any type of motorized vehicles; any roads, buildings, or other structures; and all logging, mining, and oil and gas extraction, except under rare conditions. Of course, the pre-existence of such activities in an area might disqualify land from wilderness designation, but government officials, politicians, and activists searching for suitable "wilderness" did not want to exclude lands being grazed—such as Leopold's original "wilderness area" on the Gila. The advocates of wilderness did not always like the practice of livestock grazing—some, like John Muir, hated it—but they recognized that it had long been practiced on landscapes that they wanted for the wilderness system. As a political necessity, they agreed to "grandfather" the practice into the law. In the wilderness areas, however, ranching would face various restrictions: like other activities it could be done only on foot or horseback, given the strict prohibition on motorized vehicles.

What would happen to the Blue Range Primitive Area? The Wilderness Act directed that all seventy-six Primitive Areas receive additional study to determine their suitability for wilderness status, and the Forest Service started this process. In many cases, local opposition arose to prevent areas becoming official wilderness; such was the case on the Blue. Especially opposed to wilderness designation were the ranchers. The Blue community mobilized, wrote letters, signed petitions, and lobbied their Arizona congressmen against wilderness designation. The ultimate decision would be up to Congress, which usually accepted the recommendation of a state's congressional delegation.

One of the leading opposition figures was Fred Fritz Jr. (1895–1985), owner of the Three Xs Ranch (XXX), which his father had pioneered in the 1880s. Educated only on the Blue, he nevertheless was an articulate spokesman for the region and for ranching interests. He was elected to the Arizona legislature many times and served as both Speaker of the House and President of the Senate. He had also been President of the Arizona Cattle Growers Association. As the controversy over the wilderness issue heated up, he was interviewed in an article in the December 17, 1967 issue of *Arizona Magazine*, "The Cattleman and the Wilderness" (Dedera 1967).

> Fred Fritz, Jr. . . . in boots . . . is 5 feet 4. He's wiry, true, and extraordinarily active for a man of 72. He is not shy about speaking his mind and he believes his rights are rooted in the most basic of human justice: that a man who has labored all his life should not be forced to give up what he has fairly earned. . . .
>
> The [Fritz] range is 62,000 acres of Apache National Forest due east of Phoenix on the New Mexico border. Fritz' Herefords, with a mother herd of about 450 cows, graze up and down the Blue River and far back into the crags and canyons, slopes and slides, green meadows and grassy mesas. It is a country so stunningly lovely that men can only blink in appreciation, their puny words sticking in their inadequate minds.
>
> Half of the Fritz range lies in the Blue Range Primitive Area, established in 1933.
>
> [Fritz Jr.'s] dad came into the Blue country in the mid-80s and fought Indians, disease and drought and ferocious animals to establish his ranch. After one Apache raid, the elder Fritz was one of only three white men left alive along the river. What finally got him [years later] was a grizzly bear, in desperate hand-to-paw combat that ranks among the sagas of the West. Fritz never

recovered from the mauling and his death years afterwards was blamed on the bear.

The article explains the restrictions to be imposed on lands designated "wild and primitive": all the work would have to be performed by saddle transportation, without machinery.

> Most of the ranchers running cattle on 17 allotments in the Blue Range Primitive Area believe the wilderness rules will hurt— maybe even drive some out of business. They have instinctively turned, as they have in the past to Fred Fritz, Jr. as spokesman and champion. . . .

Fritz Jr. explains their opposition:

> "I have always recognized the public nature of these lands, and the rights of other users of the forest. In fact, I didn't invent the term, multiple use, but I've preached it all my life. I haven't killed a deer in 20 years, myself, but I welcome hunters and I usually throw in some guide service free.
>
> "The government says multiple use is good for most of its public lands, but not for wilderness, and that's a contradiction that doesn't make much sense to me.
>
> "I've built 17 water catchments, little dams that I won't be able to maintain without power equipment. I put out salt in 40 places and it's used by my stock and by wildlife, and I can't pack in all that salt on muleback.

Fritz Jr. points to ecological problems with the U.S. Forest lands that will only grow worse with wilderness restrictions.

> Some of my best grass is being seriously invaded by juniper, and I think some experiments are in order, for the conversion of some of these thickets back to grass. But that calls for bulldozer. I can't do it with an ax.
>
> "The Forest Service has made its share of mistakes. Before the Forest Service, fire was one of nature's tools, and frequent small fires kept the fuel down. The Forest Service has put out every fire it could for the last 50 years, and now this Blue Range is prime for a bad fire. And you hear some so-called wilderness lovers say that "fire is a part of the wilderness—let it burn."

"I tell you, if we let some of it burn now, there won't be much left.

The fires he predicted would in fact come later to the region. He also questions whether the public will benefit in any way from the wilderness designation.

They say wilderness will preserve nature for the public. Let's take a hard look at what wilderness designation is going to mean for the Blue. If you're rich enough to hire a guide and a pack-string, you might see it.

"Not many hunters will walk that far. The country will simply be out of reach for ninety-nine percent of our people.

"I hear there is a population explosion. It's said that land has to be set aside as wilderness for posterity.

"Well, as a working cowman, I believe somebody had better start worrying how we're going to feed those masses that are on the way. We ranchers grow food. We make the land produce. Many of us suspect that the long-range goal of the conservationists is to phase out the cattle operations on the wilderness areas, as soon as the wilderness areas are locked up. Then the picture will be complete—the wilderness won't be visited by many people, so it won't be seen. It won't produce. Not even the game herds can be harvested properly. My water developments will deteriorate and the brush will come in so thick a terrible fire is almost assured. There's your wilderness, as I see it. . . ."

"I wouldn't want to live to see that," he said. "It has been the guiding rule of my life that I would never knowingly do anything to this country to hurt it, and that I would leave it in better condition than I found it."

THE WILDERNESS PROPOSAL AND COUNTY ROAD 10

As expected, the Forest Service proposed all its Primitive Areas be designated official Wilderness. A "Proposal for a Blue Range Wilderness in the Apache National Forest" appeared in the late 1960s (USFS: ca. 1969) and a longer revised proposal in 1971 (USFS 1971). Almost all of the Primitive Area, 177,239 acres, was to be included in the Wilderness. After a prologue summarizing Blue history, the Proposal begins its rationale for wilderness designation:

Recommendations for future management of the Blue Range rest on the primary importance and value of its wilderness resource. The deep rugged canyons, the steep timbered ridges, the sweeping reaches of stark, broken country, the outstanding solitude and the sense of being close to creation, make this area unique in its setting.

Here in the Blue a pleasing mix of all the resources is combined to make the area outstanding as a Wilderness, where the mark of man and his activities is relatively obscure, where a visitor can virtually isolate himself from the stresses of modern civilization and gain spiritual refreshment through self-evaluation.

Limited motorized travel has invaded the area along the Blue River, but frequent flooding has almost obliterated signs of this invasion. (USFS ca. 1969)

Here the Forest Service proposal finesses a problem related to the criteria for official wilderness: Leopold's original idea of roadlessness. The problem was obvious enough to be picked up immediately by wilderness opponents: "limited motorized travel" had historically cut the proposed Blue wilderness in two, down the middle, along County Road 10 (or Forest Road 281).

In the early pioneer days a road ran the length of the Blue River. Carrying more than local traffic, it connected Alpine, Arizona, and Luna, New Mexico, with Clifton, Arizona, to the south. As described in chapter 3, big floods early in the twentieth century took out the riverbed road south of the Fritz XXX ranch on the lower Blue. As an alternative to the Blue River road, the mountainous US Route 666 (now 191), "the Coronado Trail," was built along the western edge of the Blue watershed in the early 1920s and became the means for almost all traffic between Clifton and Alpine. Ranchers on the lower Blue, including the Fritz family, built another road, F.R. 475 or the Juan Miller Road, leading off Route 666, which they used to get in and out of the Blue. On the upper Blue, however, the old Blue River road survived and was maintained as F.R. 281. It ran south from near Alpine deep into the center of the Primitive Area to serve the ranchers and others living along the route.

By the late 1960s, no one was living between the Fritz XXX ranch and the end of the Blue road at the old Toles Cosper ranch, the Y Bar Y. Between these two ranches, about twelve miles apart as the crow flies, lay the unmaintained remnants of the old County Road 10, which Fritz and others wanted restored as a "corridor road."

One permittee on the Blue, Dennis Stacy, recalls:

> When my grandfather was alive, and my aunt and uncle bought that ranch on the upper Blue, Greenlee County used to run a 'dozer or a cat and a roadgrader, and they would blade a road right up the river bottom, connecting the lower Blue with the upper Blue. And my aunt and uncle and a lot of the people used to drive, not four-wheel pickups but their old Model T cars on that road. . . ." (Stacy 1998)

How long this connecting road remained passable is unclear; county maintenance apparently ended in the 1940s. Some ranchers like the Fritzes continued to use portions of the old road into the 1960s to reach parts of their allotments. The last rancher to use the old road thinks that after the Primitive Area was established in 1933, the Forest Service closed it to anyone who did not have property there (Goodwin 2000). The Forest Service today claims it had no part of the road closure on the lower Blue. It contends that the County had "no need to continue with keeping the road open. . . . Due to periodic flooding over the years, the Road closed itself and the costs to keep it passable were too steep to keep it open" (Bedell 2001).

County Road 10 became an issue again in 1969 due to the proposed wilderness designation. Opponents of wilderness cited it as evidence to disqualify the Blue from being a roadless area. By the same token, the Forest Service was just as determined to let the road be effaced by continued neglect. The Greenlee County Board of Supervisors formally petitioned the Forest Service on July 24, 1970, opposing creation of a wilderness area out of the Blue, and asking that a corridor be provided along the River with "provisions for a roadway as existed along said river since 1896" (USFS 1970). According to some residents, the Forest Service then blocked the road to prevent the County from unilaterally restoring it.

Permittee rancher Dennis Stacy remembers,

> Around 1969 or 1970, the Forest Service decided to block the road off. . . . I remember the Board of Supervisors was pretty angry about it, and I remember some of those meetings with the Forest Service at the Greenlee County courthouse. They wanted

to do away with that road and make it into a wilderness area. And that's when we were collecting all those petitions [against wilderness designation]. (Stacy 2000)

Dennis Stacy cites a photograph in the Clifton Ranger Office of the road at a point within the proposed wilderness area,

> and it shows where a grader has gone up that river, with cobble on each side, and a ranger with packhorse riding right down that bladed road.
>
> What's interesting to me, is that if you look at the criteria for someplace to be a wilderness area, it says that if a piece of land was ever trammeled by man, or if a road was ever put in by mechanical means, then it cannot be considered for Wilderness designation. And that Blue Range Primitive Area had a road put in by mechanical means and maintained by mechanical means. There's old sawmills down there [too].... [The Forest Service] kind of changed the rules to fit their needs. (Dennis and Douglas Stacy 1998)

In its wilderness proposal, the Forest Service simply ignored the old road. As for the road still being used from the upper Blue into the heart of the Primitive Area, connecting the parcels of private property and homes of people living there, the proposal simply "cherry-stemmed" it. "Wilderness" would begin at roadside but exclude the road and the inholdings it connected. Wilderness boundaries would thus be gerrymandered around these to include only the remaining "roadless" Forest Service land. Cherry-stemming technically achieved the criterion for wilderness, but people on the Blue regarded this practice as an aggressive stratagem that presaged their expulsion one day from the wilderness area.

In any case, Dennis Stacy raised a pertinent question: how "untrammeled" and "primeval" is the Blue?—to use words from the preamble to the 1964 Wilderness Act. The Forest Service's citation of the "frequent flooding" that "has almost obliterated signs of this invasion" of motor vehicles points to the erosion discussed in chapter 3. But paradoxically this erosion and the concomitant flooding caused by humans is evidence of the transformation of the Blue Valley from whatever "primeval" state may have existed before 1880. Once it had been the contention of Aldo Leopold and the Forest Service that flooding caused by livestock and other human activities had "ruined" the Blue, altered the river, and destroyed the road. Obliteration of that road was now being cited as evidence of qualification for wilderness status because it was still unspoiled by humans! Or, in words from the Forest Service wilderness proposal, the Blue is "where the mark of man and his activities is relatively obscure."

Ironically, at the time, this contradiction was unacknowledged—perhaps unrecognized—by both the Forest Service and the ranchers. Each for their own reasons had no desire to portray the Blue as spoiled by humans.

Pyrrhic Victory for the Opposition

The "Proposal for a Blue Range Wilderness" summarizes other information about the Blue around 1970.

> Many opportunities for outdoor recreation are available. About 1000 people venture into the Blue Range every year, primarily for hunting and fishing. Hunting with hounds for bear and lions is a popular sport. As populations and social pressures increase, more people will probably turn to the Wilderness for outdoor recreation. There are no developed recreation sites and no need for any in the foreseeable future. (USFS ca. 1979)

Two primitive campsites had been developed along the upper Blue River during the CCC days and a half dozen more created along Route 666. They all lay close to the boundaries of the proposed new Wilderness.

> All or portions of 17 grazing allotments are involved in the proposed Wilderness. The acreage of land actually used for grazing varies considerably between the allotments. Browse is the staple forage for livestock during the fall and winter grazing season. There are 15 grazing permittees whose cattle use the 17 allotments; of these, three families live year-long within the Primitive Area, but outside the proposed Wilderness, along the upper Blue River. (USFS 1971)

Other permittees lived either on the Blue, outside the proposed Wilderness, or in surrounding ranches and communities. Aside from ranchers, a number of retired persons lived then (as now) yearlong within the Primitive Area, plus some summer residents.

The Forest Service estimated,

> About 1600 cattle spend 18,615 months grazing within the area.
> Grazing capacity varies considerably between allotments. Range
> developments in the area include 140 miles of fence, 46 corrals,
> 8 earthen stock tanks, 22 developed springs, 5 cabins, and por-
> tions of two hard pipelines. Fences are of wood and steel posts,
> with barbed wire. Springs were developed by installing concrete
> or rock masonry catchment basins, steel or wooden drinking
> troughs, and plastic or galvanized pipe.
>   Grazing use will continue where it is compatible with the
> Wilderness and the ability of the forage resource to sustain itself.
> (USFS ca. 1969)

In its 1971 revised proposal, the Forest Service made more exact
its figures for the number of cattle actually permitted for allotments
within the proposed Wilderness: 1,524 with 17,592 Animal Unit Months
(AUMs) of grazing (USFS 1971).

In its bureaucratic style, the 1971 proposal seems to draw directly
from the range analyses of the period, and gives the Forest Service view
at the time regarding the problems surrounding ranching on the Blue,
without clarifying how these relate to wilderness designation.

> Range analysis and wildlife studies reveal there is considerable
> competition for browse between cattle and big game, especially
> during winter months. This condition would exist with or with-
> out wilderness designation. The future management objectives
> will be to reduce this conflict to the extent practicable.

The "big game" in this case means elk, which had begun to compete seri-
ously with cattle for the grass. Whether the Forest Service would favor
the elk or the cows in this competition is not mentioned. Here is a typical
Forest Service summary of range conditions on the Blue that could have
been taken directly from their files.

> Large portions of the range allotment are unsuitable for grazing
> due to steep slopes, dense timber and brush stands and rocky and
> barren areas. Some of the suitable range was excessively grazed
> in the past. Range condition varies considerably with the major-
> ity of the suitable range in fair to poor condition. Improper dis-
> tribution is a major obstacle to good management.

Some opportunities exist to improve forage condition through use of better range management grazing systems which are compatible with wilderness.

Ranchers might become uneasy reading these remarks, especially a phrase such as "compatible with wilderness."

As required by law, the Forest Service held meetings and solicited public comment on the proposed Wilderness. The 1971 proposal dutifully sums up the responses.

In public reaction, responses in 3-day period totaled 3,422 against and 1,600 in favor of the Blue Range Wilderness. Of these, 2,659 against and 22 in favor were xeroxed or mimeographed form letters. Review of responses showed that many individuals made more than one response to the proposal. Local government reaction was strongly against any wilderness. Ten of 14 County Boards of Supervisors of Arizona submitted resolutions against the proposal. . . . [The opposition] cited the need to determine mineral potential, the need to develop the area for all forms of recreation, the need for increased timber harvest, the need for more range improvements, the need for access for many purposes including all forms of economic development, the need for access for emergencies, the need to increase water yield, the need to hold back increasing governmental restrictions, the desirability of multiple use over single use as a land management ethic, and the lack of need for an additional wilderness because of the proximity of many other such areas.

In the end, the Blue Range Primitive Area did not become wilderness. The Blue was not included in the bill that Arizona congressmen put before Congress designating wilderness areas in their state. This was peculiar: of the seventy-six primitive areas in the United States, only the Blue Range Primitive Area was not converted into official wilderness. The other primitive areas became the core of the U.S. wilderness system, while even today the Blue retains the odd distinction of being the only designated "primitive area" left in the U.S. Forest Service System.

Why did the Blue remain an anomaly? Local opposition, especially from ranchers, was intense, and Fred Fritz Jr. certainly had political ties to Arizona congressmen. But wilderness designation faced similar opposition in many parts of the West. Some observers have suggested that mining interests were decisive, especially the Phelps Dodge Copper Company, which had a huge open pit mine in Morenci. These interests were guarding present and future water and mining rights in the lower Blue. (Flader 1974:42–42, n. 9.)

Don Hoffman, the present-day director of the Arizona Wilderness Alliance, worked on the wilderness "inventory" on the Blue for the Forest Service and lives there now on the "Dry Blue" creek across the New Mexico line. His organization is still lobbying for wilderness designation for the Blue. When asked why the Blue failed to make wilderness status in the 1970s along with the other primitive areas, he cannot point to any certain cause.

> Good question. Quality-wise, it's as high as any of them in terms of the quality of the wilderness. In fact, right now the Blue is probably the highest quality nondesignated land set in the lower 48. At 700,000 acres it's the largest Forest Service chunk in the lower 48 that's not protected as Forest Service Wilderness. It probably has to do with the politics of the area. It's not like this is the only rural area where wilderness issues are contentious. This was true throughout the west. So why this [exception] happened is really difficult to say. (Hoffman 2002)

He thinks that the environmental groups may have made mistakes. If they had to compromise on wilderness areas in a statewide bill, it was easy to compromise on the Blue, because it would be administered as wilderness, anyway.

The Forest Service decided to administer the last remaining Primitive Area virtually the same as a wilderness area, according to the same rules. Ironically, the victory of the Blue wilderness opponents was entirely Pyrrhic, as later events would clearly show.

8

Returning the XXX Ranch to the Wild

Many of us suspect that the long-range goal of the conservationists is to phase out the cattle operations on the wilderness areas, as soon as the wilderness areas are locked up.

FRED FRITZ JR. (Dedera 1967)

Down here at the Greenlee County Courthouse, they have a map, and that map was sent to the Board of Supervisors by John Bedell when he first came here [as head of Apache-Sitgreaves National Forest]. He came down to meet with them, and at that time my brother-in-law Jack Savios was a Supervisor, and Mr. Bedell said, "If there's anything I can do to help you guys, let me know," and my brother-in-law said, "I'd like to have a map from the Forest Service of all the private land in Greenlee County that the Forest Service wants to acquire."...About a month later this map came...and if you want to see that map and all the land the Forest Service has marked in yellow, go down to the Greenlee County Courthouse in Clifton and ask Kay Gale, and she'll show you the map with all the patented land the Forest Service wants to acquire. And our piece and the Marks', and everybody on the upper Blue is on it, all of the old Three X is on it, a lot of the patented land on Eagle Creek is on it, the lower Blue is on it.

DENNIS STACY (Dennis and Douglas Stacy 1998)

THWARTED IN ITS PLANS to declare the Blue area official wilderness, the Forest Service nevertheless persisted in creating the conditions for wilderness, regardless of designation. The "corridor road" that Fred Fritz Jr. and Blue residents wanted reopened to connect all the ranches along the Blue was flatly rejected by the agency, and the County did not have the resources to go to court on the issue.

However, the main method the Forest Service has used to create conditions for wilderness is to acquire when possible the inholdings of privately owned land and ranches within the Primitive Area, or adjacent to it and surrounded by National Forest land. This has been a public policy openly pursued. The Forest Service has criteria of what are "desirable lands" to acquire, and many of these potentially apply to most private land on the Blue: "valuable watershed lands without extensive improvements"; "high sediment producing lands"; "isolated tracts that do not have extensive improvements"; "abandoned homesteads"; "lands on which the resource management is being improperly handled"; and finally, "lands suitable and needed to supplement wildland, public-recreation developments" (USFS ca. 1980).

As noted in the epigraph at the head of this chapter, the Apache-Sitgreaves Forest Supervisor was quite forthcoming in providing Greenlee County with a map of desired acquisitions. A letter accompanied it.

Dear Ms. Ruger:

Enclosed is a map that depicts the tracts of private land within the National Forest and Greenlee County that we consider desirable for acquisition for National Forest purposes. As you can see, nearly all in-holdings are considered desirable for National Forest uses.

There are major advantages to the County of not having widely scattered private development within the National Forest with the attendant demands for County services that far exceed the tax revenue that they provide. The National Forest is a valuable county asset that can only become more valuable as time passes and populations increase.

JOHN C. BEDELL, Apache-Sitgreaves National Forest Supervisor (letter sent June 8, 1990, together with the map, to Ms. A. Lynn Ruger, Greenlee County Economic Development Coordinator, Greenlee County Courthouse, Clifton, Arizona)

The letter and the map are still kept in the courthouse by the county clerk to be shown to anyone who asks. The map's existence is well known on the Blue because everyone's private real estate there—or in Mr. Bedell's words, "nearly all inholdings"—are marked on the map in yellow as "desirable for acquisition." "All inholdings" means all settlement: all homes as well as the "base property" needed to ranch. If the Federal Government did acquire this land, there would no longer be private land for people to live on the Blue. There would be no Blue community. The fact that this map and accompanying letter exist confirms the Blue residents' worst apprehensions about the future. They have it on paper: the way they see it, the U.S. government considers their elimination as a population "desirable."

Nearly ten years after the map was sent to the County, Mr. Bedell, still Apache-Sitgreaves Forest supervisor, confirmed again the policy in a letter to me (USFS 2000b). "The isolated tracts of land along the Blue and San Francisco Rivers are classified as desirable for acquisition through the land exchange program. . . ." Although the words "isolated tracts" makes them seem marginal, these pieces of land are the once-homesteaded private properties on which the entire population of the Blue now lives. They are "isolated" because laws in the past limited private acquisition of public lands so that private property in ranching country was predestined to be small islands within a sea of federally owned land.

In his letter, Mr. Bedell stressed that land acquisition has been "strictly voluntary based on private land owners," that land acquisition has nothing to do with "our current efforts to balance livestock with capacity," and that "it is in no way a part of our current NEPA decisions associated with Allotment Management. . . ." By this he means the deep reductions of livestock enforced on many allotments in the 1990s, a process that will be described in subsequent chapters.

Local ranchers believe that motives surrounding the would-be wilderness area help explain the Forest Service push since the late 1960s to reduce stocking numbers, retire permits, and buy out private holdings within or bordering the Primitive Area. But the Forest Service denies any connection between the wilderness issue, land acquisition, and agency decisions regulating the permittees' allotments—how many cattle they can run, and when and where. Ranchers on the Blue, however, remain skeptical of this alleged lack of connection. They see the issues as linked and believe it all reflects one goal: to phase out ranching and maybe eventually even people living on the Blue.

THE XXX FOR SALE—OR TRADE?

The case of the Fritz XXX ranch is cited today on the Blue as the earliest evidence for the theory that ranching is to be "phased out," in Fred

Fritz Jr.'s words, in favor of wilderness. With the oldest ranch on the Blue, pioneered by his father, and himself a lifelong rancher, Fred Fritz Jr., as noted in chapter 7, was a community leader and influential in Arizona politics. But he and his wife

> had only one little girl, and she died at a very young age, and they were never able to have any other children, and there were no nephews or nieces or anybody who wanted the ranch, and when it came time that Freddie was up in his 70s and couldn't run it anymore, there was nobody around to help, and there was nobody for him to give it to or will it to, and let them run it until the time came it was theirs. . . . I can remember how I felt that was the most heartbreaking thing I'd ever seen, watching Freddie have to go through this. I'd known him ever since I was a little tiny kid. (Mona Bunnel, a neighbor [Bunnel 1998])

The large "Sandrock" allotment of the XXX stretched into the heart of the Primitive Area, where it included the former allotments of two earlier ranches, the "Bell" and the "HU Bar." Fritz owned the patented (private) lands of these two homesteads inside the Primitive area. Late in 1968, while the potential wilderness designation for the Blue was being considered, the Nature Conservancy approached the Forest Service about purchasing the Bell and HU Bar patented land, along with another nearby former homestead, the "Smith Place," owned by a neighboring rancher, Herschel Downs. No one was living any longer on these three properties; they were abandoned homesteads.

The Forest Service usually has very limited funds to buy land; instead, it often trades land for land. To obtain inholdings or other land the agency wants, it will swap U.S. Forest holdings near urban areas, land valuable for development. Often these trades are accomplished through middlemen, and sometimes the third parties have been environmental groups, especially the Nature Conservancy. The latter specializes in buying private land to "save" it for conservation purposes. In some cases it administers the land itself, but often it trades the land it wants conserved to the federal government in return for other land it can sell for development to make money to buy still more land it wants to conserve.

Who initiated the idea to buy the three old homesteads within the Primitive Area is unclear. But John T. Koen, Assistant Regional Forester in the Albuquerque office, responded by letter on January 10, 1969, to a

Nature Conservancy inquiry by giving data about the Smith Place, Bell Ranch, and HU Bar Ranch, including estimated worth and the names of the owners.

> The three tracts of land to which you refer are all considered to be of high priority by the Apache National Forest and would rate among the top priority cases in the Region because they are within the exterior boundaries of the Blue Range Primitive Area. The lands are classified as desirable for acquisition and would be incorporated into the Blue Range Primitive Area Management Program if acquired. (USFS 1969a)

Another letter on January 21, answering Nature Conservancy questions, admitted,

> We are not aware of any further details as to the personal feelings of the landowners with whom you will be dealing other than what you have already outlined. We do not know the financial status of the landowners. . . . We wish you success in your endeavor to acquire these lands for incorporation into the Blue Range Primitive Area. We certainly appreciate your interest in striving to help us place these lands in Federal ownership. (USFS 1969a)

This attempted acquisition was unsuccessful, and the properties remained in the hands of Fritz and Downs. Probably Fred Fritz Jr., like other ranchers on the Blue, preferred to pass his ranch and allotment to another rancher, not to the Forest Service to be retired to wilderness.

In the early 1970s Fritz, in his seventies and no longer feeling up to ranching, was looking for a prospective buyer. Any proposed sale would need to be discussed with the Forest Service, as they would have to approve transfer of the Sandrock allotment grazing permit that went with the XXX. Grazing permits to particular Forest Service allotments generally change hands along with the ownership of the private "base properties" to which they are connected. Allotments and the private property, while legally separable, are treated as a whole by the buyers, sellers, and lending banks, and the purchase price for a ranch will be greatly influenced by the number of cattle permitted on its allotment. So the terms of the new permit must be spelled out by the Forest Service before a purchase can occur.

A formal discussion between a permittee and a Forest Service official is often summarized in a letter sent by the latter to the former. Sometimes the permittee is asked to sign a copy of the letter and return it; in any case, the summary goes into the Forest Service files. From these files, and copies of documents the permittee kept, we can gather an insight into the growing conflict between the Forest Service and the rancher in this case—a conflict that would be repeated on the Blue in future years.

In November 1972, Clifton District Ranger Jerry A. Dieter wrote to confirm a recent discussion with Fritz. The letter contained some words that Fritz would not have liked to hear.

> I discussed with you the Suitability Standards that have been developed which deal with the soils, slope, vegetative cover and erosion. These standards will be applied to the Sandrock Allotment. The Sandrock is considered a marginal range land for yearlong grazing along with several other allotments with similar geology. There is a considerable amount of nonsuitable range land on the allotment, which was determined during the 1968 analysis. The suitability standards when applied to your allotment will no doubt increase the nonsuitable range. This, as you stated, would lead to a reduction in capacity and livestock numbers. I felt it imperative that these points be discussed with you before a prospective buyer be brought to the office to process transfer papers. (USFS 1972a)

While the summary is couched in the bland, bureaucratic, quasi-scientific terminology favored by the Forest Service, the discussion must have been bitter to the old rancher. To be told that the ranch that had been his home for seventy-seven years was considered "marginal range land," much of it unsuitable for grazing, was to question what his life and that of his father had been about. And the ominous forewarning of a mandated reduction in livestock numbers would be the last thing Fritz wanted to hear as he searched for a buyer for his ranch.

Ranger Dieter goes on to spell out how, while Fritz then had a permit for 542 head of cattle yearlong, 135 of those were based on temporary permits that might not be transferred to a new purchaser; also, how after further studies were made, the numbers might be reduced even lower. Then the ranger summarizes the rest of the meeting in diplomatic language that concedes Fritz's adverse reaction at the meeting.

You have had moderate success in operating the ranch as you felt it should be. It has taken you a life time to obtain the knowledge of the country in order to do this. A new buyer however, will not have the benefit of your experience to continue operating it the same way you have, and adjustments would have to be made, either in the system, numbers or both.

You mentioned that this reduces a person's incentive when they have only something like this to look forward to and felt that this would make it very difficult for you to sell the place. You stated that you did not agree with many of the Forest Service policies, that you were not satisfied with results of the analysis, and that you were pretty discouraged to see this happen after putting a life time of work into it. You felt that this was another step toward removing all grazing from public lands, either by total elimination or by making it economically unfeasible. . . .

I explained again that I felt it important to talk with you about this before you sold because it would be discussed with the prospective buyer when the time came. (USFS 1972a)

Fritz brought the issue to Ranger Dieter's superior, the Apache National Forest Supervisor, Hallie L. Cox, who answered Fritz by letter in December 1972. Cox supported his ranger, citing 1963 and 1968 range analyses, indicating that

of the 62,500 acres within the Sandrock Allotment, approximately one-half is forage producing and suitable for grazing. In relation to your term permit this would be about 5 acres per cow month, which is less acres per cow month than the stocking on several allotments in the Blue river area. (USFS 1972b)

All indications were that the Forest Service had decided to reduce the number of cattle on the XXX on transfer to a new owner.

A year later, in December 1973, the District Ranger met again with Fred Fritz Jr. and, in Dieter's words, "asked if you would consider trading your private land holdings to the government, through a tri-partite land exchange." Fritz could keep forty acres at his XXX ranch, the minimum base property needed for an allotment, but the Forest Service wanted the Bell and HU Bar properties lying in the Primitive Area.

You would be able to realize a pretty good return from the land and still have the allotment to work as long as you feel you are able. During this time you might want to consider gradually phasing out your operation since lack of help will be an increasing problem. (USFS 1973)

Fritz said he would "play it by ear" for a year or so and see what happened. He was feeling better and thought he could still work the ranch.

A year later, in November 1974, the Forest Service increased the pressure on Fred Fritz Jr. at a meeting on his annual permittee plan for 1975. The issues that the Forest Service insists are never connected—land sales and stocking rates—nevertheless appear cheek by jowl in Ranger Dieter's summarizing letter.

I asked you if the Bell Place was still available for a land exchange. You indicated you have decided not to do anything with it at this time. You felt that because of the mining activity in the area that you would like to keep the place, since the value could increase if minerals were found.

I discussed the general findings of our study that was conducted in April of 1974. On the basis of the soils information we gathered, there is a little over 10,000 acres (10,400) out of the 62,670 acres in the allotment, that is suitable from a soils and watershed standpoint. We plan to start an intensive soil and hydrological study this coming spring which will give us more information about the needs of the watershed.

As a result of our study I am not in a position to recommend a transfer of the permit in the event the need should develop. For the same reason, we cannot justify continuing the temporary permit past the end of the next year, December 31, 1975.

You expressed your concern about the trend of grazing practices on public lands. You felt that you would be leaving the ranch in better condition than it was when you got it. I explained that we were not questioning this point. The problem being that you are looking at it from a standpoint of grazing and we have to look at it from a watershed standpoint. (USFS 1974)

The Ranger and the rancher certainly had diverging perspectives. Fritz would never deny that overgrazing could hurt the land (see his words at the beginning of chapter 3). He had seen the damage early in the century when he was growing up. Therefore throughout his career he had supported the principle of Forest Service grazing regulation. It was a matter of self-interest for the rancher: overgrazing eventually would reduce the capacity of the land to produce healthier cows and more and heavier calves, and this would hurt the rancher. But Fritz knew his land better than anyone in the Forest Service, and to him it did not look overgrazed in the 1970s—in fact, he believed it had improved from earlier in the century. He was running many fewer head of cattle on the land than were run in the past, and he could see from their healthy condition that there was plenty of forage available.

But what could he say when the Ranger started talking about "soils information" and hydrological studies and "the needs of the watershed"? Probably to him these were abstractions that made little sense. In any case, he was not in a position to argue with "studies." In returning a copy of the Ranger's letter with his signature, he added some bitter remarks saying how much he disagreed with the Ranger's statements. At a loss for ecological arguments, he had to make the case in an area he did understand, economics.

> There is practically no other source of revenue to be derived from the land of Blue River except that from livestock grazing fees. The loss of this revenue will affect our school districts and the economy of our communities.
>
> You stymie any sale for our ranch.
>
> Your policy and study eliminates livestock grazing or reduces it to a point where we cannot financially operate.

(signed) Fred B. Fritz (USFS 1974)

The Ranger's statement that he could not recommend "a transfer of the permit" (for the same number of cattle Fritz was running) to a new owner was a serious threat. Fritz next appealed to the Region 3 (Southwest) headquarters of the Forest Service in Albuquerque. Copies of his letter are unavailable, but the files contain a long letter in reply from W.R. Fallis, Director, Range Management, beginning "Dear Freddie." Fallis supports the Ranger and gives Fritz a short lecture on how drought and overgrazing can result in unsatisfactory range and watershed conditions leading to erosion and flooding.

I know these points are not news to you, but they are mentioned only to emphasize the importance of stocking at conservative levels and employing a management system which provides periodic rest from grazing. This gives grazed plants the opportunity to recuperate and maintain themselves. If this is not done, deterioration tends to accelerate, especially in periods of deficient moisture. When this occurs, watershed, wildlife, wilderness and related resources all suffer.

In reply to Fritz's arguments from economics, Fallis states, "the economic losses associated with reduction of permitted livestock on the National Forests are serious. Nevertheless, management which does not meet the requirements of the Multiple Use and Sustained Yield Act, Environmental Policy Act, Wilderness Act and related laws cannot be justified." He is diplomatic:

> Your long tenure in the Blue River country and the investments you have made for range improvements are greatly appreciated. It has been said many times, Freddie, that only you could have successfully run livestock in that country. Through many years of hard work, you developed a successful operation, but changing interests and objectives of our society make it necessary to reevaluate some of our past management practices on public lands.

As for future permitted numbers, Fallis reasserts the authority of the Forest Service to change them, and that

> the studies being conducted by Ranger Dieter will provide a basis from which to establish a tentative grazing capacity that will meet all resource needs. I believe you will agree that a thorough evaluation of resource needs, your economic interests and those of future operators is the only fair way to approach such matters. (USFS 1975)

We can only surmise Fritz's reaction to this bland assurance of "scientific management." But he must have realized he was helpless in the face of the interpretation the Forest Service would put on their studies. The ultimate fate of his ranch was in the agency's hands, which not only held practically all the cards but could change the rules of the game, citing laws, science, and "changing interests and objectives of our society."

Less than a century after Fritz's father exulted in the "Land O' Milk and Honey," the Forest Service had declared it marginal, barely productive.

THE XXX AND EROSION

Some things might change, but some things remained the same. Erosion on the Blue, as we have seen, was not a new concern but one first raised by the Forest Service at the time of the big floods of 1904–06 (Hunt 1905). In fact, Fred Fritz's XXX ranch was part of the "Clifton Addition" to the Apache National Forest after the floods, justified by the necessity for the Forest Service to do something about erosion and flooding on the Blue and San Francisco watersheds. But as discussed in chapters 3 and 4, erosion and flooding continued. There was the large flood of 1916, and as we have seen, Aldo Leopold was dismayed by the situation in 1922 (Leopold 1949). Leopold made many recommendations as to what could be done, most of which fell into two categories: grazing control and "artificial erosion control works" (Leopold 1921a). It is not clear from the records what was achieved in the case of the latter. In terms of grazing, the number of cattle on the land was radically reduced from earlier in the century (when the Fritz ranch alone had 2,500 cattle). And as recounted in chapter 5, grazing came to be better managed in ways that better protected the land. But the problem of erosion and flooding persisted.

Records available in the Alpine and Clifton Ranger districts and Forest headquarters in Springerville often show concern with erosion. Analyses of soil conditions on allotments began in the late 1920s and were conducted sporadically over the subsequent decades up to the present. These analyses often did not have past baselines against which to measure—certainly any from earlier in the century. Carried out by different persons at different times—usually by range technicians, rarely by soil experts—the studies may reflect subjective differences in judgment in rating soil conditions and may therefore be difficult to compare or evaluate. In any case, what one finds in the records is a plethora of small verdicts that add up to no single conclusive picture—except, of course, that erosion remained a problem. To what degree recent livestock grazing was responsible for this situation remained unclear.

From the 1930s up through the 1990s on the upper Blue, with a few exceptions, allotments tended to have soil conditions rated "fair"; "good" or "excellent"; and "stable" or trending upward. A series of "Erosion Problem Area Reports" done in late 1939 on a number of upper Blue allotments found some erosion connected with overgrazing, but put most erosion in "Class I"—the least serious. Some of the reports emphasized the steep nature of the country and that "an important cause of erosion here is geology." "Much of [the erosion] is normal geologic erosion" (USFS 1939a). "The principal cause of erosion in this area is geologic" (USFS 1939b).

A Forest Ranger in 1970 commented on an allotment analysis,

> Soils in the Blue area are quite unstable, as evidenced by the tremendous floods which occur periodically on the Blue River. . . . In some areas the poor soil condition is a geological phenomenon over which man has little control. In other areas, the soils are deep and fertile, and overlying vegetation will respond to proper range management practices, thus stabilizing the soil. (USFS 1969b: Introduction)

In this rugged country, such areas might alternate within the same allotment. And though many reports recognized the "erosive" character of much of the land, there were few recommendations for reduced grazing on particular pastures.

If erosion conditions on the upper Blue for the most part looked tolerable to the Forest Service since the 1930s, evaluations of allotments on the lower Blue often were much more critical. Whether this difference reflects varying geological conditions is unclear. It might be partly due to the lower altitude and less rainfall of the lower Blue (the Fritz ranch, for example, had an average of fifteen inches a year, compared with twenty inches to the north). Another factor that may have made a difference is that most of the lower Blue is part of the Clifton Ranger District, while the upper Blue is under the Alpine District.

In 1942 W.G. Koogler, a Senior Range Examiner, issued a general report on the "Watersheds of the Apache National Forest" in which he made the distinction that

> the orderly water yield and streamflow regulation afforded by the high forested and well grassed plateau bears striking contrast to conditions on the lower Blue and Frisco watersheds. . . . Notwithstanding local overgrazing and problem areas on the upper Blue, conditions there are relatively good compared to the lower basin. (USFS 1942:5, 20)

The Fritz's Sandrock allotment was on the lower Blue. Many comments citing soil erosion can be gleaned from Forest Service records on this allotment from 1929 up through the 1960s. Also, comments of forest officers who thought the allotment overstocked (USFS 1964; USFS 1968b; USFS 1983a). But what was the relationship between the two? Overgrazing certainly could cause soil erosion, but how much of the erosion evident was due to the grazing of XXX cattle after 1920? Would fewer livestock now mean less erosion? Some of the erosion may have been normal geologic erosion, as noted on the upper Blue. Still other erosion was due to the replacement of grasses by piñon, juniper, and other trees and shrubs inferior to grass in retarding erosion and retaining soil moisture. This process, discussed at the end of chapter 3, has been a historical trend throughout the Southwest. Initiated by the heavy overgrazing at the turn of the century, it was accelerated through most of the twentieth century by the Forest Service policy of fire suppression. The absence of periodic natural fires or fires set by Indians allowed the junipers and piñon pines to spread unchecked, and prevented the return of grass even without grazing (see USFS 1979).

Juniper invasion was prominent throughout the Sandrock allotment (USFS 1964). They could be uprooted and destroyed using a bulldozer through practices called "chaining" and "pushing," sometimes encouraged by the Forest Service. However, motorized equipment was prohibited in the Primitive Area, ironically preventing the restoration of the land there to natural conditions more closely resembling those before settlers and livestock. The 1973 meeting of Ranger Jerry Dieter and rancher Fritz dealt with this topic. As Dieter summarized in a letter,

> You [Fritz] felt that Congress would act on the reclassification of the Primitive Area by the end of 1974, and you wanted to see what would result. We talked about the need for juniper pushing and reseeding in areas such as the VT's. The removal of the VT area from the Primitive Area would allow this kind of work to be done. (USFS 1973)

If juniper and other erosive factors were difficult or impossible to control, the Forest Service could at least control grazing, especially by limiting the number of livestock. The Forest Service had begun in November 1972 to indicate they would limit Fred Fritz's livestock and soon began to cite as justification erosion along with hydrological and soil studies. Probably it is not coincidental that another significant flood involving the Blue had occurred throughout the Gila watershed in October 1972, putting pressure on the agency again to do something.

A New Owner: The XXX and AD Bar Combine

In 1976, bowing to Forest Service demands, Fred Fritz entered into a "non-use agreement" to reduce his herd temporarily from 542 to 300 head for a six-year period to see how the land responded and to allow the Forest Service to do more range and soils analysis. "We also agreed that the new permittee would be expected to comply with the results of these studies" (USFS 1976).

Within a few months, there was a new permittee. Fred Fritz had found as buyer a neighboring rancher, Sewall Goodwin. In 1973, Goodwin had bought the 6K6 Ranch, whose "AD Bar" allotment bordered the XXX Sandrock allotment to the north and was mostly within the Primitive Area. Like the Sandrock, the AD Bar was very rough country with poor soils, heavily invaded by juniper and piñon. In 1917 the allotment had a permit for 443 head of cattle and in 1930 393 head. But by 1951 it was reduced to 213 cattle yearlong, which was still the number when Goodwin bought the ranch. Economically, this was a very low number for a ranch, but combined with the reduced permit of 300 for the Sandrock, Goodwin considered his expanded ranch viable.

The Forest Service was still trying to acquire the private parcels in the Primitive Area. In addition to the old Bell and HU Bar homesteads he bought from Fritz, Goodwin had acquired with the 6K6 another old homestead, the "Burns place," also in the Primitive Area. But like Fritz, Goodwin was uninterested in parting with rare patented land.

Goodwin had been warned before buying that range conditions on the Sandrock allotment were in bad condition but replied to the Forest Supervisor,

> I have carefully inspected the majority of the range improvements on the Sandrock allotment and have come to the conclusion that on the whole they are in a lot better shape than your letter indicates. We are also not interested in selling any of our patented land. (USFS 1976)

Goodwin, in his 50s and an Arizona rancher all his life, thought the land was in better condition than the Forest Service was claiming—

otherwise he would not have bought the ranch. But, as with Fritz, he was reading different natural signs than those read by the Forest Service. Ranger Dieter was warning Goodwin that ecological conditions were bad on both the Sandrock and AD Bar range, hinting ominously that the permitted number of cattle would probably have to be lowered, depending on the results of "ongoing studies."

In late 1977, Gary A. Davis, a wildlife biologist from Forest headquarters, began to survey the Sandrock allotment. After his first visits he conveyed conclusions to the District Ranger in language unusually indignant and pointed for a Forest Service memo. He deplored the erosion he found as well as the condition of the riparian habitat. "In my opinion...we are violating our own laws by allowing the continued degradation of the land. The problem of overgrazing by domestic livestock on the Sandrock Allotment has been recognized for many years." He cited excerpts from agency documents on the allotment from 1929, 1933, 1934, and 1968, critical of range conditions and blaming overgrazing. The rhetoric of the modern environmentalist movement appears in his exhortation to the Ranger.

> It's obvious that we as an organization have realized for 50 years
> that this allotment has been overstocked. We are committed by
> law to protect and enhance the growth and vigor of the vegeta-
> tion that constitutes the life support system for earth's living
> creatures, man included. Apparently this commitment has been
> given a low priority in this particular situation—expediency,
> temporary needs or financial difficulties experienced by permit-
> tees, and political pressures dictate land use policies. What's best
> for the land and the American people as a whole has apparently
> been ignored.

It was Davis's "personal opinion that in order to alleviate the deplorable conditions existing on this allotment, we need to eliminate grazing by domestic livestock"—six years in the future when the permit would be up for renewal (USFS 1977).

But remarkably, two years later when Davis concluded his study, "Wildlife Habitat Analysis, AD Bar Allotment," submitted in October 1979 to Apache-Sitgreaves Forest Headquarters, his tone had greatly changed. He was still critical of the Forest Service, but instead of advocating the elimination of grazing, he had an entirely new proposal.

He found habitat conditions had deteriorated over the past century for most species, including cattle. His opening general observations were: "1. Soil loss due to lack of cover is obvious in many areas. 2. Encroachment by juniper and piñon trees has contributed, along with overgrazing, to a reduced forage base from the pre-white man era (supported by tree ring data collected)" (USFS 1979). Even with 213 cattle since 1951, the forage base (grass and browse species) was decreasing, and juniper and piñon trees were continuing to encroach, and he thought that the area was approaching a stable "climax condition" in which piñon and juniper woodland would dominate. This would not only lead to more erosion, but also provide less food for most wild species as well as for cattle. As for current grazing, this was not the nub of the problem.

> We, as an agency, are responsible for the loss of productivity on this Allotment. Our management objective ought to be to return the area to a productive successional stage which will support diverse viable populations of wildlife and an economic cattle operation. We have a responsibility, within the capability of the resources, to keep the permittee in business while we restore the Allotment. . . .
>
> Fire and rest are needed as management tools to once again create the productive successional stage which occurred prior to settlement by white man. We typically attempt to manage this country by building improvements, devising grazing systems which will improve distribution, or reducing numbers. We continue to attempt to manage a forage base which would probably continue to decline even if all the livestock were removed. Without fire as a tool, junipers and pinyons will continue to push the site towards climax. In my opinion our range improvement dollars should be spent restoring this area through burning followed by rest, rather than improving distribution to harvest the remainder of a declining forage resource. Rest-rotation systems will, in theory, maintain for a period of time the existing forage base but they cannot restore an area taken over by juniper or pinyon back to a productive grass site. (USFS 1979)

In other words, the land could be restored through fire and a resting period to a condition nearer to that existing prior to the coming of white settlers. Fire could reverse the juniper and piñon invasion, and restore grass and other forage; this would benefit most wildlife *and* make it possible eventually to graze more cattle on the land. Both the land and the rancher would benefit.

Davis's proposal was bold. Perhaps too bold—it was not tried. Nor has the Forest Service been willing to use controlled burning as a tool elsewhere on the Blue to fight the juniper and piñon and restore earlier grassier conditions. The reasons for the Forest Service reluctance to set fires may lie partly in its historical role of "Smokey the Bear," forest fire preventer. But the main reason today, as well as in 1979, may simply be bureaucratic caution: the risk of fire getting out of control.

Decision Time for the Sandrock

In 1982 the six-year study period was coming to an end, and the Forest Service continued on its path. As a last resort, Sewall Goodwin had his congressman make inquiries at Forest Service headquarters in Washington, D.C. The official reply stood behind the case developed in Clifton: "This allotment is in an area of extremely rough terrain. Approximately 83 percent is considered unsuitable range for grazing cattle." Grazing areas had been overused, and studies indicated that "additional adjustments in stocking" were necessary, and "prospects at this time do not appear favorable for any substantial amount of grazing on the Sandrock Allotment" (USFS 1982a).

On seeing a copy of this letter, Fred Fritz wrote a short note to Goodwin and his wife, commenting that, "This Forest report is *most ridiculous,* to say 83% of the XXX allotment is nonsuitable for grazing. What have those cows and I done all these years?" (Fritz 1982).

In 1982 the new Forest Supervisor Nick McDonough met with Sewall Goodwin and his wife Lois, and laid out four options. "My first priority is, and continues to be, the purchase or exchange for private lands option." The Forest Service was still intent on acquiring the inholdings in the Primitive area. The other three options were

1. combining the Sandrock and AD Bar allotments in one management plan. "The grazing capacity would be 180-head year-long, including the horses"—down from the combined 517 head of cattle when Goodwin had bought the ranches;

2. if the allotments were sold independently, the AD Bar would be reduced to 50 head yearlong (down from 217), and Sandrock to 120 (down from 300);

3. the two allotments could be combined but only for winter use: then 300 head might be permitted on the two. Goodwin would have to find other pastures for the stock in the summer. (USFS 1982b)

Goodwin was backed into a corner. He could not make a living on the fewer than 180 head of cattle he would be allowed in renewing his permit. Nor could he borrow much from the bank on the basis of that permitted number to pay an extra large "balloon" payment due that year on the purchase price. He felt compelled to think of selling the private lands he owned, and of finding some way to rescue his capital from an untenable situation.

In January 1983 Goodwin met with Greg L. Gray, Range Conservationist acting for the Clifton District. From the letter summarizing the meeting, we learn there was disagreement over how much the private land was worth. Also,

You stated that you felt that the Forest Service was trying to get the private land; and if they couldn't get it by buying, they were trying to force you to sell it by reducing your permit and therefore your income. We explained that the studies conducted on the allotment had nothing to do with the private land and the reductions indicated were in no way related to forcing you to sell your private land. (USFS 1983a)

The Forest Service could always deny an intended connection, but Goodwin believed that in effect a connection existed.

Furthermore, by cutting the combined allotments so sharply, the Forest Service was breaking with an established tradition in regard to its permittees. It was abandoning any commitment, as expressed above by Wildlife Biologist Gary Davis, "to keep the permittee in business." Cuts in permits were not unprecedented, but cutting the number of livestock to where a family could not make a living? This was shocking in the history of the Forest Service on the Blue.

Ranchers started protesting. The Greenlee County Supervisors called a special meeting where people could express their disquiet and anger.

The retired Freddy Fritz commented that his former allotment had been called "Sandrock" for a reason: during his lifetime it had been bare in many places, with no vegetation—"it'll never have much production." He attributed damage to what had been done in the days of the open range, prior to his taking over the ranch in 1917. But he thought it could still run 300 cattle, as he had been doing the years before he sold out (USFS 1983b).

Forest Supervisor McDonough presented the Forest Service case, recapitulating the history of overgrazing, erosion and flooding on the Blue. He conceded that the stock reductions the Forest Service wanted would "remove or very nearly remove these allotments from any serious consideration for further grazing." Yet "[T]hese conclusions are not arbitrary or capricious but are based upon 'state of the art' soil, water and range analysis." He concluded,

> It is my belief that the bulk of the flooding occurring on the Blue River at this time, is occurring within the depleted portions of the Sand Rock, AD Bar, Strayhorse, Alma Mesa, and Raspberry-KP allotments. Other allotments, though contributing initially to this problem, have now been corrected with stocking and management adjustments. (USFS 1983b)

All five "problem allotments" were within the Primitive Area on the lower Blue. No one noted the irony that the Primitive Area thus held not the rangeland changed least by man, but the land changed most, by erosion and piñon-juniper invasion. "Primitive" here did not mean "pristine," but rather its opposite.

The meeting ended in suggestions that participants meet again with the Arizona congressional delegation. McDonough mentioned that environmentalist groups like the Wilderness Society and the Wildlife Federation would also want to be involved (USFS 1983b). A story in the Clifton *Copper Era* newspaper on May 25, 1983, noted: "One veteran rancher seemed to sum up the cattlemen's view of the situation, when he stated at the meeting, 'Anyone that's got enough guts to live up there and ranch in that rugged country, well, we should just leave him alone and let him do it.'"

More meetings occurred, but Goodwin finally caved in. He explained,

> The contract showed that there was a balloon payment [an extra large payment] on the sixth year. They knew about the payments,

and the sixth year was when we started having trouble with the Forest Service. They cut our allotment from 300 to 120 head, and they said they were going to cut the 6K6 [the AD Bar allotment] from 200 to 50. I've got that in writing. . . . We could see the handwriting on the wall, and it's kind of hard to fight the government. . . .

I feel they used the cuts as a tool to get us out and to acquire that patented land. They were going to cut us so bad we couldn't stay. . . . When you get one cow to the section [one square mile], that's what it amounted to.

So for some time there has been a Government program to buy up the Primitive Area. We didn't sell the Three X's to the government. We sold it to some investors, and they turned around and traded it to the Forest Service for some land in Show Low [next to developed land]. And we took the cattle off. . . It's cute the way they do things, but they just squeeze you out. (Goodwin 2000)

On December 20, 1983, a news release from the Apache-Sitgreaves National Forest office announced that the Sandrock allotment would be closed to livestock grazing for an "indeterminate period" in order "to allow the watershed to recover through the natural increase of vegetation" (USFS 1983b).

But the pressure on Blue permittees would not end with Fred Fritz and Sewall Goodwin. In the fall of 1988, officials from the Southwest Region offices of the Forest Service in Albuquerque took a field trip with Clifton District personnel over the allotments of the lower Blue. The field trip report, prepared by the Regional Ecologist Reggie Fletcher, found the erosion problems "immense" and trending downward in condition.

Much of the District is extremely steep and rugged. . . . Soils are generally shallow. . . . Such soils are extremely difficult to improve when degraded. Erosion rates are extremely high with bedrock exposed in many areas. . . . The fragility of the range ecosystem in its ability to sustain livestock has been underestimated in virtually all of our actions. The permittees are now generally fearful the Forest Service will completely remove livestock from many allotments in the District. . . .

> For the remote and rugged ecosystems such as cover most of the Clifton Ranger District, productivity is low and erosion has been extreme. (USFS 1989a)

The report recommends that the Forest service follow the example of the Sandrock allotment and "modify existing livestock use."

> Much of the District is to be considered in the no capacity category and most of the rest will be difficult to manage for livestock. However, during the field trip all present agreed it was imperative we avoid talk of closing allotments to grazing. Our objective should be to balance capacity with permitted, and leave it to the permittee to decide on the economic suitability of permitted AUM numbers [animal units per month]. (USFS 1989a)

In other words, the way to end grazing was not simply to stop it on an allotment—this would lead to political uproar. The smarter way to end grazing was to reduce the permitted number of cattle low enough to make a ranch economically unviable—as had happened in the Sandrock case. In the 1990s this strategy was indeed followed, selectively on allotments in the Clifton District, but wholesale in the Blue portion of the Alpine District. The rationale in the latter District, however, had little or nothing to do with erosion but instead was based on other ecological issues, primarily endangered species, and was partly in response to environmental activist lawsuits.

In an ironic way, Aldo Leopold's vision of a Blue Valley "ruined" economically was finally coming true. The ranchers' ruin had come not from floods or from trying to "possess" the wilderness, as Leopold had imagined. Their ruin had come from a political and cultural climate radically changed from that of Leopold's day. The Forest Service was now less interested in protecting the livelihood of the ranchers who depended on it than in attempting to return the land, changed by man as it was, to a state nearer a wilderness ideal, an ideal pioneered by Leopold. Bowing to the claims of environmental activists, overgrazing—or any grazing—was seen as an obstacle to this wilderness goal.

A few postscripts will complete the story of the XXX and 6K6, Sandrock, and AD Bar. Goodwin and his wife Lois eventually gave up and sold the 6K6 ranch to a real estate man from Phoenix. They bought a new ranch near Alma, New Mexico.

Fred Fritz died in 1985 in Clifton, and over a thousand people attended his funeral. Tributes of love and respect were paid to the memory of this old cattleman and civic leader. But he died knowing his ranch was defunct.

The Sandrock allotment has never been reopened to grazing. The XXX ranch buildings have fallen into disrepair. Hunters and others occasionally camp in them. Sewall and Lois Goodwin interested the Arizona State Parks in preserving the Fritz Ranch as well as the old Cosper Ranch as "National Register" historical sites. However, the Forest Service would not cooperate with these nominations, and the effort lapsed (Arizona State Parks 1990).

Nowadays, residents on the Blue consider the Sandrock area a "dead area." Not only are people and cattle missing, but also the deer. Goodwin comments,

> This ranch that we had on the Blue River, when we took all the cattle off, the wildlife went also, the deer left, because they liked to be with the cattle. The deer like the salt we leave for the cattle, and they feel protected from predators with cattle around. Mind you, this is 120 sections, and we had to take the cattle off piece by piece, because you had to drive the cattle a long ways—a rough ranch—so we camped out there with pack mules, and took these cattle off. As we took the cattle off—it took two years to get all the cattle off—we'd go back and look for tracks to see if the cattle were there. The wildlife would be gone. (Goodwin 2000)

9

Ranching and the
Environmental Movement

Ranching as a land use, and ranchers as a culture, have been with us
for more than four hundred years, dating back to the early Spanish
colonists who struggled northward over El Paso del Norte and found
a home for their livestock near present-day Espanola, New Mexico.
Today, more so than at any time in its history, the ranching culture is
under assault. If what I have presented in this essay is true—that ranch
lands are compatible with our region's natural heritage and that herbiv-
ory is a necessary ecological process in the restoration and maintenance
of healthy rangelands—then why are ranchers and livestock grazing so
vilified? Why have scores of environmental groups banded together for
"a prompt end to public lands grazing"?

RICHARD L. KNIGHT, "The Ecology of Ranching" (Knight 2002:135)

To UNDERSTAND THE FATE of the ranching on the Blue, one must consider it in the context of the raging controversy in the 1990s over
ranching on federal or "public" lands in the West. Of course, the environmental effect of ranching on these lands was controversial even before
the creation of the Forest Service; in fact, concern to protect land from
overgrazing was one rationale for federal regulation of Western rangelands. Throughout the twentieth century there was no lack of criticism
of grazing practices (Rowley 1985:27–35). Aldo Leopold, as we have
seen, was one critic. From at least the 1930s, organized hunters, foresters, and wilderness advocates all chastised ranchers for their influence
over National Forests grazing policy. In the 1940s the celebrated writer
Bernard DeVoto wrote a series of columns in *Harper's* attacking ranchers
for the damaging effects of their livestock on the public lands. The foundation was laid early for polarized politics on the issue of public grazing, with organized ranchers versus the conservation movement. This

polarization was merely augmented and more widely publicized by the growth of the environmental movement in the 1970s and 1980s (Merrill 2002:171, 192–93).

The American conservation movement had always contained two tendencies, the utilitarian and the preservationist. Teddy Roosevelt and Forest Service head Gifford Pinchot represented the former: they wanted to use natural resources wisely to benefit the American people. The preservationist tendency, exemplified by the writer John Muir, differed sharply: its ideal was to preserve wild nature unspoiled as a good in itself, to *not* use it, except for spiritual or recreational purposes. This latter orientation was strengthened during the twentieth century by the many struggles of the conservation movement to create new national parks and an American wilderness system.

A more extended expression of the preservationist philosophy gained currency in the 1980s throughout the environmentalist movement, expressed in the new concepts of "deep ecology" and "biocentrism." Instead of seeing the natural environment as primarily a resource for humans ("anthropocentrism"), the deep ecology approach views all nature as having intrinsic worth, independent of human use. "Biocentric equality" means that "all things in the biosphere have an equal right to live and blossom and to reach their own individual forms of unfolding and self-realization within the larger Self-realization." Of course, "in the process of living, all species use each other as food, shelter, etc.," and humans must do this also, "but we should live with minimum rather than maximum impact on other species and on the Earth in general." Other species, and also ecosystems, have as much moral stature as human beings (Devall and Sessions 1985:67–69).

This philosophy, initially embraced by self-styled "radical environmentalists" like the "Earth First!" organization, came to influence the assumptions of many others in the contemporary environmental movement. Biocentrism has shaped the principles this movement wants enforced by law and regulation. To paraphrase Wallace Kaufman (Kaufman 1994:93), these principles are: (1) nature is good, if not sacred; (2) altering or destroying any part of nature is bad; (3) nature has a balance that humans always disrupt; therefore (4) humans should do as little as possible to change natural conditions in order to avoid damaging nature.

To this way of thinking, cattle ranching in Western landscapes is not a problem to be solved through more regulation, new ranching methods, or fewer livestock: it is instead a practice that is unnatural and illegitimate in principle. (Commercial logging and mining are similarly regarded.) Predictably, by the early 1990s a political movement had emerged among environmentalists, initially in the Southwest, to rid *all* public lands of *any* livestock grazing. Certainly in its historical and sociological contexts this was a radical demand. The initial slogan was that the West should be "Cattle Free by '93." The movement attracted much publicity in the 1990s, especially in the West, but also nationally. A host of environmental groups and individuals have been involved, and an organization named "RangeNet" was founded in 2000 to link activists wanting to end all grazing on public lands. In 2001 the Sierra Club, through a membership ballot and with support from its leaders, joined the anti-grazing coalition, signaling the acceptance by much of mainstream environmentalism of what was originally an extreme idea.

THE CASE AGAINST GRAZING

The political movement to eliminate grazing on public lands has generated a large literature devoted to making its case, from Lynn Jacobs's early, sprawling, self-published *Waste of the West* (1992) to a recent coffee-table tome, *Welfare Ranching: The Subsidized Destruction of the American West* (Wuerthner and Matteson 2002). Probably the most scholarly and comprehensive representative of this literature is Debra L. Donahue's *The Western Range Revisited: Removing Livestock from Public Lands to Conserve Native Biodiversity* (1999). Donahue, who holds degrees in law and wildlife biology, cautions readers to beware of the claims and generalizations of range scientists and range managers.

> Attempting to use the literature to generalize about current range conditions, or about the individual contribution of livestock, is problematic not only because vegetation, soils, and climate vary widely and because historical and current land uses and thus disturbance factors differ. Investigators' methods, objectives and predispositions can also dramatically influence results. Results may be portrayed carelessly or even misrepresented, intentionally or otherwise, by the investigators or others. Both academics and the land management agencies may be culpable. . . .

> The public lands grazing debate is fueled by misrepresen-
> tations or biased characterizations of range condition and other
> grazing-related issues. . . . Much of the range science and range
> management literature exhibits "a defensive tone" or an obvious
> pro-livestock production bent. . . . (Donahue 1999:61–62)

Donahue may be correct, but by the same token we also cannot
depend on the objectivity of anti-grazing literature. Generally, it com-
bines frank advocacy with a tendency to "cherry-pick" data for anything that supports its cause and fits its outlook, ignoring any evidence
to the contrary. Donahue herself admits to an ideologically "biocentric"
approach (1999:161), and her book may be seen as an advocate's brief
against livestock grazing on the federal lands. The purpose here, however,
is not to judge the arguments put forth, but simply to summarize them
for readers unfamiliar with the debate.

Most of the environmentalist case against livestock centers on the
need to protect natural values, in particular "biodiversity." In Donahue's
words, her book argues that

> the strongest justification for removing livestock from, or at
> minimum reducing drastically their use of, [federal] lands is to
> restore, where possible, the natural ecological functions of range-
> land ecosystems in order to protect and conserve their native
> biodiversity. (Donahue 1999:ix)

Anti-grazing advocates have claimed that livestock grazing is the "most
insidious and pervasive threat to biodiversity on rangelands" (Donahue
1999:115).

The concept of biodiversity encompasses the gamut of life forms,
from plants to insects to vertebrates; activists charge that livestock grazing has negatively affected a great many species. They argue that the
introduction of a "large-bodied herbivore" (the cow) has had dramatic
effects on plant communities in all types of western North American habitat. By altering the environment, livestock has harmed a wide
range of animals: fish, tortoise, snakes, lizards, birds, and small mammals
(Fleischner 1994), including many endangered species. Because domestic
cattle are an exotic species that evolved in the wetter, greener, and cooler
environment of Europe, they are out of place in the drier, hotter areas of
the American West. Cattle especially damage riparian areas and species

because they tend to concentrate near streams and other sources of water and shade (Belsky 1999; Fleischner 1994:635; Oppenheimer 1996).

In addition to claiming that livestock grazing has overall indirect negative effects on wildlife, anti-grazing activists are especially incensed at the deliberate killings of predator species by ranchers and government agencies in order to protect livestock. Mountain lions, black bears, and coyotes are targets today, as well as wolves and grizzlies in the past. Prairie dogs too have been objects of extermination, as they destroy grass and dig holes that break the legs of horses and cattle. Finally, livestock are accused of having spread diseases decimating native wildlife species (Wolff 1999:9). "The livestock industry is the last wildlife-genocide program in the United States," one activist has stated. "All-out war is declared on a diversity of species every day to benefit a single industry" (Oppenheimer 1996).

"The deleterious effects of livestock on native ecosystems are not limited to changes in species composition. Grazing also disrupts the fundamental ecosystem functions of nutrient cycling and succession," conservation biologist Thomas Fleischner charges. Livestock destroy macrobiotic soil crusts in arid regions, disrupt ecological succession, alter the ecosystem structure, degrade soil stability, increase erosion and soil compaction, and harm water quality. They have aided the spread of other exotic species. The fencing and roads that go with ranching have also altered the rangeland ecology (Belsky 1999:10; Fleischner 1994:633; Freilich 2003).

Knowing that in a political debate, they must appeal also to the "anthropocentric" in people, activists further argue that ranching is a less valuable use of the public lands for humans than hunting, recreation, and watershed conservation and that ranching in fact diminishes these other uses (Donahue 1999:280). Donahue argues that arid public rangelands, if retired from ranching, could be converted into biodiversity preserves, which would still be "used" to maintain "the protected area's ability to provide ecological services."

> Another "use" is the preservation of the area's historic and prehistoric resources. Other, more obvious land uses that could be accommodated, and perhaps enhanced or expanded, include low-impact recreational activities, such as hiking, hunting, catch-and-release fishing, dispersed camping, water sports, spelunking,

amateur archeology, and photography. These activities would
bring dollars into the local area. In addition, reserves would provide field laboratories in which scientists could do much-needed
research. . . . (Donahue 1999:189)

Activists have also appealed to taxpayer sentiment by attacking governmental support for ranching as undeserved subsidies, even "welfare."
They have claimed the grazing fees charged ranchers are far lower than
market value and do not cover government management and maintenance costs on federal rangeland. Also indicted are the costs of other
federal programs that benefit ranching, such as "animal damage control"
(predator killing) and emergency feed programs for livestock in drought
conditions (Donahue 1999:278–79; Oppenheimer 1996; Wolff 1999).

Anti-ranching advocates charge that these subsidies are being spent
on what is only a marginal wing of the livestock industry, for public lands
contribute only "a tiny fraction of national livestock production" (Donahue 1999:4). Two percent is the figure often seen in activist literature.
But estimates vary. Wolff claims that "Federal public land in the eleven
western states contributes only 3–5% of the beef produced annually in
the U.S." (Wolff 1999:2). Donahue cites a 1977 federal study of grazing
fees that reported "about half of the livestock in the western states, or
9 percent of all U.S. livestock, spent some portion of the year on public
lands," and that "the national forests and BLM lands provided only 3 to
5 percent of the feed consumed by U.S. beef cattle in the 1970s." She
quotes also a 1994 calculation by the Department of Interior Rangeland
Reform task force that all federal lands provide "about 7 percent of beef
cattle forage and about 2 percent of the total feed consumed by beef cattle
in the 48 contiguous states" (Donahue 1999:252).

The anti-grazing argument has minimized the economic importance
of public lands ranching, while emphasizing its cost. Other socioeconomic
aspects of ranching are also criticized. Sometimes anti-grazing literature
assails ranchers as being privileged and wealthy, and cites examples of
corporations and other wealthy entities that own ranches to take advantage of subsidies and tax benefits (Wolff 1999:2; Donahue 1999: 263–68).
On the other hand, sometimes data are presented to show that many if
not most ranches using federal land are such marginal operations that
they are economically unsustainable. Their owners must take second jobs
off the ranch, or they derive incomes elsewhere and are only "hobby

ranchers." In either case, such owners do not really depend for their livelihood on public lands—another reason to end grazing on these lands (Donahue 1999:263–268).

Anti-grazing activists see a need to undermine the common rationale for continuing federal grazing policies, which is to preserve the family ranch and its associated way of life. On one hand, the critics stress that public land ranching is a marginal way of life dying out on its own. But on the other they attack the "way of life" argument itself, either by claiming "there is no single ranching 'culture' or way of life," or by frontal attack "demythologizing the ranching mystique" (Donahue 1999:269; 88–113). Edward Abbey, the writer who inspired so many biocentric activists, led the way by portraying the cowboy not as the traditional Western hero close to nature, but instead as a vulgar, ruthlessly utilitarian, violent destroyer of nature (Abbey 1986). Not only is this opinion privately but widely held by anti-ranching activists but sometimes they argue it in public venues in an effort to de-romanticize the cowboy image.

In Defense of Ranching

Under attack, livestock grazing in the West has found defenders. This includes ranchers themselves, of course, and their rural neighbors but also range scientists and other specialists from the natural sciences, inside and outside of academia. Furthermore, during the 1990s, a whole segment of the conservation movement emerged to defend ranching against anti-grazing fundamentalism. Two recent works that best summarize the defense of ranching are Richard L. Knight et al., *Ranching West of the 100th Meridian* (2002), and Nathan F. Sayre, *The New Ranch Handbook* (2001).

Ranchers espouse an anthropocentric worldview without apology. They believe that their work is good, because it provides valuable products—meat, wool, leather, and the hundreds of other livestock byproducts—that people want and need. A rural Western publication argues this view.

> Western rangelands are not usually suitable for crop production, and the plant roughages found on most rangelands cannot be digested by humans but are ideal for ruminants. . . . Sheep and cattle, therefore, convert otherwise wasted forage to food and fiber. And since the federal government owns about 170 million

acres of the land used for grazing, productive use of these lands benefits ranchers, consumers, taxpayers. . . . (*Resource Roundup* 2004)

From the rancher's perspective, our nation would be utterly perverse to forego the use of a renewable natural resource such as grass and other forage. This perspective is

> a common worldview in the ranching community, a view that goes all the way back to the settlement of the West and the ideas of John Locke: That which is not put to good use for the benefit of people is waste. . . .
>
> For the rancher, grass grazed is grass put to good use. For the environmentalist, missing grass is a sign of devastation. In general, then, it might be said that for many with an environmental perspective, to use a natural resource is to despoil it. For those with a more agricultural orientation, not to use it is a crime. (Huntsinger 2002:83)

Ranchers and others with an "agricultural orientation" reject the charge that the public rangelands of the West are marginal to America's needs. They scoff at the "2%" and "3%" statistics given out by environmental activists as misleading propaganda, taken from calculations at slaughter. A pro-grazing advocate from Tucson explains,

> It has long been a contention of grazing foes that western grazing produces an insignificant amount of our total beef, and that we could easily get along without federal lands grazing. But the small production percentage is a myth. It just depends how you count. Western ranches generally do not produce cattle for the slaughter house, but instead raise yearlings to approximately 500 pounds by feeding them natural forage which is indigestible by humans. The yearlings are then shipped east to Midwestern farmers' fields where these "solar energy converters" feeding on crop residue, fatten to about 800 pounds. From there they go to feedlots and gain another 300 pounds or so on corn, molasses, and crop residue. These cows get counted at the slaughter house and the Midwestern farmers get the credit for beef production. In reality, 20% of the nation's beef is produced in the west. (DuHamel 2002)

Recent Department of Agriculture statistics do show about 20% of all beef cattle, and a slightly higher percentage of calves, in the U.S. at any one time are grazing in the eleven Western states (USDA 2004) where altogether about half the rangeland is "public." Not all of these cattle graze on public lands, but a breakdown between public and private is difficult to estimate due to the very nature of public lands ranching: public land must be combined with private land in a single ranching or agricultural operation. The estimate given by the Public Lands Council is that between three to five million of the six million beef cattle in the eleven Western states would depend for at least part of their lives on public rangeland (Public Lands Council 1999). This would mean ten to seventeen percent of American cattle have their origins on public-land ranches. The percentage of marketable lambs coming from public lands is much higher.

Proponents of public land ranching also argue that

> because the West is a patchwork of state, federal and privately owned lands, ranchers require a mix of private and federal lands in order to survive. Rural economies depend heavily on public lands grazing—each dollar created from cattle and sheep sales generates another $5 to $6 in business activity. (People for the USA 1996)

Further, ranching is the social and economic backbone of many small communities and rural counties throughout the mountain West, and "grazing on public land is essential to the viability of western ranching" (Sullins et al. 2002).

Public land ranchers bridle at the charge they receive "welfare" from the government. They work hard to produce a commodity people want, and they sell it on the open market. They do not see the government as supporting or subsidizing them. On the contrary, they see the government and its regulations as an imposition. In what other business do you have the government as a partner with ultimate say over your operation? They view the government as a very demanding landlord.

True, "the lease rate for grazing on private lands is higher than on public lands. But the difference is like renting a furnished apartment compared to an unfinished one" (People for the USA 1996). Public lands are also biologically less productive.

Many of the lands in the public domain are those not taken by homesteaders a century ago because they are only marginally fertile. Ranchers with federal allotments are responsible for fencing, water development, maintenance, and miscellaneous cost that they would not be responsible for on privately-leased lands. Too, in contrast to privately-leased lands, public grazing lands are still open to the general public, and ranchers must contend with the problems...gates left open (necessitating time spent to gather livestock), and trash (hamburger wrappers, beverage cans, old tires, and refrigerators) that they must remove. Such problems can greatly increase a rancher's cost of operation. (*Resource Roundup* 2004)

Pro-grazing advocates also cite the few economic studies attempting to compare the costs of private and public forage, as showing a "wash" (Knize 1999:57).

Economic arguments in the grazing controversy, however, are secondary. The attack on grazing has mainly been based on environmental concerns, on the alleged damage to the land and wildlife by livestock. Ranchers, including those on the Blue, have reacted strongly to these charges. Often they counter that they must keep their grazing land in good shape or it would cease to provide a living for them. Many will admit that sometimes poor ranching practices and overgrazing have damaged the land, especially around the turn of the twentieth century when the range was unfenced and herds were too large. But ranchers today insist that they are good stewards of the land.

Forest Service and Bureau of Land Management data over the years do indicate general improvement of range conditions, but environmental groups have read the same data as an unsatisfactory portrayal (Knight et al. 2002:123; Knize 1999:5). A scientific panel set up by the National Academy of Sciences found it "impossible to determine if the range was stable, deteriorating or improving" (Marston 2002:6).

All national assessments [of rangeland health] suffer from the lack of current, comprehensive, and statistically representative data obtained in the field. No data collected using the same methods over time or using a sampling design that enables aggregation of the data at the national level are available for assessing both federal and nonfederal rangelands. Many reports depend on the opinion and judgment of both field personnel and authors rather than on current data. The reports cited above attempted to combine these data into a national-level assessment of range-lands, but the results have been inconclusive. (National Research Council 1994:26, cited in Knight 2002:139)

Whatever the damage done in the past to the range, defenders of grazing argue, the answer is better grazing practice. Ending grazing is not the answer. Removing all cows from public land might be advocated in the name of ecology, but it makes no ecological sense. "Nature does not run backwards" (DeBuys 1999). Simply taking the cows off does not result in the restoration of the land to some "pristine" state. In fact, over-resting the land can be as damaging as overgrazing (Savory 2002:158–60). Articles, with photographs, appear consistently in the pages of *Range* magazine ("The Cowboy Spirit on America's Outback") reporting on the benefits of controlled grazing and documenting the harm of no grazing (e.g., Dagget 2005a, b; Rich 2005a–c).

A body of research shows that controlled grazing results in more ecological benefits than no grazing. This research is summarized in a report whose main author, Jerry Holechek, is recognized as one of the most prominent range scientists in the U.S.

These studies provide evidence that controlled livestock grazing may enhance rangeland vegetation by altering plant succession, increasing plant diversity and productivity, and reducing plant mortality during drought. . . . [M]oderately grazed mid seral rangelands support a higher diversity of wildlife species than those lightly grazed in near climax condition. Riparian habitat improvement has occurred under carefully timed grazing at light to conservative intensities. . . . (Holechek et al. 2004:1)

The key here is "controlled" livestock grazing. But the evidence used against grazing usually comes from studies of the effects of *uncontrolled* grazing. Holechek has commented,

It's an unethical and unscientific process. They use studies which document the effects of unmanaged livestock. That's not an honest comparison at all. You see the same set of studies quoted over and over, whenever they attempt to close allotments. Which is very ironic, since most of those findings were eliminated from

our review because of bad study designs and unscientific meth-
odologies. When you add that to the fact that they're not relevant at all unless the federally created grazing systems mandate
unregulated livestock, it's a pretty sordid business. (Rich 2004:1)

A new ecological view is that rangeland grazing is not only natural
but necessary.

> Rangelands are disturbance-prone ecosystems that evolved
> with natural regimes of fire and grazing. . . . Grass and shrubs
> coevolved with herbivores, species that grazed and browsed their
> new growth. The West has always been defined by large popu-
> lations of herbivores, although their identity has changed over
> the centuries. Whether it was mastodons and sloths, or bison and
> pronghorn, or grasshoppers and rodents, grass and shrubs need
> the stimulating disturbance brought about by large, blunt-ended
> incisors clipping their aboveground biomass. Not to mention the
> dung and urine incorporated by hoof action facilitating more
> efficient nutrient cycling. . . . [W]e have learned that grazing by
> livestock, when appropriately done, contributes to the distur-
> bance that rangelands require. Perhaps we have come to the point
> where we measure land health premised on disturbance rather
> than just rest and realize there is no "balance of nature" but only
> a "flux of nature." (Knight 2002:127)

In this view, grazing managed correctly not only benefits the land,
but also promotes biodiversity. Ranchers have always argued that their
care of the range, particularly through the water sources they develop for
their livestock, benefit wildlife and cite game statistics as proof (*Resource
Roundup* 2004). But now some wildlife biologists are claiming that, as
part of an "intermediate disturbance hypothesis," disturbances such as
grazing tend to create species diversity, and "recent research indicates
that biodiversity is enhanced by intermediate grazing regimes. . . ."
(Huntsinger 2002:86; Sayre 2001:17; Starrs 2002:16).

Does livestock grazing threaten or endanger certain species? Each
instance must be analyzed in its specifics, but grazing defenders claim
there are actually few cases where it can be demonstrated—as opposed
to being hypothetically posited—that cattle or sheep are a menace to an
endangered species. And sometimes such species are actually helped by

the presence of cattle (Budd 2002:116). Numerous examples have been cited, especially in the past issues of *Range* magazine. One of the most striking and best-documented cases is that of the Southwestern willow flycatcher. Listed as an endangered subspecies, the largest population of these birds currently thrives on the private lands of the U Bar Ranch near Gila, New Mexico, in a riparian area that has historically been intensively farmed using irrigation and grazed by cattle. On Forest Service land upstream and downstream from the U Bar, where cattle have been excluded for a number of years, the flycatcher does not nest at all. (Yet perversely, the U.S. Fish and Wildlife Service and the Forest Service have often used the presence of the bird, or of habitat it supposedly prefers, as a reason to reduce or eliminate cattle on federal allotments.) The U Bar also hosts large numbers of two endangered fish species, the Spike Dace and the Loach Minnow. Obviously, the anti-grazing assertion that cattle, by definition, threaten endangered species cannot be true (Ogilvie 1998; Sayre 2001:19, 85).

The Rancher-Environmentalist Alliance: "Cows vs. Condos"

Numerous arguments can be made for the ecological benefits of livestock ranching, if managed correctly. However, what has led increasing numbers of Westerners with environmental concerns to rally in support of ranchers is their perception of the manifest alternative to the ranch: urban development. "The greatest threat to Western landscapes today is not livestock grazing but urbanization, a land use that feeds on the economic decline of ranching" (Sayre 2001:91).

The argument is simple, and actual examples abound in the developing West. If environmentalist pressures cause federal agencies to cut the number of cattle allowed to graze federal allotments, ranching will become less and less viable as a livelihood for families that depend on public land. Forced to abandon ranching, and living in rural areas usually with few other economic possibilities, they will be compelled to sell their private land. This land, the heart of their ranch, typically was limited by the homesteading laws to an acreage too small to ranch successfully by itself. But the private land has great value if sold, as it will gravitate in the market towards lucrative real estate development, including subdivision into smaller properties ("ranchettes" or condominiums) much in demand in the New West. Thus, the slogan encapsulating this stark choice: "cows versus condos" (Sheridan 2001, 2007).

Common sense would indicate, and recent research (Knight 2002) confirms, that pockets of housing development strewn over Western rangelands result in much greater, much more undesirable ecological change than any effects associated with ranching.

> The upshot of the biological changes associated with the conversion of ranch land to ranchettes is an altered natural heritage. In the years to come, as the West gradually transforms itself from rural ranches with low human densities to increasingly sprawl-riddled landscapes with more people, more dogs and cats, more cars and fences, more night lights perforating the once-black night sky, the rich natural diversity that once characterized the rural West will be altered forever. We will have more generalist species—those that thrive in association with humans—and fewer specialist species—those whose evolutionary histories failed to prepare them for our high population densities and our advanced technology. . . . (Knight 2002:135)

According to the Nature Conservancy, ranchers are now seen as a "last line of defense against developers; that if ranches fold, there will be no use for the land other than residential use, which breaks up the landscape and taxes the water supply" (Kiefer 2000).

> Put ranchers out of business and we lose open space, access, wildlife habitat, riparian corridors and scenic views to developers. Subdivisions and homes *will* spring up where these ranches once stood. With them will come noxious weeds, overgrazed horse paddocks, access restrictions, vegetation conversions and barriers to wildlife movement. (Bean-Dochnahl 2000:16).

In the 1990s, as the conflict over public-land grazing grew, a section of the environmental movement recognized the probable result of forcing ranchers off the land and reacted to create a whole new approach to ranching. Paul Starrs, geographer and historian of ranching, summarizes the beginnings of this movement.

> To use or not to use: This was the polarization betwixt proponents and opponents of grazing. . . . The debate, Manichean in philosophical terms, is polarized black versus white and lodged against the detents of reason. The splits are extreme: full use or

none, wild or domestic, city slickers or rural rubes, federal or private, small or big, endangered species or livestock. In these terms, the hand dealt is typically all-cows or no-cows. But this doesn't need to be so—as a number of entirely reasonable conservation and biodiversity groups have made clear by meeting ranchers and other western interest groups more than halfway. Innovations are happening in support of not just biodiversity but also working landscapes and a central terrain of shared use and purpose. . . .

There are intriguing programs designed to use the steward ship practices of ranchers—and the actions of grazing animals, and habitat they use, for part or all of the year—for larger aims. These aims may be personal goals, open-space goals, ecological goals, watershed goals, fuel-hazard-reduction goals, economic goals, community goals, government goals. . . . (Starrs 2002)

In other words, it was an effort to combine, even fuse, the goals of ecology and ranching.

The Nature Conservancy, not an activist group but the largest of all U.S. environmental organizations in terms of its endowment, had long acknowledged ranching as sometimes the best use of land—a "working landscape" compatible with natural values if managed right. It has a long record of supporting ranching in selected areas to keep out development, while promoting conservationist approaches in land management. One example is the Gray Ranch of the New Mexico boot heel, an early effort at a new ecological approach (Clifford 1998; Daggett 1995:12–23). For its pragmatic philosophy, the Conservancy has been attacked by radical environmentalist groups, with little result (Kiefer 2000).

In the mid-1990s, a bitter split developed in the Santa Fe chapter of the Sierra Club (essentially its New Mexico branch), precisely over the question of livestock grazing and the cows versus condos dilemma. Nationally, the Sierra Club members eventually voted to endorse a purist anti-grazing position that put them in line with the anti-grazing campaign in the West. But before this occurred, a couple of conservationists and a rancher member of the Santa Fe chapter emerged in 1997 to found their own organization, the Quivira Coalition, devoted to promoting the concept that "ecologically healthy rangeland and economically robust ranches can be compatible" (Quivira Coalition 2003:1). The new organization succeeded in bringing together on its board of directors representatives of groups that had often been in contention—ranchers, environmentalists, public land managers, range scientists, biologists—uniting them around a set of common goals. Soon it had upwards of a thousand dues-paying members reflecting the same backgrounds.

What distinguished the new group was not only its diverse constituency but also its rejection of the polarizing rhetoric, confrontational litigation, and political activism of the "old movement." In the words of Courtney White, Quivira Coalition Executive Director,

> A new movement should eschew the extremes. It needs to focus on pragmatic solutions that solve real problems—and that means mobilizing the middle . . .—anyone dedicated to restoring ecological and economic health to this country, and doing so collaboratively, and with meaningful measurements of our success. It is in the middle—the Radical Center—where the work can begin. (White 2004:15)

The Quivira Coalition's practical work has involved numerous hands-on demonstration projects to restore land in the state of New Mexico. Also, it has sponsored an ongoing series of outdoor classes, workshops, tours, and conferences in New Mexico and Arizona to educate ranchers and others in aspects of rangeland health and "progressive" ranch management. The Coalition's "New Ranch" model is featured in their quarterly newsletter, and detailed in *The New Ranch Handbook* (Sayre 2001) it commissioned and published.

The Quivira Coalition attracted much favorable press, not only publications favorable to ranching, such as *Range* magazine (White and Winder 1999) and *American Cowboy* (Brown 1999), but local media of the Southwest, such as the *Santa Fe Reporter* (Goldberg 1998), the *Albuquerque Journal* (Robinson 2002), and the Albuquerque *Weekly Alibi* (Domrzalski 1999). The spreading of the new viewpoint had an immediate impact. As the story in the *Santa Fe Reporter* put it, "The Quivira Coalition is changing the grazing debate—and not everyone likes it"—referring to anti-grazing groups such as the Sierra Club and the Santa Fe-based Forest Guardians. These groups now found themselves on the defensive against the sophisticated ecological arguments of fellow environmentalists and natural scientists. Sometimes they were reduced to sputtering insults. "The Quivira Coalition...are the Benedict Arnolds of the Sierra Club and environmental movement" (Goldberg 1998:14).

Whatever the outcome of the Quivira Coalition's ambitious attempt to reform ranching in order to save it, they had indeed changed the terms of debate. They had come to the timely help of ranchers in the arena of public relations. The "man bites dog" story of ranchers and environmentalists uniting even reached the New York Times in November 2001 (Brown 2001).

Similar collaborative efforts embracing the philosophy of the "radical center" have emerged in other Western states. A few include the Malpai Borderlands Group and Sonoran Institute in Arizona, the Trout Creek Mountain Working Group in Oregon, the Montana Land Reliance, the Colorado Cattlemen's Agricultural Land Trust and the West Elk Livestock Association in Colorado (Bradford and Allen 1999; Knight et al. 2002; Knize 1999; McDonald 2001). But individual ranches have also been carrying out their own innovative "New Ranch" approaches, demonstrating how natural conservation and land restoration are compatible with sustainable ranching. "[T]here is growing recognition that improved management can rebuild most western riparian zones and uplands and still maintain cattle at or near current levels" (Wilkinson 1992:109). Examples have been featured in virtually every issue of *Range* magazine since the 1990s, while ten notable ranches around the West were portrayed with beautiful photography in *Beyond the Rangeland Conflict* by Dan Dagget, one of the earliest environmentalists converted to work with ranchers rather than opposing them (Dagget 1995).

Many ranchers, traditionally conservative, regard this new movement with caution, if not skepticism and suspicion. But other ranchers are being drawn into it. Elements of the Forest Service are also sympathetic to the "radical center," the more so because they also have felt the brunt of the polarized debate. At the least, the New Ranch movement offers individual ranchers a way to adapt to the changing times.

It's odd that a lifeway whose supporters are so given to espousing tradition is, in fact, completely dependent on tacking before countervailing political, ecological, and economic winds. Ranchers tend, pretty much of necessity, to be ultimate pragmatists....

Because ranching requires access to so much land and because its incomes are at best small, ranching has rarely had a strong built-in economic constituency in places of power. Instead ranchers have through the years had to make cultural converts. And they continue having to do so, with surprising and ongoing success. (Starrs 2002:5)

Part of the ongoing cultural conversion is the recognition by urban environmentalists and others that most ranchers do genuinely care for the land they ranch and for the wildlife on it. The great majority of ranch families are committed to staying on the land if they can survive economically; it is not profit that drives them but the way of life, a cultural choice (see Starrs 1998). Moreover, they are the people with the closest ties to the land they ranch, and with the most experience of it. They are the people with the most developed practical skills and knowledge for actually working on the land. If the goal truly is to restore rangeland health, who better to enlist in the effort as stewards? But ranchers cannot be enlisted if they are forced off the land.

Blue Range Primitive Area.

Bill and Barbara Marks at home.

Wolf and Coyote in Alpine Ranger Office, Alpine, Arizona.

The Blue River.

Rose Awtrey (*right*) roping a calf for branding, helped by Dustie Harper (*left*), and Brittney Joy (*center*). Photo copyright 2015 by Jenny Yates, In My Dreams.

Rose Awtrey (*left*), Barbara Marks (*center*), and Dustie Harper (*right*) cowpunching. Photo copyright 2015 by Jenny Yates, In My Dreams.

Rose Awtrey on cattle drive along Beaver Creek.
Photo copyright 2015 by Jenny Yates, In My Dreams.

Rose Awtrey at shipping corral. Photo copyright 2015 by Jenny Yates, In My Dreams.

Ranchers attending a meeting.

Tim Robart and family at home.

10

A New Regulatory Regime

The 1995 NEPA Cuts on the Blue

The Congress...declares that it is the continuing policy of the Federal
Government...to use all practicable means and measures...in a manner calculated to foster and promote the general welfare, to create and
maintain conditions under which man and nature can exist in productive harmony, and fulfill the social, economic and other requirements of
present and future generations of Americans.

THE NATIONAL ENVIRONMENTAL POLICY ACT OF 1969
(U.S. Congress 1970)

T HE ENVIRONMENTAL MOVEMENT'S onslaught on grazing in the 1990s
was not just a public relations war to turn opinion against ranching.
It was also a war fought in the courts and through government agencies.
Certainly the election of Bill Clinton as President in 1992, with Al Gore
as Vice President, advanced the agenda of mainstream environmental
groups who had become a virtual constituency of the Democratic Party.[1]
These groups maintained an especially close relationship with Al Gore,
who had conspicuously tried to identify himself with the environmental movement. Gore, it was reported, played a key role in his administration's choice of new appointees to lead the agencies responsible for
managing federal land in the West: the Department of Interior and the
Department of Agriculture, which included the Forest Service. Some of
the new appointees had a history of ties to the environmental movement;
others were rumored to be sympathetic to its goals. Although policy
shifts in large government agencies can take time, a crystal ball was not
needed during the Clinton-Gore administrations of the 1990s to predict
that natural resource industries in general would be increasingly on the
defensive against initiatives from Washington, D.C. And so it proved.

These industries—timber, mining, ranching, fishing, and some forms of outdoor recreation—had also come under increasing attacks in the courts. Congress had passed an array of environmental legislation in the late 1960s and early 1970s, mostly under President Nixon. By the 1990s lawyers and activists of the environmental movement became increasingly bold and adept in using these laws, especially the Endangered Species Act, to bring suits against productive activities that might have an "environmental impact" on nature. The laws had been written so that activities on federal lands were especially liable to lawsuits.

The environmental movement gained an enormous, well-publicized legal victory early in the 1990s when its lawsuits forced the Forest Service to suspend most logging in the Pacific Northwest—the nation's richest timber region—on the grounds of protecting the northern spotted owl. The Clinton Administration subsequently came up with a Forest plan that basically ratified the drastic cuts in timber harvest, down to a fourth of what had been previously envisioned. Less noticed nationally during these years was a campaign of lawsuits similarly suppressing the timber industry in the Southwest, in the name of protecting the Mexican spotted owl (a cousin subspecies of the Pacific Northwest owls). In Arizona and New Mexico, timber harvests were reduced by eighty percent, with an estimated loss of 2,400 jobs and $60 million annually (Pendley 1995:41–47, 92).

In 1993, timber harvesting was halted in the Apache-Sitgreaves National Forest. The halt damaged the Greenlee County economy, costing the county government shared revenues from timber harvests of about $200,000 annually (Greenlee County 1994). Ending logging also would hurt Blue ranchers who held summer allotments in the heavily forested mountains: the cutting of thick stands of timber had periodically opened up new pastures for their livestock. But the real concern of the ranchers, who had been closely watching the progress of the environmental movement, was that the same laws and legal tactics used against logging would be used against them. The Blue region abounds with habitat (potential or actual) for a number of species officially listed as endangered or threatened, or considered by the Forest Service as "sensitive." These species include the Mexican spotted owl, the northern goshawk, the American peregrine falcon, the bald eagle, the lesser long-nosed bat, the Southwestern willow flycatcher, the Apache trout, the loach minnow, spikedace (another minnow), and the Mexican gray wolf. To challenge ranching on the Blue under the Endangered Species Act, all that was needed were biological opinions linking these species' fortunes negatively to cattle grazing.

Environmental organizations in the Southwest existed to do just this: dig up biological research papers and turn them into lawsuits. The Forest Guardians of Santa Fe, the Southwest Center for Biological Diversity (later simply the Center for Biological Diversity) of Tucson, and affiliated legal groups such as Earthjustice had played a large role in shutting down logging in New Mexico and Arizona. On a roll from that victory, they turned their sights increasingly on the ranching industry. Drawing on the biocentric philosophy and no-compromise stance of Earth First! described in chapter 9, they were fundamentalist in their total opposition to grazing and frank lack of any sympathy for ranching families they might put out of business and force off the land.

Kieran Suckling, the director of the Southwest Center, told one reporter in regard to ranching: "Yes, we are destroying a way of life that goes back 100 years. But it's a way of life that is one of the most destructive in our country. . . . Ranching is one of the most nihilistic life styles this planet has ever seen. It should end. Good riddance" (Kenworthy 1998a). (Actually, cattle ranching in the Southwest goes back more than 400 years to the early Spanish settlers.) Suckling's biocentric outlook appeared in another interview when he was asked whether he was bothered by the anguish of the ranch families losing their incomes through his Center's suits. "I hear you talk about the pain of the people but I don't see you match that up with the pain of the species. . . . A loach minnow is more important, than say, Betty and Jim's ranch, a thousand times more important" (Walley 1999). "'What if humanity were down to a few hundred people?' Suckling asked. 'We'd be concerned. But we're down to a few hundred Southwestern willow flycatchers, and we have people crying Chicken Little because we're trying to protect them'" (Davis 1994). (Suckling and the Center have never acknowledged that the largest population of this songbird subspecies is thriving on the U Bar Ranch near Gila, New Mexico, on private land continually used for agriculture and grazing for over a hundred years [Ogilvie 1998; Sayre 2001:19, 85].)

Working together with their lawyers and other environmental organizations, the Southwest Center and Forest Guardians perfected the "legal train-wreck" strategy that had first emerged in the West in the struggle to stop timber cutting. First, barrage the Forest Service by appealing its actions; when the desired results are not forthcoming, file lawsuits so numerous that the agency is forced to bend. A legal observer who witnessed this process commented critically,

> The U.S. Forest Service is a virtual sitting duck for environmental groups making nit-picking appeals regarding the endless USFS documents required to harvest timber: forest plans, new forest plans, interim forest plans, proposed timber sales, proposed salvage sales, and on and on. Under USFS rules anyone can appeal a decision of the USFS, and it appears that almost anyone does. . . . (Pendley 1995:31)

Ranching under the Forest Service, like timber harvesting, is also wrapped in documents and plans, bureaucratic procedures, agency decisions on numbers of stock permitted, seasons of use for each allotment, and so on—details of which are publically available and may be appealed.

> Anything can serve as the basis for appealing a decision by the USFS: not enough data considered; wrong data considered; improper data admitted into the record; not enough alternatives considered; not enough public hearings held; public hearings not held in the right place; insufficient time for the public to comment; and on and on—a list that is limited only by the imagination of those filing the appeal.
>
> Even when it is over, it isn't really over. Unsuccessful appeals can become lawsuits. Most environmental statutes. . .allow private citizens to file lawsuits if they believe the U.S. government is not performing its job under the federal statute. Needless to say, with the abundance of "feel good" language that has clogged our federal laws to satisfy the demands of the various environmental groups, there is almost always a statutory basis for asserting that the law is being flouted.
>
> Once again, process is also a cause of action. Under the Administrative Procedure Act, failure to attend to the minutest detail is a basis for litigation. . . . Similarly, the National Environmental Policy Act (NEPA), which requires the agency to set forth its decision-making process for "major federal actions" that "significantly affect the quality of the human environment," has become the source of endless delays, appeals, and successful lawsuits. (Pendley 1995:32f)

The National Environmental Policy Act (NEPA), that became law on January 1, 1970, was perhaps "intended by many of the legislators who voted for it to be little more than a fuzzy and unenforceable policy statement," enunciating high principles in ringing phrases. Yet courts interpreted the seemingly innocuous provision that required "detailed statements" for federal actions to mean that the government must provide *very detailed* environmental impact statements, or EISs. This requirement subsequently applied to a wide variety of government actions. "Grazing on the public lands, for example, was never mentioned in NEPA's relatively sparse legislative history, but court-mandated EISs have played a role of considerable importance in modern federal grazing policy" (Wilkinson 1992:95).

One consequence of environmental impact statements and laws like NEPA that attempted to set up rational federal land use planning was to redistribute political power. "Environmental and recreation groups were able to manipulate the legal and procedural handles created by planning to obtain greater influence over public land decisions" (Nelson 1995:173). A second consequence was to turn land management more and more over to the courts.

> For most of public land history few of the important decisions were made by the judiciary. All this changed, however, in the 1970s. As in other areas of environmental policy, the judicial branch began to rival the Congress and the executive branch in influence over public land policy. (Nelson 1995:151)

Public land ranchers would correspondingly lose much of the power and influence they had previously enjoyed when decisions emerged from their direct relations with the agencies.

NEPA 1995 UNFOLDS

The new dispensation heralded by NEPA took time to work itself out. There was reluctance within the agencies to divert their personnel and budgets into the very expensive and time-consuming processes of creating detailed EISs. A student of the Bureau of Land Management's experience commented:

> The pouring of money into grazing EISs, combined with a shaky base of knowledge about rangelands and with a natural resource

of modest economic value at stake, raised at least some eyebrows. One range scientist considered that the EISs were "pure busy-work carried out in the name of decision making, but serving only to divert energy, attention and effort from management functions to useless paperwork." (Nelson 1995:111)

Legal challenges early on compelled the Bureau of Land Management to do EISs, but the Forest Service relied into the 1990s on its traditional production utilization studies and range analyses in reissuing permits (Bedell 2005). This situation changed due to the legal offensive of environmental activist groups and the listing of more and more endangered and threatened species in the West's forests. The Forest Service decided it now had to reissue permits under the NEPA process, knowing from its timber experience it needed to arrive at results that could be defended in court.

A forest service employee, and member of the 1995 NEPA team on the Alpine District, explains,

> But [the NEPA reissuance of permits beginning in mid-1990s] was the first time the Forest Service went through a public process doing allotment management plans, which they were supposed to have done since the National Environment Policy Act of 1970. They were supposed to be doing this through a very public process, and they never really did. "Well, this is what you had before," and it seemed like everything was okay, and so when they renewed permits they weren't going through the NEPA analysis they were required to do. (Hoffman 2002)

Grazing permits under the Forest Service are issued for up to ten years, at which time they need to be reissued. Beginning in 1995 reissuance was to be regarded as a "major federal action" under NEPA, requiring an "environmental analysis" (or "EA") to determine if a larger scale EIS is needed. The NEPA EA would include a range analysis to evaluate "forage resources," as well as a biological analysis to determine what measures might be necessary to protect threatened and endangered species. New permits were to be issued (or not) specifying the permitted number of animals, seasons of use, allowable "forage utilization" (amount of grass that can be grazed), and "facilities needed to mitigate adverse impacts" (i.e., fencing or some other action to comply with the Endangered Species Act).

There were so many permits expiring in 1995 that a crisis developed. Mitchel White, leader of the Forest Service ID (interdisciplinary) team that was put together to do the 1995 NEPA analysis in the Alpine Ranger District, explains:

> If I remember right, we had 27 allotments on the Alpine Ranger District to be permitted for NEPA. The last NEPA document prior to my coming there was eight years in the making. It took them eight years to go through a NEPA document for range analysis. Well, the Forest Service didn't have eight years in 1995 to do NEPA on 27 allotments. We had to get them done because the permits were expiring, and we couldn't hold up the issuance of a grazing permit because we didn't have the NEPA done.
>
> So, Congress passed the Rescission Act, which gave us legislative relief in that we could go ahead and issue a grazing permit in lieu of having NEPA done, as long as we scheduled NEPA for completion in a reasonable time frame... But within that law they said that we still had to do 20% on the [Apache-Sitgreaves] Forest.... More than 100 permits were going to expire, so the Rescission Act...meant we would have to do 21 or 23 on this Forest in 1995.
>
> Well, it turned out that those allotments on the Alpine District were the highest priority, based on our Forest Plan, because of cold water fisheries, T & E [threatened and endangered] fisheries and some other legal requirements that were going on at the time. It fell on the Alpine District that we had to do the bulk of allotments on the Forest. I think Alpine had 13 [out of 27]. (White 2004)

The Supervisor (head) of the Apache-Sitgreaves National Forest at the time also stressed that litigation was driving his Forest to focus the 1995 NEPA analysis on the allotments that might be challenged under the Endangered Species Act (ESA).

> It was a critical resource issue, primarily driven by threatened and endangered species, and the effects that domestic livestock have on those. On the Apache side of the Forest, we got the fifth largest cold water fisheries in the National Forest system and we've got endangered species in all these streams. That was something we had to deal with, primarily driven by lawsuits.

We needed to do a lot of analyses. What we were threatened
with was an injunction. An injunction to take the livestock off
the Forest completely...We were out of compliance with the
ESA and the National Forest Act. So that was the driving force.
Primarily it was associated with riparian [areas], by streams. Primarily it was fish related. (Bedell 2001)

The upper Blue River in the Alpine District had four yearlong permits that would expire at the end of 1995, with eight allotments among
them; and three one-season permits with four allotments. Permits are
issued to the ranch owner for the allotments he uses—usually at least
two allotments, one for winter grazing and another at a higher altitude
for summer pasture. The Blue allotments that would be the target for the
1995 NEPA analyses had the following permittees:

1. Herschel and Ramona Downs, with their daughter and son-
   in-law Mona and Bill Bunnell: Raspberry and KP allotments.
   This family lives on the Blue;

2. The Lazy YJ Ranch owned by William Quinsler: the Bobcat/
   Johnson and Beaver Creek allotments. Quinsler, a utility
   executive with a home in Phoenix, had the Lazy YJ allotments ranched on his behalf for years by Blue residents Rose
   Coleman and her former husband Charles Coleman;

3. Rose Coleman: Fish Creek, Steeple Mesa, Fish Hook, Hannagan allotments—shared jointly with the Robart family (a
   vestige of the common allotments of the early Forest Service
   era prior to fencing). Rose is the granddaughter of Blue pioneer Toles Cosper and has lived on the Blue nearly all her
   life;

4. Marian Robart, with her son Tim and his family: joint use
   of Fish Creek, Steeple Mesa, Fish Hook, and Hannagan allotments. Their home ranch where they were living, at the
   end of the road down the upper Blue, is at the site of Toles
   Cosper's early ranch;

5. Glen McCarty of Reserve, NM: Turkey Creek and Coyote/
   Widmer allotments. McCarty, from an old-time ranching
   family, has other permits and allotments on the bordering
   Gila Forest of New Mexico;

6. The Powder River Ranch, owned by several individuals from the Phoenix area: the Lower Campbell Blue allotment. Its other allotments and "home" ranch, the AD Bar (once owned by Fred Fritz and then Sewall Goodwin), lie in the Clifton Ranger District on the edge of the lower Blue watershed;

7. Dan Heap of St. Johns, AZ: the Lower Campbell Blue allotment. His other allotments and home ranch lie near St. Johns, outside the Alpine District.

On April 28, 1995, the Alpine District Ranger sent out letters asking for comments on all the allotments, not only from the ranchers involved but also any other members of the public. These would be persons who had expressed any concerns about an allotment in writing in the past or had asked to be notified of any actions taken on a particular allotment. This was part of the "public process" mandated by the NEPA. The letter was accompanied by a "scoping report," as the Forest Service calls it, which describes—in general terms, and with several alternatives—the "proposed actions" being contemplated in regard to the permit. For the four yearlong permits on the Blue, the proposed actions were nearly similar and included:

1. issuing a "variable head" permit to "keep stocking within the numbers needed to meet Forest Plan standards and guidelines and the permit objectives";

2. implementing "mitigation measures" to protect the loach minnow and Apache trout and their habitat, mainly by discouraging livestock from certain riparian areas while fences were being built to exclude them;

3. limiting grazing "utilization" (consumption) to forty-five percent or less of grass and forbs (brush or herbs other than grass), a limitation seen as protecting the fish and the northern goshawk as well as preventing overgrazing.

The suggested "preliminary alternatives" were

1. issue a new permit that is the same as the current permit;

2. issue a new permit but with different permitted numbers and/or season of use;

3. mitigation combined with 1 or 2 above to comply with the
   Endangered Species Act, the Clean Water Act, the National
   Historic Preservation Act, etc.

Another alternative would be not to reissue a new ten-year grazing permit. Comments were invited on these proposed actions and alternatives, to be submitted by May 15, and the projected date for a decision was given as September 10 (USFS 1995a).

"Scoping" Comments

How many parties were solicited is uncertain; but thirteen scoping comments were received and saved in the Range NEPA files, analyzed as part of the NEPA process (USFS 1995b), with someone for the Forest Service responding to the comments. Perhaps these comments played little part in the final decisions, but they are of interest for what they reveal about the views of the letter writers. One was a comment by someone concerned with elk overgrazing. Two of the letters were from individuals, outside the Blue, generally supporting the ranchers and asking that their permits be reissued without any cuts. One detailed comment was from Arizona Game and Fish. Blue ranchers submitted only four letters, a sign that they were not initially alarmed by the NEPA analysis or the "proposed actions."

One of the owners of the Powder River Ranch (the AD Bar) wrote to say simply she did not want to see a change in grazing. Rose Coleman wrote a letter complaining that

> the permittee is the first to be picked on. As discussed time and again, the elk have a definite impact on the forage, stream banks and fences. The herd size continues to grow while livestock numbers remain the same, or as proposed now, reduced.... [It] is ludicrous to think livestock have an impact on the loach minnow [or much] on the Apache Trout. We all know it is just a ploy to remove livestock.... (Coleman 1995)

Another letter came from a Blue ranching couple, Bill and Barbara Marks, who were not up for permit reissue in 1995, but who had been very active in Blue community affairs, particularly grazing issues. Their studiously polite letter had many suggestions for improving matters on the range, and pleas for understanding the ranchers' situation.

[These] grazing permits must be authorized. They meet all of the criteria—the lands are suitable for domestic livestock grazing, the livestock operators to whom you must make forage available are qualified, the economic and social well-being of the community are dependent upon this resource use, and livestock grazing is consistent with land management plans. The only changes that have taken place in the last several years are the increased numbers of recreationists and elk. Since they also contribute to the economic and social health of the community, we acknowledge their value and respect it, but to move towards economic dependency on them is folly. The livestock operators in this area cannot be expected to give up anymore than they already have, because to do so would not only mean excessive financial burdens and possible ruin to the operators but to the entire community as well. Because of the Forest Service policy you stated, FSM 2202.1, your agency must promote community stability, not destruction. (Bill and Barbara Marks 1995)

Glen McCarty's letter struck a more feisty tone, challenging the Forest Service on several points. Like the others, he complains about the elk: "I read lots of restrictions and mitigation on cattle numbers but *nothing* on elk. The Forest Service and the Arizona Game and Fish need to mitigate and control elk the same as cattle." He also protested a "variable head permit" as unheard of, too vague and putting the rancher at the mercy of the Forest Service (McCarty 1995). In responding to this comment, the Forest Service analysis claimed "the use of variable numbers and season on a permit is not new" and referred to a section of the Grazing Permit Administrative Handbook (USFS 1995b:12).

Individuals representing five environmental organizations also responded to the scoping request concerning the Blue permittees. All five were groups opposing grazing, and all had a record of participating in lawsuits against grazing, often with each other on the same lawsuits. The letter from farthest away came from the Boulder, Colorado, office of Kimi A. Matsumoto, Staff Attorney for the National Wildlife Federation. Written in legalese, most of the letter was based on misunderstandings of what the Forest Service was doing or going to do in the case of the four grazing permits, in terms of legal responsibilities. The letter's particular concern was that endangered species protection be provided for the

Apache trout. Kimi Matsumoto had probably never been to the Blue; at least, nothing in the letter made any reference to local conditions (Matsumoto 1995).

Perhaps the National Wildlife Federation was enlisted in the cause by its affiliate, the Arizona Wildlife Federation, based in Mesa, near Phoenix. A letter from its head, Rick Erman, also did not mention local conditions on the Blue. Instead, he questioned whether livestock grazing was compatible with ecosystems in the Southwest and argued that wildlife needs must have primary consideration over cattle (Erman 1995).

The letter from the Southwest Center for Biological Diversity regarding the four allotments was a long list advising the Forest Service what it must or must not do to remain in compliance with the law. The writer complains that he knows nothing about the Blue.

> It is difficult if not impossible to provide any specific comments regarding these allotments when virtually no information is provided in the scoping document. At the very minimum, an outline of current and desired conditions should be included. What are management problems? Are TES [threatened and endangered species] present? What are the preliminary alternatives? (Hogan 1995)

The Forest Service comment evaluator dismissed this complaint. "Contact points for additional information were given. This is not a significant NEPA issue" (USFS 1995b:6).

The Southwest Center had admitted it did not even know whether endangered species were present on the Blue allotments. That this group should know little about local conditions on the Blue would not be surprising to those familiar with its modus operandi. Its staff members rarely go into the field themselves. Sited in university towns, group members cull data from academic sources, but they especially rely on documents obtainable from the government agencies they sue, such as the Forest Service and the U.S. Fish and Wildlife Service. On the basis of their library research, they launch their appeals and legal actions. Their comments, appeals, and lawsuits tend to be wholesale and indiscriminate, aiming at all potential targets in a particular category. As the Southwest Center was commenting on the NEPA studies on the Blue, it was also issuing nearly identical comments on many dozens, perhaps hundreds, of other allotment analyses being conducted across the Southwest. The same approach appears to have been taken by the two wildlife federations mentioned above. The result resembles a form letter in its generality.

Another letter in this vein was received from the "Forest Conservation Council, Southwest Regional Office" in Santa Fe. Unlike the two wildlife federations and the Southwest Center, this group appears to have had little in the way of membership, and its name can be found in Internet research only in conjunction with lawsuits filed by the Forest Guardians of Santa Fe. Since the Forest Guardians did not send comments on the Blue allotments, perhaps the Forest Conservation Council was acting as its surrogate. In any case, the outlook of the two parties is similar: "cows should be viewed as exotic pests on the landscape," and "we feel that domestic livestock grazing should be eliminated from the Apache-Sitgreaves National Forest." The Council writer lectured the Forest Service in terms close to those of the Southwest Center on what it could and could not do legally (Cameron 1995).

A letter from Rex R. Johnson Jr., of Southwest Trout, Inc., differs from the other environmentalist comments in its specificity of detail and actual familiarity with the area being analyzed. He states that he and his group examined streams in the Apache-Sitgreaves Forest "where we feel coldwater fisheries are at risk or where they have disappeared and might be restored," including streams on the Blue grazing allotments going through the NEPA process. Johnson would later write a fly-fisherman's guide to Arizona trout (Johnson 1999). In the mid-1990s he was also associated with Gila Watch, a Silver City, New Mexico environmental activist group working closely with the Southwest Center. Southwest Trout also appears as a joint plaintiff in anti-grazing lawsuits organized by the Southwest Center. Therefore one would expect Johnson's NEPA comments to be highly critical of ranching on the Blue River, and in fact he finds its watershed system to be "extremely degraded."

> The streams in the Blue Range lie in steep, highly erosive watersheds highly susceptive to damage caused by sudden summer rainstorms. The lower elevations of these streams make them subject to high summer temperatures when riparian conditions are substandard, threatening their trout populations. (Johnson 1995).

Leaving a discussion of riparian areas, Johnson repeats an assertion often made by anti-grazing activists, though it is not true—certainly not for permittees on the Blue.

> We also note that ranching in this area is changing from that of a family-based homestead to one of absentee business interests. Most permittees in the Clifton and Alpine Districts no longer live within traditional "base properties" and ranch on the corresponding forest permit. Quite to the contrary, today's permits are more like "trading cards," bought, sold, and exchanged, often by businessmen with non-ranching backgrounds. (Johnson 1995)

Such a generalization might ease the conscience of activists, who like to think of themselves as nobly opposing rapacious businessmen and not driving poor ranch families off the land. However, in 1995 Johnson's comment applied to very few permittees on the Blue; actually, the great majority of permittees had ranching backgrounds and lived on ranches or in small towns near their allotments—land they worked with their own hands. Of the four permits on which Johnson was commenting (numbers 1 through 4 above), only one belonged to a nonrancher: Mr. Quinsler, the utility executive from Phoenix. But all evidence is that his investment in the ranch was not primarily to make a profit—for little money could be made on Blue allotments—but instead to have a summer mountain residence for his family.

Johnson notes that

> within the past ten years we have seen former ranch base properties along the Blue River acquired by the Forest Service and the corresponding allotments re-assigned or retired—all in the interest of recovering the watershed and promoting wildlife and recreation within the Blue Range Primitive Area.... [We] hope that all allotments within the Blue Range Primitive Area (including several of those in the current proposal) will be given the same emphasis. (Johnson 1995)

Actually, the only allotment that had been retired from grazing at that time was the Fritz Sandrock allotment, but a number of "base" properties—private properties that once held ranches—had in fact been acquired by the Forest Service. (This process and the Sandrock example are discussed in chapter 8.) The environmental vision here, of phasing cattle off the Blue Primitive Area in order to reclaim it as wilderness, would tend to validate the ranchers' suspicions of Forest Service and environmental activist motives.

Johnson quotes extensively from the Apache-Sitgreaves National Forest Plan of 1987. Forest plans are always written with admirable goals, and Johnson uses their own "management objectives" to criticize the Forest Service for not meeting them in the case of the Blue allotments. For example, the plan prescribes

> allowable use for the riparian zone will not exceed 30 percent [of grass eaten]. Maintain at least 80 percent of the potential overstory crown coverage. Maintain at least three age classes of woody riparian species, with at least 10 percent of the woody plant cover in sprouts, seedlings, and saplings. . . . Maintain at least 80 percent of the potential stream shading from June to September along perennial cold and cool water streams. Maintain at least 80 percent of the potential emergent vegetation cover from May 1 to July 15 in key wetlands. . . . Manage for stream temperatures not to exceed 68 degrees F. on cold water streams. . . . Manage for or maintain habitat capability for Apache trout, rainbow trout, brook trout, brown trout, loach minnow, and Little Colorado spikedace at least 60 percent of potential. . . . (USFS 1987:159–162, quoted in Johnson 1995)

And so on, in great detail. Many of these conditions might be impossible to meet with or without cattle, but they allowed Johnson to hoist the Forest Service on its own petard. Johnson cites two dozen streams on the eight allotments that

> we have examined in the years 1991, 1992, 1993, and 1994 and know to contain trout [and other fish] populations and to be in clear violation of nearly every one of the prescriptions we have quoted above from the forest plan. . . . Thus all eight allotments have at least potential Apache trout habitat. In addition, we have actually found Apache trout in Beaver Creek. . . .
>
> It is not clear to us how you are going to address this basic lack in present management. . . .
>
> You are so fundamentally out of sync with your forest plan in the management of these riparian areas that it is unthinkable to us that you would re-issue the current grazing permits

for another 10 years without a thorough re-assessment of what
you're doing and where you're going. . . . (Johnson 1995)

Johnson cites a number of streams on the various allotments that he
believes are in violation of Forest Service regulations, including a few he
thinks in "atrocious" condition.

His "scoping" commentary may be compared to what he says to a
different audience in his *Arizona Trout: A Fly Fishing Guide*. There he
also complains about grazing, but

> on balance, [the Blue] is still a fair stream holding wild browns
> and some rainbows in its upper 50 miles [out of 75 miles
> length]. . . . I've caught many nice trout in these same upper
> reaches. . . . I've managed to catch a fair number of 14- to 16-inch
> browns and rainbows over the years. . . .
>
> Besides the 50 trout-bearing miles of the mainstem, Blue
> drainage holds by my count no fewer than 20 trout-bearing trib-
> utaries and sub-tributaries. (Johnson 1999:56)

Therefore, by his testimony, plenty of trout remain in the Blue, but not
the Apache trout. Johnson's fishing guide does not blame this situation
on grazing; instead, he agrees with the thinking of local ranchers on the
subject.

> Once the major game fish of Arizona, and essentially the state's
> only game fish, the Gila and Apache trout have gradually disap-
> peared from nearly all their original range. Both are now listed
> under the Endangered Species Act. . . . Both forms readily inter-
> breed with the rainbow trout, and it is mainly the repeated stock-
> ing of rainbows since the turn of the century into nearly every
> suitable source of cold water that has led to the disappearance of
> the natives. (Johnson 1999:7)

The planting of hatchery rainbows and also, for a time, brown trout, led to
the dominance of well-adapted rainbow and brown- and rainbow-Apache
hybrids and the near extinction of the pure Apache trout, which is now
less desirable to fishermen. Today, trying to reverse the process, federal
agencies are reintroducing the Apache in areas like the Blue watershed.

The attempt to keep cattle off the streams in the name of protecting
the Apache trout should be seen in this context. Whatever the impact of

grazing on the riparian areas, it seems a distant factor in the decline of the Apache trout. For this, Arizona state agencies catering to fishermen's demands were primarily responsible.

THE NEPA ANALYSES

During the summer of 1995, the Alpine District office Interdisciplinary (ID) Team, led by Mitchel White, worked on NEPA analyses of the twenty-seven allotments (twelve on the Blue) that they had decided to do that year. White describes the process.

> So actually we went back to Range Science 101, and developed a process for determining what grazing capacity was on those allotments. The two issues were balancing permitted numbers with the capacity of the land, and proper season of use. . . . We went and looked at the criteria for assessing grazing on Forest land. That's all we did, was apply our handbook and manual directions. We didn't create anything new. We developed the methodology using standard Forest Service procedure, and using principles of animal behavior and water availability. Like I said, it was Range Science 101. (White 2004)

The handbook was the Region 3 (Southwest) Allotment Analysis Handbook, which in the words of the Forest Service "provides broad guidelines for the collection analysis of resource information" to be used in NEPA analysis, though specific methods may vary at the local level (USFS 1996b).

For data the Forest Service keeps records of their "production/utilization studies" (grass and forb [non-grass herb] growth and consumption), soil analyses, and other observations periodically carried out on allotments. However, this data in the Alpine and Clifton Districts has been collected only at irregular intervals, sometimes years apart, by different personnel, and sometimes using different methods. To go into the field during the summer of 1995 for a thorough study of each allotment's condition was beyond the capacity of the Alpine District's limited staff. Mitchel White claims his ID team did go often into the field to verify their findings and procedures. Ranching people on the Blue say they saw very little of the ID Team outdoors during that summer. But both parties agree that the bulk of the NEPA analysis was done using computers in the Ranger District office.

Standards and Guidelines in the [Forest Service manual] direct the Forest to "utilize the Forest's Geographic Information System and Terrestrial Ecosystem Survey information...to evaluate grazing capability based upon watershed condition.... The methodology applied by the Forest utilized existing data on vegetation and other basic resource components such as soils, water, slope, in the production/capacity determinations. Once the basic resource information was assimilated, the data and methodology was applied to the individual allotment via a Geographic Information System based on the specifics of vegetation type, canopy closure, soils, slope, and water, for each acre. (USFS 1996b)

The Geographic Information System and Terrestrial Ecosystem Survey were based on satellite mapping data that could purportedly give the Forest Service an "accurate determination of the acres which can realistically contribute to the grazing capacity of the allotments" (USFS 1996b). These computer models could be programmed to take account of terrain, vegetation types, soils and erosion rates, and other factors that would affect grazing capacity. Available field data, such as past estimates of range conditions, could be entered.

The ID team had to make certain critical assumptions about where to set the parameters of their model. For example, for cattle grazing purposes they decided to count only land less than one quarter of a mile from water on the grounds that cattle would travel farther from water only if they have overgrazed the first quarter mile. They also decided that cattle would only consume grass on slopes of less than thirty percent grade, being too lazy to climb steeper grades (though elk would go up to fifty-five percent). The team also estimated 1,000 pounds of forage per month per animal. Other assumptions were made as to how various types of tree canopies influenced grass and forb production. Restrictions on grazing due to the presence of sensitive, threatened, or endangered species had to be figured in, as well as riparian areas that were to be fenced off to protect loach minnow, spikedace, and Apache trout (USFS 1995c).

The constrictive nature of the assumptions and estimates and other factors determined by Mitchell White's NEPA team were seen in the results, which radically reduced the carrying capacity of Blue allotments from previous estimates. Did this mean that the Forest Service had been deeply wrong in the past? "Yeah, I would say we were wrong in the past," said White. "Those numbers were cut so drastically because those allotments were overstocked, based on their ability to support livestock grazing. That's it in a nutshell" (White 2004). According to Don Hoffman, another member of the team,

> Perhaps if we had been doing our job better back in the 60s, 70s, and 80s, and doing sound range management as we're supposed to, probably those numbers would have been reduced a long time ago.... For years I had watched other [range managers]...and they were just not making the hard decisions they were supposed to be making if they were doing things right. They just felt bad for the plight of the rancher, I guess.... And what happened, of course, was under the NEPA process of doing permit issuances, all of a sudden that process was done under a microscope.... We're required to do a full range analysis, and when it happened, it was not good news. (Hoffman 2002)

The head of the Apache-Seagraves National Forest, John Bedell, gives a view from a somewhat different perspective.

> It was a critical resources issue, primarily driven by threatened and endangered species, and the effects that domestic livestock have on those...and we've got endangered species in all these streams. So I think that the yardstick that was used ten to fifteen years ago, changed, with the listing of all these species, and it affected utilization standards. The capacity with the complex of endangered species reduced forty to fifty to sixty percent utilization standards to about twenty.... That was something we had to deal with, primarily driven by lawsuits [from environmental groups].... What we were threatened with was an injunction. An injunction, we felt, would have said to take the livestock off completely. (Bedell 2001)

THE NEPA ANALYSIS RECOMMENDATIONS

At a meeting in Alpine on September 8, 1995, permittees undergoing NEPA analysis were presented with the findings and recommendations of the Forest Service team. The ranchers would later say that they expected some reductions, but they were stunned by deep cuts proposed for their herds.

The most extreme proposed reduction covered the allotments of the elderly Herschel Downs, his wife, their daughter Ramona, and her husband Bill Bunnell. Their previous permit had been for 225 cows plus their calves for the year around, plus 160 yearlings (calves from the previous year) for four-and-a-half months, though their average actual use was somewhat lower. The previously permitted number of "AMs" (Animal Months) had therefore been 3,420 annually. The NEPA analysis calculated the desirable "balanced" carrying capacity to be only 546 AMs, thereby recommending an 84% reduction in permitted numbers. The Downs and Bunnells would be allowed only 46 cows with calves. This number would be far below the 300 or so cows with calves, widely considered the bedrock minimum for a self-supporting ranch operation.[2] The Forest Service decision effectively meant that the Downs and Bunnells could no longer make a living by ranching.

These figures are found in the "Summary and Explanation of Information Provided to Permittees" on the KP and Raspberry (Downs) allotments at the September 8 meeting (USFS 1995d). Also summarized are the "major explanatory factors." On the KP allotment "24% of soils are impaired, another 20% are partially impaired." Nineteen percent of the land was on slopes greater than 55%, which had been ruled out for elk and cattle, another 41% on slopes greater than 31%, so ruled out for cows. Land within one fourth of a mile of water, with slopes 30% or under and soils "fully capable" of grazing, comprised only 21% of the total allotment that was calculated left to support cattle. But other restrictions also were applied to the calculations. Ninety-three percent of the allotment was under "medium-high canopy closure," meaning less grass available in the shade. (All figures were derived from satellite mapping data and computer-programmed "equations" rather than ground-level measurements.) Eight percent of the KP allotment was within goshawk territory, 40% within Mexican spotted owl habitat. The KP contained only 0.1 miles of loach minnow streams but 23 miles of Apache trout streams. All of these species required "mitigation measures" in terms of some form of grazing restriction.

The smaller Raspberry allotment (named after one of the original Blue pioneers, killed in the Apache raid of 1886) received a similar analysis based on satellite data, with 94% of its soils estimated as "unsuitable" for grazing. All of the above factors, combined with other assumptions in the Forest Service computerized model, led to the final recommendation that the number of cattle permitted for the Downs-Bunnell family should be slashed by 84% (USFS 1995d, 1995e, 1995f).

Hit nearly as hard as the Downs and Bunnells were the allotments of two other Blue permittees: Rose Coleman and the Robart family. These two shared in common four allotments (two summer, two winter) between them. The "animal months" on their winter (low-country) range were cut by 84% also, leaving Coleman with only 35 head (down from 230) and the Robarts with 16 head (down from 114) from mid-October to mid-June. The Steeple Mesa allotment was determined to have only 8.9% of its total area "fully capable" for grazing, on less than 31% slope and within a quarter mile of water; Fishhook allotment only 12.1%. Miles of loach minnow streams and Apache trout streams also needed "mitigation," contributing to reduced carrying capacity in the Forest Service analysis (USFS 1995g, 1995h, 1995i).

Coleman's and the Robarts' summer allotments in the high country suffered 73% "animal month" cuts, resulting in a loss of permitted head for Coleman from 177 to 54, and for the Robarts from 72 to 23, for mid-July to mid-October. No animals were to be permitted to graze from mid-June to mid-July as had been allowed previously, purportedly to allow the grass to recover as the summer rains began. This meant the ranchers would have to feed their animals on their own small amounts of private land, either growing or buying cattle feed.

Apparently the two summer allotments did not have soil problems or distance-from-water problems, but only 62% of one and 67% of the other were less than 31% slope. Mexican spotted owl habitat covered the whole allotments, plus there were 20 miles of Apache trout stream. The northern goshawk also led to acres of reduced grazing (USFS 1995g).

Just as with the Downs and Bunnell allotments, the Robart and Coleman operations no longer made any sense in terms of subsistence ranching, let alone profits. Rose Coleman, along with her former husband—they had just divorced in 1995—had also managed the cattle of the neighboring Quinsler ranch, the Lazy YJ, for a percentage of the profit. The NEPA outcome for this allotment would materially affect Rose more than the Quinslers, who had an urban income and owned the ranch primarily as a summer home.

The Forest Service analysis of the Quinsler high-country allotment, Beaver Creek, resulted in an animal month reduction of 40% during a four-and-a-half month summer season, meaning cattle would be reduced from 235 to 179 head for only three-and-a-half months, mid-July to the end of October. However, the problem would be where to take most of cattle during the longer winter season, November to mid-June, for the analysis of the Quinsler winter Bobcat-Johnson allotment on Blue bottomlands resulted in an animal month reduction of 81% a reduction of 215–235 down to 42 head.

Additionally, cattle were to be kept off both allotments from mid-June to mid-July, to be fed by the owner on his own property. The explanations for the reductions were the same as for other winter pastures—large areas of impaired soils, land ruled off limit by steep slopes, miles of loach minnow streams, and 76% of the allotment in proposed critical habitat for the Mexican spotted owl (USFS 1995j, 1995k).

The above NEPA decisions have been detailed because they directly affected people living and working on the Blue. The other Blue allotments mentioned earlier in the chapter also received cuts in permitted livestock, not as great as the Downs-Bunnells or the Robarts or Rose Coleman, but nevertheless severe. Across the Alpine District the cuts varied, but the Blue was hardest hit in this first round of NEPA cuts. Blue ranchers who had not been subjected to this round of NEPA analyses, believed with some fatalism that over the coming few years, as their permits expired, NEPA analyses would deal them similar blows. Their fears would be borne out.

Notes

1. By "mainstream" I mean widely recognized environmental organizations, each with tens of thousands of members and tens of millions of dollars in yearly income. Some "mainstream" organizations are not involved in grazing issues, but those that are include the Sierra Club, the National Wildlife Federation, the World Wildlife Fund, the National Audubon Society, the Natural Resources Defense Council, the Environmental Defense Fund, the Wilderness Society, Defenders of Wildlife, and the Environmental Law Institute. All these groups, influenced by "biocentric" ideas, share similar views on the environment, including a generalized hostility towards most human commercial activity utilizing the natural resources of public lands. They want either to restrict or end public-lands ranching. The Nature Conservancy, which might in some ways be reckoned a "mainstream" group, differs from the other groups in its thinking and practice regarding ranching, as explained in chapter 9.

2. "Two hundred fifty cows" was the figure usually given by ranchers and Forest range managers to my question of how big a herd a family operation needed to main-

tain in order to stay in business—without any outside income. Paul Starrs gives that number in *Let the Cowboy Ride* (Starrs 1998:205). But Larry D. Butler, in "Economic Survival of Western Ranching," says, "Today's western family ranch with a cow-calf operation typically needs more than 300 mother cows to be considered a viable economic unit" (Butler 2002:197). Jerry Holechek, author of the widely utilized *Range Management* textbook (Holechek et al. 2011), believes that, "depending on many factors," between 300 and 500 "animal units" is the minimum (personal communication).

11

The Ranchers Resist

Appealing the Cuts

"We're going to stick together," she said. "We're going to help our fellow permittees."

BARBARA MARKS,
quoted by the *White Mountain Independent*, September 29, 1995

BLUE RANCHERS LOST little time in sharing the news with other federal land ranchers in the Apache-Sitgreaves Forest and beyond. By telephone, fax, and Internet, which ranchers were beginning to use, they could quickly span the distances that separated their homes. In less than two weeks, a large general meeting of permittees and others across the Forest was organized.

> A group of nearly 100 ranchers and permittees met at the Apache County road department yard near the rodeo grounds Wednesday [Sept. 20] to discuss the situation and possible responses.
>
> Barbara Marks and Rose Coleman, both from ranching families on the Blue, said they called the meeting because of the proposed loss of grazing lands.
>
> Marks said she realizes some permittees have not yet been affected, but the time will come when their permits expire. (*White Mountain Independent* 1995a)
>
> Barbara Marks...said that getting the ranchers together to form a unified front may be difficult at first, but it is something necessary.
>
> One of the problems is the vastness of the national forest, and the fact that not all grazing permits expire at the same time. (*White Mountain Independent* 1995b)

Different methods had been used in different parts of the Forest to determine new allotment restrictions. Some ranger districts had suffered more and deeper cuts than others. The Alpine district including the Blue had suffered worse cuts than the other districts, including the Clifton district on the lower Blue. These differences fueled the old suspicion that there was some larger plan or tendency afoot to clear ranching out of the Blue Primitive Area. This theory was strengthened by the pattern of cuts on the New Mexico side in the Gila National Forest, where the severest NEPA cuts were also occurring in the allotments located within or adjacent to the Gila Wilderness area (Taylor et al., n.d.).

The fact that the Blue was especially hit hard might also explain why two Blue ranchers—Rose Coleman, granddaughter of pioneer Toles Cosper, and Bill and Barbara Marks from another early Blue family—were leaders in organizing the permittees, along with Earl Baker, a rancher from near Springerville. Barbara Marks, in particular, would become the articulate and indefatigable spokeswoman for the Blue ranchers over the coming decade in all the battles to be fought over environmental issues. Her family's permit was due to come up for renewal in 1998.

Not only ranchers attended the September 20 meeting. Speakers of various backgrounds had been invited to advise the permittees: a range expert retired from the University of Arizona; an economist from Western New Mexico University; and the director of the Arizona/New Mexico Coalition of Counties—an organization formed to fend off the increasing environmental restrictions costing rural counties. In their struggle, the ranchers knew they would need to rely heavily on outside expertise. After sharing information, the meeting created the "Apache-Sitgreaves Allottees Association," with Earl Baker as president and Rose as secretary. Barbara Marks was the spokeswoman for a committee formed to work on a strategy to resist the proposed livestock reductions.

"We're still in the information gathering stage," Marks said. . . .

She said the focus will be on the social and economic impact of the grazing permit restrictions, an area which must be covered [by NEPA mandate] but, even according to some personnel of the Forest Service, was not dealt with in detail.

The ranchers, both those being affected immediately and those with permits expiring next year, are also concentrating on the cumulative effects on public services which will have their budgets cut as revenues from forest users decrease. (*White Mountain Independent* 1995b)

The same newspaper stories quoted the Alpine District Ranger, Charles Denton, who allowed,

> "I did know there would be some cuts, but I didn't realize how bad they would be," he said.
>
> Denton said the next 30 days will be the most important for permittees, requiring them to respond with solid data instead of emotional comment. . . .
>
> There are presently three alternatives: the first would be no grazing allowed; second is reissuing the same permits, with the same numbers, same season of use and land management program for utilization; and third, using all of the available books to come up with an arbitrary [*sic*] decision with little subjective reasoning involved.
>
> "That's why there's a drastic change," Denton said. "Now we're using a different yardstick to measure with." (*White Mountain Independent* 1995b)

The Forest Service stood by this rationale: their decisions were simply the outcome of an impersonal process based on range science. The ranchers, however, saw the decisions as utterly political, caving in to urban environmental pressure groups. They were exhorted at the meeting to contact their elected officials, but they knew from the experience of the logging industry that politicians, no matter how friendly to rural interests, might not be able to come to their rescue. In any case, they realized they had to present the "solid data" that Denton requested to make their own scientific case.

Comment

The affected parties and any other interested persons were, by Forest Service regulations, allowed thirty days to comment on the proposed actions before a final decision by the agency. In effect, they were given the opportunity to argue why the Forest Service should revise its Draft Environmental Assessment (EA) justifying the cuts in livestock (USFS 1995p). They had from September 12 to October 12, 1995.

Eventually the Alpine Ranger District received comments from forty-three parties, a few after the formal deadline. Many of the "commentors" (in Forest Service jargon) submitted more than one letter or document.

The affected ranchers as a matter of course submitted information and arguments contesting the Forest Service findings. But so did other ranchers from the Blue, notably the Markses, as well as ranchers from beyond the Blue and beyond the Alpine District. Some comment letters supporting the ranchers were from friends and other local residents. Official support also came from the Greenlee County Board of Supervisors, the Apache County [Springerville] Board of Supervisors, the Arizona State Legislature, and the governing board of Catron County—the New Mexico country bordering Greenlee County and the Blue, where the NEPA process had also come down hard on various ranchers. The New Mexico State University Range Improvement Task Force, which had a history of supporting ranchers in that state, also submitted comments on the Arizona ranchers' behalf. On the other hand, the Arizona Game and Fish Department and the Department of Environmental Quality (concerned with water) entered comments that were largely technical but could be seen as backing the Forest Service findings. Finally, there were five letters and two faxes from the National Wildlife Federation and one letter from the Southwest Center for Biological Diversity, which argued that the Forest Service had not gone far enough to restrict cattle. The Center, in particular, wanted all cattle taken off the allotments (USFS 1995m; USFS 1995n).

Along with their personal comments, all the affected ranchers and a few of their supporters submitted copies of the NMSU letter. They also submitted one or two anonymous documents to which they appended their signatures. These documents, which the Forest Service labeled the "Lakeside form" and the "EA form," each contain very detailed objections on legal and scientific grounds. The Lakeside Form is twelve, single-spaced pages raising forty-nine points of criticism. On Rose Coleman's form she adds a point "fifty" with her own questions and comments regarding her allotment and that of the Quinslers, which she managed. But the other forty-nine points are relevant to all the allotments in the Alpine and Springerville Districts. Other people submitted fifty, forty-nine, thirty-nine, or thirty-five points, but all came from the same document, word for word, which is probably why the Forest Service called it a "form."

The "EA Form" was similar but even longer: forty single-spaced pages of small print that challenged the Forest Service's environmental assessment in a host of ways, citing federal laws and Forest Service regulations but mostly relying on range and other scientific data.

Years later, ranchers could not recall who wrote these "forms" helping them contest the Draft Environmental Assessment. It is highly unlikely that the ranchers themselves composed them, as the documents reflect expert legal and scientific knowledge. Possible authors would include a law firm specializing in environmental lawsuits; someone from one of the Arizona universities; or a consultant, hired perhaps by Apache County.

One other expert opinion identified by name was that of Phil R. Ogden, a retired Professor and Range Extension Specialist from the University of Arizona, who wrote on behalf of the Downs and Bunnell allotments, which he had been hired to evaluate in a previous dispute with the Forest Service. In a different form, the Greenlee County Board of Supervisors separately submitted Dr. Ogden's criticisms of the Draft Environmental Assessment.

The Forest Service had an obligation to consider all comments, and a "List of Draft EA Comments and Commentors" indicates how they approached this task (USFS 1995n). Representatives of the different ranger districts of the Apache-Sitgreaves met with two members of the Forest Supervisor's staff in November 1995 to review the comments and decide how to address each. Since many of the comments duplicated others or made the same point, they were consolidated into one set. Comments specific to particular allotments, "about 100 each for Alpine and Springerville districts," could be addressed by each district. But the team identified 175 different comments that raised more general concerns that needed to be addressed at the Forest level. These comments the team broke down into major topics with subtopics. Thus organized, the comments could be addressed—or not.

Thirty-six of the comments the team found "Outside": "outside the scope of the project and the decision to be made, and for which the only response is that it is outside of the scope." Twenty-one of the comments were considered "Covered": already addressed by the Environmental Assessment or other documents "part of the project record, and for which it is therefore not necessary to initiate a separate response." Twenty-four comments were regarded as "Statements": "a statement of a preference, or an opinion, or a disagreement without either specificity or information such that a response could be made." Finally, seventy-eight comments (forty-five percent of the total) were categorized as "Respond," denoting that they would be "individually responded to in an appendix of the final EA" (USFS 1995n).

The 175 composite comments could be listed, but many requireed detailed explication. Here is a brief summary.

The first major category of comments the team addressed came under the topic "NEPA—Failures, Shortcomings." Such comments argued either that NEPA should not apply to the reissuing of grazing permits, or that the way the environmental assessment was conducted did not accord with the law or Forest Service regulations. Most of these criticisms can be found in the Lakeside and EA "forms" which doggedly cited federal laws, regulations, and court cases to attack in lawyer-like fashion the "Draft Environmental Assessment" and the procedures that produced it. A frequently criticized aspect of the EA was its failure to take into account social and economic effects, ignoring impacts on ranching and associated communities involved—matters mandated by federal law and Forest Service policies (USFS 1995n:1a–1f).

Many comments questioned the "range science" behind the Forest Service analysis. The methodology of the Interdisciplinary (ID) Team that had issued the EA was attacked from every angle. Their model of "production/capacity" was disputed in such matters as how far cattle would travel for water, how steep a slope they would climb, how much they would eat, what soils and plants would provide forage, and so on. The purported effects of cattle on the land were contested, as well as the effect of grazing on streams, vegetation, and wildlife species. The ranchers had their opinions on all these questions, but the "forms" they submitted, as well as the comments from Professor Ogden and the NMSU Range Improvement Task Force, supported them by arguing a different version of "range science." The Forest Service had to respond specifically.

Another large category of complaint was the failure of the NEPA analysis to take into consideration the large numbers of unregulated elk that roved many of the Blue allotments. Commentors argued that high elk traffic might be responsible for some of the environmental effects blamed on cattle and cited elk research by the Forest Service.

Critics claimed the ID team was biased. It was accused of being weighted with fish and wildlife experts who were too deferential to state

and federal fish and wildlife agencies and unsympathetic to cattle grazing. Although they were usually too politic to say so outright, most
ranchers considered the ID team stacked with "environmentalists" and
their sympathizers, and they hinted at this in their comments. Underlying many comments was a sense of the hurt and anger ranchers felt
toward the Forest Service breaking with its traditional policy of supporting family ranchers and their communities. As one disgruntled rancher
put it, the National Forest was now being run by Kieran Suckling (head
of the Southwest Center for Biological Diversity), as the agency bowed to
the threat of environmental law suits.

The Final Decision

The Alpine Ranger District took almost two months to issue the "Final
Environmental Assessment" for each allotment. It came on December 5,
1995. Although particulars differed by allotment, the language justifying the assessments was largely the same for each permittee and with
few changes followed word for word the earlier "Draft Environmental
Assessment." The main difference was an appendix responding to comments selected by the Forest Service. In virtually all cases the methods
and assumptions and conclusions of the ID Team were upheld and justified. As the "Decision Notice" accompanying the Final EA stated, "Input
received from 43 respondents aggregated to over 200 separate comments.
Comments to the draft EA were addressed in Appendix H of the final
EA. These comments resulted in a number of corrections and clarifica-
tions but did not result in any substantial changes to the final EA" (USFS
1995r:3). In other words, the Forest Service was not changing its mind.

The EAs had put forth in all cases three alternatives for each allotment. "Alternative A" was, "No livestock grazing." Apparently this
"alternative" was new to the ranchers, judging from their comments, but
it matched the demands of the radical environmentalists. "Alternative B"
was, "Imbalance with capacity"—and matched the number of livestock
that had been allowed under the previous permit. "Alternative C" was,
"Balanced permitted numbers with capacity" and was denominated the
"preferred alternative." It also listed the "mitigation measures" to protect the different endangered and threatened species on the allotment. In
the case of fishes such as the Apache trout and loach minnow, this meant
restricting cattle access to riparian areas and stream bottom pastures. In

the case of birds such as the Mexican spotted owl and the goshawk, it meant limiting grazing in areas considered their ".critical habitat."

To present a sense of the preferred alternative C, I quote at length the "Decision and Rationale" for the two allotments of the Downs-Bunnell grazing permit, the "KP," and "Raspberry."

> Based on the results of the analysis documented in the Environmental Assessment (EA), it is my decision to implement Alternative C. . . . Implementation of Alternative C which balances allotment capacity with permitted use includes:
>
> 46 cattle (cow/calf), January 1 to December 31
>
> Applicable Standards and Guidelines . . . as follows.
>
> —No more than 45% utilization by weight on riparian forage and browse
>
> —No more than 40% utilization by weight on upland forage and browse
>
> —No more than 20% utilization average by weight in forested areas within goshawk territories on grasses and forbs
>
> —No more than 40% utilization average by weight in forested areas within goshawk territories on browse, and
>
> —No more than 20–40% utilization by weight on forage and browse within Mexican Spotted Owl (MSO) critical habitat
>
> Other Terms and Conditions of the permit as follows:
>
> —No mineral supplement sites and no herd-size gathers or trailing done with MSO protected activity centers (PACs) unless authorized, and
>
> —Regular rotation of mineral supplement sites in suitable MSO habitat outside of PACs (addressed in Annual Operating Plan)
>
> —On the KP Allotment, cattle gathered in the summer country (upper KP) and moved to the winter country (lower KP and Raspberry) and vice versa will not utilize KP Creek drainage as a driveway.

Mitigation measures for Loach minnow—Exclude Oak Creek Pasture and Raspberry Holding Pasture from livestock grazing within the Raspberry Allotment

Mitigation measures per USFWS [U.S. Fish and Wildlife Service] 10/27/95 Biological Opinion (BO) for the threatened Apache Trout (incorporates BO on Apache Trout Habitat Improvement Plan)—KP Creek drainage will no longer be used as a driveway between summer and winter country and vice versa

—Fence Reach 5 on Bear Wallow Creek to eliminate livestock grazing

Rationale for selecting Alternative C is that this alternative incorporates legal requirements into the grazing authorized...[and] also authorizes grazing at a level and in a manner that 1) brings environmental impacts to below significance per National Framework for Permit Issuance direction (January 1995) and 2) perpetuates satisfactory resource conditions and improves unsatisfactory conditions. All of the above are practicable means adopted in order to avoid or minimize environmental harm from the selected alternative.

The final rationale for my decision to select Alternative C is that while implementation may affect the human environment by causing economic impacts to livestock operation, the economic and social effects are not significant in the context of 40 CFR 1508.27 at the local and regional level. (USFS 1995r:3)

Of course the economic and social effects on the ranchers in this case were very significant. The Downses, their daughter Mona, and son-in-law Bill Bunnell subsequently had to give up ranching while trying to hold onto their private land. They offered to rent cottages as a "guest ranch" and guided hunters in the fall; Mona kept working as part-time Postmistress of Blue; and Bill went away to Tucson to train as a prison guard (see chapter 15).

Alternative C was chosen for all Blue allotments that had gone through the NEPA process. Making the final decision was Forest Supervisor John C. Bedell, who signed the Decision Notices on December 5, 1995. Alternative C may have been positioned to seem a moderate, middle way between Alternatives A (no cattle) and B (existing permitted numbers), but its effect on the ranchers was radical, cutting livestock numbers below those necessary to sustain a livelihood in ranching.

Later, Supervisor Bedell claimed that he had no choice, given the environmental lawsuits the Forest Service faced. If the Forest Service didn't act, a judge might issue an injunction removing all the cattle from its lands.

> It was a critical resource issue, primarily driven by threatened and endangered species, and the effects that domestic livestock have on those. . . .
>
> A regulatory agency, like the Fish and Wildlife Service, will tell the environmental community, when they ask for their information, that we [USFS] are not in compliance [with the Endangered Species Act]. . . . We're out of compliance with the Biological Opinion [of the US Fish and Wildlife Service], so therefore we're out of compliance with the Act. . . .
>
> I can't even estimate how many lawsuits we have. I think there are nine or ten, and they're all tied to non-compliance with the ESA. . . .
>
> It was a tough hit. I think that if we hadn't done what we did, we would not have *anything* left in terms of cattle. (Bedell 2001)

In the eyes of Bedell, the Forest Service was caught ineluctably between the demands of two communities—the environmental movement and the ranchers—and still had to do its duty under the law. The Endangered Species Act in particular, as interpreted, favored the environmental activists.

> [The ranchers] blame the Forest Service, but it's really not what they claim. We have the responsibility to deal with whatever the appropriate use is, and the appropriate use today is different than the appropriate use yesterday, and I say it's due primarily to the protection of listed species. (Bedell 2001)

Appeals to Albuquerque

Appeals of local decisions by a National Forest are possible under the agency's regulations. In this case the ranchers could appeal to the Southwestern Regional office of the Forest Service in Albuquerque. Although extremely skeptical that officials in Albuquerque would be sympathetic to their claims, they were required to exhaust the appeal process before taking matters into court. Also, appeals would delay the implementation of the livestock cuts. To handle their appeal and anticipated court case, thirteen permittees from the Apache-Sitgreaves National Forest—seven with allotments on the Blue or its connected summer pastures—engaged the Budd-Falen Law Offices of Cheyenne, Wyoming. This firm was well known for its defense of ranchers' rights in other Western cases, including ones involving the Endangered Species Act.

The extended nature of the appeals process was summarized by Deputy Regional Forester, John R. Kirkpatrick, in his final decision on the appeal delivered to the Budd-Falen Law Offices on May 29, 1997.

> Your appeal of this decision was received in this office on February 13, 1996. Under the provisions of 36 CFR 251.94 the Forest Supervisor prepared and mailed to you a copy of his written responsive statement to your appeal on April 15, 1996. [Your] response to the Forest Supervisor's responsive statement...was received in a timely manner in this office on May 8, 1996. On June, 1996, you made an oral presentation on [the] appeals via a conference call with this office. On June 21, 1996, I received a written summary of the information presented in your June 12 oral presentation.
>
> By letter dated August 12, 1996,...I indicated my review decisions...would be made by October 1, 1996. Because of demands placed on this office having to do with litigation and other appeals, my review decision...has been delayed until this time [May 29, 1997].
>
> A total of 4 other appeals were filed by various individuals, organizations, and entities, of this decision under the appeal regulations at 36 CFR 215. My review of these appeals was conducted...with decisions rendered on March 28, 1996. (USFS 1997)

These four other appeals were not from the ranchers whose permits had been cut, but from other parties not directly affected: Bill and Barbara Marks on behalf of their fellow ranchers, and three environmental organizations including the Southwest Center for Biological Diversity. Because they fell under different regulations, the appeals could be dealt with in a more summary fashion in March 1996.

The Markses had appealed, first, against what they saw as NEPA procedural violations, including failure to analyze adequately cumulative economic, social, and other effects that impinged on permittees and their communities. The Deputy Regional Forester, John R. Kirkpatrick, dismissed their argument on the basis that these effects had been addressed. The Markses had also contended that the Forest Service analysis was based on faulty data and flawed analysis procedures, or bad "range science." Their contentions were largely a reiteration of what the permittees and their allies had argued in their responses to the Draft Environmental Assessment. Not unexpectedly, Kirkpatrick rejected them one more time, defending Forest Service methodology and data. He upheld the Forest Supervisor's determination—a bad sign certainly for the impacted permittees and their lawyers, who were arguing their appeal along basically the same lines as the Markses (USFS 1996a).

The environmentalists' appeals alleged that the Forest Supervisor's decisions had not gone far enough to remove cattle and as a result the Endangered Species Act had been violated, particularly in regard to the "federally threatened Apache trout." Deputy Regional Forester Kirkpatrick replied by finding that "the proposed actions will not cause a downward trend in the population of Apache trout"; nor would it "further degrade recovery habitat"; nor would incidental take be exceeded. Kirkpatrick added, "The Forests have not violated ESA nor the Arizona Trout Recovery Plan. I affirm the Forest Supervisor with respect to this issue" (USFS 1996b:3). The environmental groups additionally claimed violation of the Clean Water Act, but Kirkpatrick rejected this too and denied their appeal (USFS 1996b:4).

Meanwhile, the main appeal, from the ranchers whose permits were cut, went slowly ahead on the time track indicated above. It is useful to see the Budd-Falen law office's response to the Forest Supervisor, mailed May 6 and received May 8, 1996 (by certified/return receipt), as it summarizes concisely the ranchers' case against the Forest Service. At the outset it states bluntly,

> The Appellants contend that the EAs [Environmental Assessments] and Decisions are fundamentally flawed in their entirety. The EAs and Decisions are based on faulty assumptions, misapplied scientific literature and theory, and the *ad hoc* perceptions of agency personnel. The EAs and Decisions are not supported by

any on-the-ground biological or scientific data. As such the EAs and Decisions are arbitrary and capricious and must be set aside.

Unfortunately, the agency NEPA processes and the appeals processes have not afforded the Appellants a meaningful opportunity to challenge the Decisions and the underlying EAs. . . . Thus, Appellants renew their request for adjudicatory, trial-type hearings. Such hearings are the only permissible means by which the Appellants can effectively refute the agency Decisions and EAs. Moreover, given the extreme importance of the allotments to the Appellants' livelihoods, basic requisites of due process command such a hearing. . . .

The "oral presentations" that the agency plans to conduct after receipt of this Reply will not suffice to provide the process due the Appellants. The Forest Service cannot reduce the Appellants' grazing permits by forty to eighty-five percent (40% to 85%) without granting a trial-type hearing in front of an independent hearing officer or administrative law judge. (Weisz 1996:3–4)

After a number of arguments contesting the Forest Service procedures, the ranchers' lawyers reach the nub of their case.

The Forest Service seems committed to the "rights versus privileges" argument [despite] the fact that the judiciary of this Nation long-ago abandoned this distinction in the due process arena. *See, e.g. Goldberg v. Kelly,* 397 U.S. 254 (1970). Indeed, the manner in which the agency views a grazing permit is reflected by the short-shrift that the EAs and Decisions gave to the economic and social impact of the Decisions on the Appellants' livelihoods, area economies, and social stability. By calling a grazing permit a "privilege," the agency feels justified in subjecting the permits to the arbitrary discretion of agency personnel.

The Appellants are entitled to due process. The agency NEPA process and this appeal process do not provide due process. The allotments and grazing permits that they hold are of extreme importance; many of the Appellants derive their entire livelihood from their grazing allotments and permits. Indeed, many of the appellants hold allotments utilized by their ancestors decades before the lands at issue were withdrawn as National Forests.

The very culture and custom of this area developed and evolved around livestock grazing. To say that there [is] no "right" to a grazing permit should not mean that the Forest Service may arbitrarily revoke or modify a permit; to describe something as a "privilege" does not meet the problem of due process. *See Garner v. Public Works,* 341 U.S. 716 (1951). (Weisz 1996:3–4)

No one expected the Forest Service to change its mind. However, when the appeal process was completed, the matter could be taken to the Federal Courts. In fact, the ranchers' lawyers had already served the Forest Service with a "Notice to Instigate Litigation" on March 18, 1996.

12

In the Courts

The Las Cruces Trial

A loach minnow is more important, than say, Betty and Jim's ranch, a thousand times more important.

KIERAN SUCKLING, environmental activist (Walley 1999)

WHILE THE FOREST SERVICE appeals process dragged out until May 1997, ranchers with allotments in the Apache-Sitgreaves National Forest joined forces with their counterparts from the neighboring Gila National Forest in New Mexico. Permittees of both Forests had been harmed by the NEPA process, although the Blue district of the Apache retained the distinction of receiving the deepest cuts in livestock. With their lawyers' help, a group of ranchers formed a "Federal Lands Legal Consortium" to bring suit against the government and prepare for their day in court, which would not come for another year.

After the Forest Service had upheld all its own decisions, the Federal Lands Legal Consortium filed a lawsuit in the U.S. District Court for the District of New Mexico. The Consortium filed on behalf of its members, Apache and Gila Forest rancher permittees affected by the 1995 NEPA decisions. They were joined in the suit by Catron County in New Mexico and Apache County in Arizona. (Greenlee County, containing the Blue, declined to participate.) Individual ranchers cited as plaintiffs in the suit included a number who lived in or near the Blue or had allotments there: Rose Coleman, the Downses, the Drachmans, Dan Heap, Glen McCarty, the Robarts, the Wiltbanks, the Lazy YJ Ranch, and the Quinslers.

The plaintiffs contended that the defendants—the United States of America and the chain of authority from the Secretary of the Department of Agriculture down to the Forest Supervisors—had violated the U.S. Constitution. They claimed that grazing permits are protected property interests under the Fifth Amendment and that the government had deprived them of that property without due process of law. The claim served as basis for plaintiffs to request a preliminary injunction on March 20, 1998, from implementation of the 1995 NEPA cuts on the grounds that the ranchers would suffer irreparable harm while the case moved through the courts. This common legal maneuver would force an earlier resolution of the issue. The ranchers badly needed this relief, as they could not afford to have the NEPA cuts reduce their income at the same time they were financially engaged in a lengthy legal case.

The motion required the contending parties to submit written evidence in support and in opposition, and the hearing took place in open court on May 20 and 21 in the U.S. District courthouse in Las Cruces, New Mexico, Judge Howard C. Bratton presiding.

Karen Budd-Falen delivered the plaintiffs' opening statement. A lawyer hailing from a federal lands ranching family in Wyoming, her empathy for the ranchers' cause was palpable.

> This is a preliminary injunction hearing to decide the fate of 26 ranchers. Many of the 26 ranchers have been on the land for generations. Their blood, sweat, tears, hearts and souls have gone into their ranches and into the land. These ranches have been in these families for many generations. In fact, many ranchers can trace their grazing preferences back to even before the Gila and Apache-Sitgreaves Forests were established.
>
> The ranchers involved here depend upon the land for their livelihood and for their very existence. Without full use of their allotments, they cannot survive. Under the Forest Service's decision issued in 1995, they cannot survive.
>
> The ranchers are also stewards and caretakers of the land. You will hear testimony that they invest thousands of dollars in water developments, range improvements and other activities on the federal lands to make the lands better for the livestock and for the wildlife. The ranchers have no reason to overgraze the land, because if they overgraze the land they will not survive, and they will eliminate their own livelihoods. It is simply a myth to think that ranchers intentionally or otherwise destroy the land, and the facts in this case will show that these permittees are good stewards and take care of the land. (Federal Lands 1998)

Andrew A. Smith, from the U.S. Justice Department team, presented a summary of the government's defense. He denied that the plaintiffs had true property rights in their allotments, and in any case whatever harm they had suffered had to be measured against potential harm to the environment.

> Also involved here in the balance of harms are endangered species, and the Supreme Court has said that when economic harm [to people] is balanced against protecting endangered species, endangered species have to win out. They are given the highest priority and have to be protected from jeopardy, whatever the cost, and that's from the famous *TVA v. Hill* case.

Tennessee Valley Authority v. Hill was the landmark 1978 interpretation in which the Supreme Court ruled that the noble aspirations of the Endangered Species Act as worded by Congress must be applied literally and absolutely in a way Congress certainly had not intended. In Tennessee the giant $110 million Tellico dam, ninety percent completed, with thousands of jobs at stake, was stopped in its construction by the presence of an endangered minnow, the snail darter (*Percina tanasi*). The ESA, the justices noted, says nothing about any balancing of competing values when considering the protection of biodiversity. "Whatever the cost," species had to be saved. (Mann and Plummer 1995:148–49, 163–69.)

If the government's defense ultimately rested on this interpretation of the ESA, the ranchers and their lawyers were basing their case on the "Takings Clause" of the Fifth Amendment to the Constitution, which protects private rights from being "taken" by the government without due process of the law and just compensation.

Karen Budd-Falen said she would put three of the twenty-six rancher plaintiffs on the stand: Rose Coleman, a descendant of early Blue pioneer Toles Cosper; Dan Heap, an Apache County rancher with an allotment on the Blue; and Hugh B. McKean, a leader of ranchers on the Gila Forest and also a descendant of an early Blue pioneer.

Dan Heap testified first. The number of permitted cattle on his Campbell Blue allotment would be reduced by forty-six percent. Before the 1995 NEPA process, the Forest Service had never given him an indication that his allotment would be reduced, and his cattleman's logic told him he was not overgrazing: "In the years we've had this permit, the weaning weight of our calves that come off this permit has increased approximately a hundred pounds, and that alone would tell you that the grazing areas are not being trodden down." Also, the NEPA Environmental Assessment stated that ninety-four percent of the soils on the Upper Campbell Blue were in stable or satisfactory conditions.

The Forest Service claimed that livestock trampling on the Campbell Blue allotment would generate off-site sediments that would likely adversely affect the critical habitat of the loach minnow downstream from the allotment. (There was no habitat actually on Heap's allotment for the loach minnow.)

Heap complained about the numerous elk on his allotment. The elk had been brought from Wyoming in 1929 and introduced to the Apache-Sitgreaves forest for hunting purposes. The elk graze the riparian areas the full year and have a great impact, especially in dry years. Compared with cattle? "Well, I'd say the elk are four or five times as much, because they're there year round; they're there when the grass comes new and young and tender. They're there to cut it and tromp it and all, and they stay right in those riparian areas. And they're there twelve months out of the year, while cattle are there only five months of the year, and we always wait until the grass has started growing and the season of use is at the maximum, before we ever put the cattle on" (Federal Lands 1998).

Hugh B. McKeen testified next, "My granddad first came there [the land between the Blue and Alma, New Mexico] in 1888." He said nothing in his allotment's record between 1988 and 1995 shows anything unsatisfactory. In fact, he was proud of his work to reverse the invasion of piñon and juniper on his allotment, his efforts to restore grass and stop erosion. Looking at that progress and then being told his livestock use will be cut, "It's pretty bad." If his herds get smaller, he may have to subdivide his private property and sell it off. He implied that the additional building and new human residents would in the long run harm the land and its species more than his ranching ever would.

Next, Rose Coleman testified that portions of her ranch had been in her family since 1890. She has personally relied for her livelihood on ranch allotments. In addition to her own ranch, she has managed another (the Lazy YJ) for thirty years. Now the Forest Service has proposed cutting her permitted grazing by more than eighty percent. For one month she has no place to put her cattle, since her holding pasture is in a loach minnow area. In friendly cross-examination: "What effect will this have on your ranching operation?" Answer: "It will probably eliminate it." She will not be able to feed her 220 head of cattle, she can't afford another lease, nor does she think anyone would buy her private property now because it has been devalued.

She was questioned whether elk appeared on her allotment.

A: Numerous.

Q: Would you estimate them to be in excess of the number of cattle?

A: Definitely.

Q: Do the elk have an impact on the quality of the range?

A: Definitely. Big.

Q: If you remove your cattle from the land, will that prevent the elk from doing their damage?

A: I don't think so.

Questioned as to what would be the ultimate outcome of the Forest Service action, Rose replied,

> Eliminate my operation. Eliminate my livelihood. It's pretty disturbing too to think that my grandfather [Toles Cosper] came in there and fought the Indians, and they ran him off the first time, and he had the determination to come back and make this outfit. My mom was riding a pack of salt in extremely rugged mountains when she was seventy, trying to help us, trying to eliminate some labor, trying to save the outfit for me, my children, and grandchildren, and now it's gone. (Federal Lands 1998)

Expert Testimony

As in their appeals to the Forest Service, the ranchers relied on outside, expert testimony to bolster their court case, but the experts were different individuals from before. The first to testify was Dennis Phillippi, a certified range management consultant who had visited all the actual allotments, whereas the Forest Service had done only a few spot checks for the NEPA analyses. "In my opinion," he said, "that's not adequate enough to make the decisions they are making, imposing on these folks." He testifies that the Forest Service did a "shotgun approach" to get quick results, but this is not good science. Longtime monitoring should be done to make determinations.

> Q: Mr. Phillippi, do you believe that the FS decisions substantially understate the future capacity on the allotments in question?
>
> A: Based on the way they used the methodology, I would say yes, they did.
>
> Q: Did the FS typically rely on models, equations, and formulae?
>
> A: That's the way it appears.
>
> Q: And were these the kind of determinations made in the office or out on the site?
>
> A: For the most part, the office would be more convenient to make those decisions. (Federal Lands 1998)

He did not think the allotments had been overgrazed.

The next witness was Rita Blow, an MBA who had submitted "economic loss analyses" for various permittees, in particular two of the hardest hit, Rose Coleman and the Robart family. Economic harm was not difficult to demonstrate, and Blow concluded,

> If the [Forest Service] does not wish to change its decision to reduce and restrict livestock grazing, it should follow formal procedures for exercising eminent domain power to condemn private land use (livestock grazing) in favor of a public land use (critical habitat for endangered species) and pay the Coleman ranch [Robard estate, etc.] for their losses. (Blow 1998:9)

This argument stems again from the Takings Clause of the Fifth Amendment. But the Forest Service had always refused to recognize a property right in an allotment—precisely to avoid paying the just compensation required by the Fifth Amendment.

Mary Darling, the next witness and professional consultant, addressed another aspect of the case. With a master's degree in biology as well as an environmental law degree, she specializes in fisheries. She had worked with California Fish and Game, and with the Forest Service for twelve years as a fisheries biologist. Now she owns a consulting company, Darling Environmental & Survey, Ltd., based in Tucson. She claimed she visited the allotments in the NEPA lawsuit wherever there might be habitat for loach minnows. She was able to compare these allotments with Nature Conservancy and other pastures in the surrounding area where no recent grazing has occurred and found cows had not severely impacted the habitat. There was no overgrazing, as far as fisheries go.

> I found a healthy, healthy riparian system, and could not find problems that would tell me, as a fishery biologist, that we need to reduce livestock numbers. . . . There's no data I can see, as a fishery biologist, that showed me harm to the species. And when I went on the ground, I did not see the impact that I expected to see from what I had read. . . . I believe there are no direct effects of cattle grazing on fish populations. (Federal Lands 1998).

Cattle do not eat or step on minnows. The environmental argument has been that cattle break down the stream banks, putting sediment into the water, and eat some of the vegetation that shades the stream. But while this might be an argument for trout streams, Darling said, it does not apply to minnows, which thrive in shallower or warmer water and can tolerate a fair amount of sediment. Later, she told me, "We don't have good information at all. Where I went, the riparian habitat was in good condition with or without cows. The loach minnow, if it is being affected, it's by recreation or by non-native game fish that eat them" (Darling 1998).

In testimony, she holds that the most significant threat to the minnows, as well as the Apache and Gila trout, are "non-native fish." The government would have to get rid of them to save the endangered species, but this is not what is being done. The Apache trout have been outcompeted by brown trout, brook trout, and rainbow trout (Federal Lands 1998). Later she told me,

> Game fish are the biggest threat to the minnows, which gets into a sociopolitical argument when you get recreational fishermen in this state who are buying licenses, and in the warmer waters fish for bass and catfish, and in the higher elevations fish for trout—and all these fish eat minnows, in an instant. These game fish are not native. So this becomes an argument, do you want to manage

for minnows, or do you want to manage for non-native game fish for food and recreation? (Darling 1998)

Next witness for the plaintiffs was Bill Moore, a wildlife specialist employed by the New Mexico Department of Agriculture. He addressed the issue of three bird species cited by the Forest Service to restrict grazing. The goshawk: "I would probably not conclude that the goshawk is in trouble at this time. I do not find any information that would lead me to believe, as a professional, that the goshawk populations are declining or in trouble in the Southwest." It is not listed as an endangered species either by the U.S. government or by the state of New Mexico. The Wildlife Society had concluded that there are no data that goshawk numbers are declining, threatened, or endangered. Nevertheless, the Forest Service has used goshawk habitat in setting grazing limitations.

The Forest Service cited the Mexican spotted owl as a reason to reduce grazing, but Moore was not aware of any studies showing effects of livestock on spotted owl habitat. There is no data showing the prey population for owls is declining. The owls tend to nest where there are tree canopies and a lot of debris on the ground. But these would not be grazing areas.

Moore continued. No research shows cattle having a negative impact on the Southwestern willow flycatcher (*Empidonax traillii extimus*). Indirect effects are asserted, but there are no studies that isolate grazing as a danger to flycatchers, which have always been rare in the Southwest and sparsely distributed. There are no studies showing population declines of flycatchers. In fact, Moore testified, the largest population of flycatchers in the Southwest exists on the U Bar Ranch near Gila, New Mexico, where they have coexisted for many years with 400 head of cattle grazing year round. Grazing is not negatively impacting their population (Federal Lands 1998).

The final expert witness was Catherine Cosgrove, with degrees in Biology and Environmental Resources, employed by Apache County. She submitted a report based on research funded by Apache and Greenlee Counties, with support from the Apache-Sitgreaves National Forest: "Economic Impacts of Apache-Sitgreaves National Forests Public Land Ranching" (Cosgrove 1998). The report centered on a detailed survey questionnaire mailed to each of the 96 Apache-Sitgreaves Forest grazing permittees; 29 (30%) had been returned. The data provide an interesting snapshot of ranching on Forest land, though they do not give an accurate picture of ranching on the Blue.

Two operations were based on sheep. For the rest, the survey indicated the average number of cattle owned by an operation was 525, including 253 cows and heifers, 16 bulls, and 256 calves and yearlings. (However, some operations—certainly this was true on the Blue—had fewer animals. See note 2, chapter 10.)

The amount of deeded (privately owned) property used in ranch operations averaged a little over 1,487 acres per ranch, but the average acreage of their Forest Service permits was 30,318 acres. The respondents estimated the value of their deeded property as $887,944 average per operation, while the average fair market value of their Forest permits was $221,709.

Despite these large capitalizations, gross ranch-derived income for 1996 was estimated at an average of only $62,474. Deducting expenses would lead to a fairly low net income (Cosgrove 1998:4–8). The figures illustrate the paradox general to ranching: land rich, income poor, small returns on capital.

The survey showed that the majority of ranches are mainly family operations, relying on family labor, with only eight respondents reporting hiring nonfamily employees.

The survey does not accurately reflect the Blue. Compared with many operations in the rest of the Forest, Blue ranches have fewer livestock, lower values, and less income. Few if any have had more than the 160 deeded acres allowed by the original Homestead law, and few ever employ nonfamily workers. (Cosgrove 1998:4, 8)

The comments on the survey indicated that the majority of respondents, if they could not make a living ranching on public lands, would choose to develop their base private property. In most cases "development" would mean subdivision and sale of small lots, primarily for residences and vacation homes (Cosgrove 1998:6, 10).

Catherine Cosgrove did not present all her survey findings in oral testimony, but the plaintiff's counsel wanted to cross-examine her on some aspects to elicit her opinions on the economic effects of reducing cattle numbers in the Forest. Predictably, she thought it would harm the affected counties economically, as well as bring hardship to individual permittees. She also criticized the Forest Service's methods.

Typically, what I've seen the Forest Service people...do is go out in May or June or maybe July before our summer monsoons come [typically mid-July], and look at the grass and say, "There's no grass here." Well, of course there isn't, because they're warm season grasses, and they don't come up until the summer rains. (Federal Lands 1998)

The appropriate time to do an assessment would be at the end of the rainy season, not the beginning.

The final part of the plaintiff's presentation entered into the record declarations by a number of affected ranchers who were not present to testify. These included statements from Barbara Quinsler and Tim Robart of the Blue. They reiterated that the deep cuts being made would "terminate our ability to run an economically viable livestock operation" (Quinsler) and "destroy the financial viability of my livestock operations on the 3LK ranch, consequently depriving me of my livelihood" (Robart).

A uniquely different situation emerged in the declaration of Esther Wiltbank. She and her husband own and operate a family guest ranch, the Sprucedale Ranch. This is located in the high country outside the Blue, but in the area where Blue ranchers find summer allotments. The Wiltbanks have only 160 acres of private land, but lease 47,100 acres of federal land on which to run their horses and cattle. From May to October they take in guests who like to participate in rounding up cattle and going on simulated trail drives. But on renewing their allotment, the Forest Service reduced their animal months by forty-six percent and reduced the season of uses for horses from full year to a fifteen-week permit. Thus horses and cattle can be grazed on the allotment only from July 15 to October 15, which severely curtails the Ranch's ability to serve guests in May, June, and the first half of July. Riding is curtailed, and stock must be concentrated on their private land and fed hay at an extra cost of $20,000.

The Government's Case

The government lawyers chose not to cross-examine the witnesses called by the plaintiffs. Their defense held that most plaintiff testimony was legally irrelevant and should be ignored.

They opened their defense by summarizing the history of government regulation of public lands and how the Forest Service by law is authorized to manage lands to prevent resource degradation, including overgrazing. They manage land for multiple uses, including wildlife and recreation, which much be balanced against grazing, only one of the uses.

In an unabashed denial of information presented by the plaintiffs, the government lawyers stated, "The defendants also claim there is no competent evidence in the record supporting the finding that Ms. Coleman, let alone any other plaintiff, will lose her business if the court does not issue a preliminary injunction." In any case,

> Any alleged economic harm to plaintiffs does not outweigh the potential harm to the environment and endangered species, should the court grant the preliminary injunction the plaintiffs request. . . . The intent of Congress, in enacting the ESA, was to halt and reverse the trend towards species extinction, whatever the cost.

Again the federal lawyers cited *Tennessee Valley Authority v. Hill* as the governing precedent.

The expert testimony presented by the ranchers questioning whether, in fact, species were being threatened, was simply ignored by the government lawyers. Instead they introduced as evidence the assessments of environmental damage found in the NEPA studies themselves and read it into the trial record directly from the documents. Their assumption seemed to be based on past experience in the courts, as explained to the author by Apache Forest Supervisor John Bedell: in a conflict over expert opinion, the judge would favor agency staff. Inasmuch as judges themselves do not have the knowledge to decide conflicting scientific and technical claims, they will tend, absent special circumstances, to defer to the government.

This assumption, however, had been challenged in the 1990s by environmentalist lawsuits that had in many cases convinced judges to rule for them against the federal agencies. Whether this was due to judges' sympathies towards environmental causes, or due to the new technique of environmentalist lawsuits, producing a blitz of "studies" and "experts" that overwhelmed the government side, is a debatable question. In the Las Cruces trial, however, the government lawyers seemed to fall back on the conventional presumption. They did not dignify the testimony of the plaintiffs' expert witnesses either by cross-examining them on the stand, or by referring to their arguments (Federal Lands 1998).

After entering the NEPA analyses into the record, the government then did call some expert witnesses, all from the Forest Service. The first was Leon Fager, a biologist who had no role in the NEPA process. He gave a very lengthy, detailed, almost scholarly presentation on the loach minnow and the spikedace. At the end he presented the theory of how livestock can harm riparian areas and therefore the minnow by increasing sedimentation and water temperature. This was the theory that Mary Darling had attempted earlier to rebut, at least as applied to the allotments in question. But Fager did not address her testimony and in fact had not visited the allotments in question, instead citing studies from elsewhere in the West.

Fager testified also regarding the Southwestern willow flycatcher. Here again he did not address the earlier testimony of Bill Moore questioning whether cattle threatened this bird. Fager simply repeated the assertion that flycatcher habitat can be rendered unsuitable by damage to riparian areas from large-scale livestock grazing. He cited no actual studies verifying this hypothesis and did not comment on Moore's example of the U Bar Ranch, where flycatchers thrive in proximity to cattle.

The plaintiffs' lawyers, however, did not cross-examine him on any point of his testimony.

Following Fager, Jim Copeland took the stand as government witness. He is a wildlife specialist and a member of the Interdisciplinary (ID) team that did the 1995 NEPA analyses. He contradicted plaintiff testimony by saying he sees riparian areas in the Forest in highly degraded states that might harm loach minnow. Specifically he cited Dan Heap's allotment, where he claims cattle are caving the banks. Copeland was briefly counter-examined by the rancher's attorney, on whether the presence of sediment in the water was natural or bad, with Copeland admitting some was natural but too much was bad for the minnows.

Mitchel White, rangeland management specialist for the Forest Service and ID team leader on the NEPA analyses, was the final government witness. He testified that the terms of the old permits were no longer consistent with the Apache-Sitgreaves Forest plans: cattle were "over capacity" and grazing needed to be reduced to allow "recovery of the resource."

One of the plaintiff lawyers, Michael G. Weisz, cross-examined White closely on many of the same issues that had been raised in appealing the NEPA decisions within the Forest Service (see chapter 11). He questioned the validity of the NEPA models and methodology and also questioned White on some of the parameters of his calculations, such as asserting that cattle consume much more on average than other experts think. White admitted that his team was only in the field visiting all the allotments for no more than a day and a half, visiting some for no more than an hour or not at all. He further admitted some meetings of the ID team involved just two participants—him and his wife. But White held closely to his claim that the ID team made all its decisions to meet "the Forest Plan." (Federal Lands 1998).

The Las Cruces Hearing Ends and the Verdict Comes

At the end of the hearing Michael Weisz of Budd-Falen gave a final oral presentation of the ranchers' case. He summarized many of the objections against the 1995 NEPA environmental analyses since they had been made public in the fall of 1995: the EAs were fundamentally flawed in their entirety; they used outdated theories and questionable assumptions; they didn't include ground inspection of the allotments, calling field visits "unnecessary." Thus the assessments were arbitrary and capricious.

> The agency altogether failed to gather and analyze the data necessary to make range management decisions: trend and condition data, production and utilization data. At the very minimum, the agency must gather such data over a 3 to 5 year period. Without any data on the condition, trend, production, utilization for each allotment, you can't make any grazing management determination, let alone a determination to cut grazing by 40 to 85%.
>
> The agency improperly relied on scientific literature. The agency picked and sorted among literature sources and only relied on portions of documents. Much of the literature does not apply to Southwestern range types. Much of the literature is outdated, being over 30 years old. . . .
>
> It also appears that decisions are mostly based on a paper chase, a literature search performed in the office, instead of information and specific data generated in the field. (Federal Lands 1998)

Weisz also stressed how the agency refused to consider the economic consequences of its actions, which legally it was bound to do. In so doing, it had violated due process rights.

The grazing decisions which are the subject of this appeal are an example of a very disturbing trend. It seems as if the NEPA process is being used to justify decisions that were made before the process started, rather than being used to assist agency personnel in making decisions." Better data would have led to different conclusion.

One of the agency personnel said that the Apache-Sitgreaves National Forest had made a tough decision, by weighing livestock grazing against environmental values. This statement demonstrates the real problem here. The agency is operating under the baseless assumption that grazing is incompatible with environmental needs. Such an assumption is unsound. Livestock grazing is entirely consistent with environmental needs. (Federal Lands 1998)

After Weisz, the government legal team closed their case by briefly referring to the legal points they had made earlier. After two days in court, the hearing ended.

The ranchers told me they never had much confidence that the courts would uphold their case. In a trial before a local jury, yes, they could prevail, but before a federal judge? They had recently witnessed too many cases in the West where the judges had ruled in favor of the environmental activists. Nevertheless, they believed that they should fight back legally, despite the cost.

The government had presented what seemed to be a pro forma defense, probably because they were confident they had legal precedent behind them. They were right.

Because the trial concerned a motion for a preliminary injunction— the legal equivalent of asking for an emergency decision—the judge issued his opinion fairly soon after the May hearings, on June 15, 1998. He denied the plaintiffs' motion.

Judge Bratton acknowledged the government's arguments that "livestock term grazing permits convey no rights or interests in pubic lands and resources held by the United States," which draws on the Granger-Thye Act of 1950. He did not cite the ranchers' argument that in practice, permits do help decide the value of the value of a ranching operation— both the price of the base private property when it is sold, and in determining security for a bank loan. But, "even assuming that Plaintiffs may have a property interest in their term livestock grazing permits, the Court finds the Defendants provided them due process of law" (Bratton 1998:8).

> The Court finds that the Forest Service's extensive appeals process satisfied all due process requirements. Plaintiffs have provided no evidence to support their claim that they were not provided an "impartial adjudicator." Based on the foregoing, the Court finds that Plaintiffs have not demonstrated substantial likelihood of prevailing on the merits. (Bratton 1998:10)

In other words, since it was unlikely the plaintiffs would win an eventual trial, there were no grounds for granting them a preliminary injunction.

Judge Bratton summarized the testimony of some of the ranchers, including Rose Coleman's, and he did agree that "based on the testimony presented at the hearing and the affidavits submitted, the Court finds that Plaintiffs have established irreparable harm." However, "Plaintiffs have not demonstrated that their financial injury outweighs the injury an injunction would cause Defendants or that an injunction would not be adverse to the public interest. In this case, an injunction involves potential injury to the environment." He cites a 1996 U.S. 10th Circuit Court decision precedent: "An environmental injury usually is of an enduring or permanent nature, seldom remedied by money damages and considered irreparable."

> Moreover, Defendants' experts presented evidence demonstrating the potential detrimental effects of livestock grazing on certain species listed under the Endangered Species Act (ESA) *See e.g.* Tr. 249–307 (Testimony of Jim Copeland) [the Forest Service biologist]. Each of the allotments at issue involves one or more species listed under the ESA. For claims involving endangered species, "the balance of hardships and the public interest tip heavily in favor of endangered species." *Sierra Club v. Marsh,* 816 F.2d 1276, 1383 (9th Cir. 1987) (citing *TVA v. Hill,* 437 U.S. 153, 187–88 (1978)). Accordingly, Plaintiffs' motion for preliminary injunction is denied. (Bratton 1998:12–13)

Outrageous as Kieran Suckling's statement, quoted at the beginning of this chapter, might seem to the ranchers, the courts did agree that a loach minnow really *is* more important than Betty and Jim's ranch.

Judge Bratton's decision reflected conventional environmental wisdom, embodied as it had become in law and legal precedent. The views of the biologists who testified for the ranchers were ignored, and "environmental injury of an enduring or permanent nature" was confidently assumed to be happening on the ranchers' allotments, based on the views of government personnel.

The decision was appealed to the Tenth Circuit of the U. S. Court of Appeals. The National Wildlife Federation joined the government side as amicus curiae. After more than a year, on October 28, 1999, a three-judge panel ruled on the appeal. After citing various laws and a raft of previous court decisions, they ruled that the Federal Lands Legal Consortium had not shown a "property interest in the terms and conditions of the of the ranchers' permits"—at least in a legal or Constitutional sense. The Takings Clause did not apply. The decision of the Las Cruces court was upheld (Holloway et. al. 1999).

The ranchers did not pursue the case further. Through regulation, the Forest Service was free to continue reducing livestock on the Blue to a vestige of past numbers.

13

Cattle and Minnows

Fencing Off Riparian Areas

We don't have endangered species out here. What we have are abundant
numbers of species that are rare in other places.

BARBARA MARKS, rancher (Kenworthy 1998c)

ALTHOUGH THE 1995 NEPA cattle cuts and the ensuing court case
marked a critical turn of fortune downward for the cattle culture of
the Blue, parallel developments at the time of the spring 1998 Las Cruces
trial seemed to confirm the threat to ranching there.

Activist groups such as the Southwest Center for Biological Diversity
and the Forest Guardians had been filing lawsuit after lawsuit against
the Southwestern Region of the Forest Service (Region 3, primarily New
Mexico and Arizona). The eleven National Forests of this Region include
over 1,000 grazing allotments, of which around 700 contain species listed
under the Endangered Species Act (ESA)—a goldfield for litigation purposes. In October 1997 the Southwest Center brought an ESA noncom-
pliance suit against the Forest Service for failure to consult with the Fish
and Wildlife Service on whether grazing activity threatened listed species on each of these 700-some allotments. In a follow-up suit filed in
December, the Forest Guardians joined the Southwest Center in naming
over 150 individual grazing allotments for which consultation was lacking and demanded an injunction against grazing on all of them pending completion of consultation. The Forest Guardians further requested
a more specific injunction against grazing in riparian areas on the allotments identified (Coppelman 1998).

The normally slow-moving federal agencies were forced to send
personnel into the field to do hasty analyses—the kind of on-site work
they neglected in the NEPA process—in order to defend themselves in
court. Forest Service officials did not try to contain their frustration in

interviews with the author. Phil Settles, Ranger for the Alpine District, commented,

> They appeal every decision, without knowing what they're talk-ing about. All it takes is a 32-cent stamp to appeal and tie things up. Citizen suit clause. They say there shouldn't be cattle.... They really feel that if they keep us in court long enough, they'll win the war. Not just against the ranchers, but the Forest Service too. What they want is just wilderness, for them only, for they are the chosen people.... They don't want the Forest Service. They want no management. They want their own control over it, for they know best, and we don't. (Settles 1999)

U.S. Department of Justice lawyers from the Environment and Natu-ral Resources Division in Washington, D.C., were called in to argue the Forest Service case. In addition, both the Arizona Cattlegrowers Associa-tion and the New Mexico Cattlegrowers Association involved themselves and were granted status as intervenor-defendants in the lawsuits.

The hearings on the activist lawsuits were to take place in District Court in Tucson, Arizona, in the spring of 1998. Not long before the scheduled hearings, discussions began among the parties to see whether agreement could be reached before the hearing. For whatever reason— the ranchers believed it to be a policy decision of the Clinton Administra-tion—the Forest Service moved to compromise on the activist demands, rather than to defend their agency. They agreed to do the required con-sultations during the coming summer on an emergency basis, in return for no blanket injunction against grazing. Furthermore, they agreed to exclude grazing in riparian areas as soon as these could be fenced off. They claimed that this had been their preferred policy anyway. In return for the Forest Service signing a stipulation to this effect, the environmen-tal groups would withdraw their motions requesting a broad injunction against all grazing on a large number of allotments (Coppelman 1998). In April 1998, a few days before the scheduled hearing in the federal court-house in Tucson, the Forest Service and the environmental groups con-cluded the agreement.

From the government's view, this agreement was very gratifying. Peter Coppelman, Deputy Assistant Attorney General, Environment and Natural Resources Division, U.S. Department of Justice, would later tes-tify before the U.S. House Committee on Resources,

I want to emphasize that the stipulations in effect memorialized the management practices that were already being implemented by the Forest Service. By entering into the stipulations, however, the Forest Service and the Fish and Wildlife Service were able to proceed, undistracted by continuing active litigation, towards timely completion of the ongoing consultation. At the same time, the threat of a sweeping preliminary injunction against all grazing had been eliminated. (Coppelman 1998)

From the Forest Service perspective, it was agreeing to steps it thought it would be obliged to take sooner or later and had scored a victory by avoiding an injunction against all grazing, as well as avoiding ongoing litigation.

However, to the ranchers this compromise appeared to be a capitulation. The legal intervenors in the case, the New Mexico and Arizona cattlegrowers' associations, pulled out of the pretrial discussions as they saw what the government's stance would be. The ranchers were outraged by what they perceived as the agency's treachery in colluding with activist demands certain to result in more reduction of permitted livestock. The fact that the deal was brokered by lawyers from a Clinton-Gore administration that embraced the environmental lobby only added to ranchers' distrust of the government. To the ranchers, the Forest Service had betrayed them, had gotten into bed with urban radicals who openly despised them to the point of wanting to eliminate them, and had gone over to the enemy.

Later that summer of 1998, ranchers and allies would stage an unprecedented demonstration in front of the Gila National Forest offices in Silver City, New Mexico, complete with banners, posters, speeches, chants, and a petition. One of their slogans was "Remember Tucson!"— where the treacherous deal was made—and a taunt at the rally was, "Kieran Suckling is the real Chief of the Forest Service," referring to the head of the Southwest Center for Biodiversity.

It should be noted that there was no equivalent demonstration at Apache-Sitgreaves Forest headquarters, and no residents from the Blue appeared at the Silver City demonstration.

From the ranchers' point of view, the Forest Service was abandoning its traditional role of caring for their interests, however paternalistically, allying itself with an urban, elitist movement that cared more for obscure animal species than for people. As Kieran Suckling had stated, "A loach minnow is more important, than say, Betty and Jim's ranch, a thousand times more important" (Walley 1999). Now the Forest Service was going to enforce this principle.

Caren Cowan, director of the New Mexico Cattlegrowers', commented on the new stipulation: "Over the generations, I think the beef producers have seen themselves as partners with the Forest Service, as custodians of the land. Then the Forest Service has come with new restrictions with no consideration of the livestock producer" (*Albuquerque Journal* 1998b). In the same article, John Faust, a rancher from Glenwood, New Mexico, states, "It's the beginning of the end as far as cattle ranching on the national forests." A Forest Guardian was also quoted, nicely summarizing his group's sentiments towards the struggling rancher: "That's the price he has to pay for abusing the land."

At least it was the price that Faust had to pay for having an allotment that ran many miles astride the San Francisco River. The ranchers were amazed by the Forest Service's claim before the court that "for the vast majority of the allotments identified in the Forest Guardians' motion, over 99% of the riparian habitat of the species identified had already been excluded from grazing" (Coppelman 1998). Such a statement evaded the reality. Along many miles of the San Francisco and Gila Rivers there were no fences, for good reason: the distances made fencing prohibitively expensive and difficult to maintain. The same was true of the southern part of the Blue River. On the northern Blue, on the other hand, the river areas were mostly private property, out of the jurisdiction of the Forest Service. But many of the upper Blue allotments contained stream and creekbeds that were also considered "riparian" despite the fact that water only ran during the rains.

For some ranchers the riparian exclusion from the rivers was not a problem, or not a big problem. Cattle needed water, but water could be piped from the river or cattle could be given access on private land—after all, homesteads had been established next to water sources. The ranchers had long used all sorts of wells and stock tanks—the most modern twist being the use of solar-powered pumps. But for allotments requiring miles of fencing, the question of expense arose. Even if the government provided the materials, as it sometimes did (and sometimes did not), the rancher was expected to provide the labor, not only for construction but maintenance. Ranchers with long, river allotments or many streams to

fence might be forced out of business. Therefore, the "stipulation" welcomed by the government had to be rejected by the cattlegrowers' associations.

The *Albuquerque Journal* had run an editorial supporting the stipulation, entitled "Forest Agency Must Ride Herd on Grazing" (*Albuquerque
Journal* 1998a). A later feature-length article on the situation repeated
the conventional urban wisdom:

> Although livestock groups dispute the degree to which cattle
> are to blame, there is broad agreement among scientists, fed-
> eral land managers and environmentalists that livestock grazing
> has caused significant damage to streamsides in New Mexico's
> national forests.
>
> "I don't know that that's fact," said [Caren] Cowan of New
> Mexico Cattle Growers. "I don't think anyone is taking into con-
> sideration the damage wildlife do, particularly elk."
>
> But [David] Stewart, the Forest Service's regional rangeland
> boss, said that if the cattle industry is unwilling to acknowledge
> grazing has damaged riparian areas, "they've got a problem. . . .
> One of the problems of the livestock industry is they're so darn
> traditional. If they don't change themselves. . . they will put
> themselves out of business. It's not us putting them out of busi-
> ness."
>
> Many ranchers say they are already changing the way they
> do business.
>
> Glenwood rancher Hugh B. McKeen [direct descendant of
> the Blue pioneer] says cottonwoods growing along the San Fran-
> cisco River are there because he stabilized a stream bank by
> planting trees and keeping cows away during the growing sea-
> son. But even that, he says, is not enough for the Forest Service
> or environmental activists.
>
> "If you took all the cows off for 1,000 years, it still wouldn't
> meet their standards," McKeen says. "What they're doing is
> kicking us off the land, and then they'll do the science."
>
> Environmental activists say healthy riparian areas like some
> of those on McKeen's allotment are the exception, rather than
> the rule. (Albuquerque Journal 1998b)

On the Blue, as recounted earlier, unsatisfactory riparian conditions had been noted even before the time of Aldo Leopold. But over the years, most ranchers on the Blue had learned to care for these areas and fenced them off without being told to do so. Bill Marks is perhaps typical.

> We fenced all the riparian areas ourselves, in the early 70s. You can look down at these riparian areas and see the growth that is there. We fenced it off, and it included our private land. Most of the riparian area along the Blue River is private land, with spots of Forest land. . . . The only time we use these areas is in the spring of the year, when we're calving, we bring in a small number of cows and calves here, we never bring in large concentrations of cattle. We bring in ten to twenty cows, we have a vaccination program for the cows, we'll brand the calves. For a few days. . . . But we fence them out of the river so animals won't come down and congregate.
>
> Q: So you weren't part of the Tucson lawsuit?
>
> Yes we were—and that's what offended us so much, because we've tried to be progressive here, and we've got the river fenced off, and we're taking care of our riparian area—we can prove it—but the FS made a backroom deal with the environmentalists. . . .
>
> Q: Then why were you part of the suit at all?
>
> [His wife Barbara interrupts:] Because they don't want any cattle at all, and we use these riparian areas for short durations. But they want zero.
>
> [Bill] We've run so hard with this, to try to mitigate some of these problems the environmentalists are hollering about. But they never have any solutions, they're never here to help us do a darn thing, they'll never send me a load of hay in here if I can't use my riparian pastures next spring. They just want to take advantage of the work I've done, fencing, to exclude me. It says on this document here today, "There will be no grazing on the Blue River." Period, end. Then today, they said they're concerned about April and May. That's the spawning season of the loach minnow—but that's just the season that we need the pastures. But what we'll do is rethink our end here, and fence off what's private, and continue on with what we do, and cut more hay or buy more. . . . (Bill and Barbara Marks 1998)

FENCE OFF THE CREEK-BEDS OR "KILL THE LITTLE MINNOWS"?

Though the upper Blue River was mostly fenced off from congregating
cattle, and a good portion of the lower Blue ran through the de-stocked
pastures of the Fritz XXX ranch, problems could and did arise if the Forest Service insisted on fencing off the twenty-some tributary streams
to the Blue. These run water only sporadically during the rainy season
but nevertheless are officially classified as habitat for loach minnow and
Apache trout. Fencing these semi-dry creeks had in fact been part of the
rationale for the 1995 NEPA cuts. The Bunnell-Downs family suffered
some of the deepest of these cuts (see chapter 10): an eighty-six percent
decrease of permitted stock, leaving them with an nonviable herd of
forty-six head. This decrease resulted from many small cuts, including
riparian. As Mona Bunnell recounts,

> They shut down some of our pastures because of endangered
> species, and that took in the river. . . . Our mountain country was
> hardest hit. It was a little of this pasture and a little of that pas-
> ture, and you either go in and spend thousands of dollars fencing
> these little areas where your cows can't get to them, or else you
> don't use them. . . .
>
> Q: Wouldn't they help you fence it off?
>
> Well, I think Rose went through this over on Fish Creek.
> They had some electric fences which they were bound and deter-
> mined were going to work. No one could tell them it wouldn't.
> The Forest Service was supposed to put it in, and [Arizona] Game
> and Fish were supposed to maintain it.
>
> Well, the Game and Fish found they had to be out there
> almost every day of the week to put it back up, because elk don't
> respect an electric fence. And trees that fall don't care. Every-
> thing tears out an electric fence. And cows were running out of it,
> and everything was a problem, so they said they'd have to put up
> at least a four-wire, maybe a three-wire fence around these areas.
> And they were cutting off essentially all of Rose's water in that
> Fish Creek area. . . .

The Forest Service had originally hinted it would leave small "water
loops," access points for cattle to drink, but fenced off so they couldn't
move downstream. Now with an eye to environmental lawsuits, they
eventually decided not to allow these.

They were also supposed to put in regular fences, when electric ones didn't work, but now they claim they don't have money enough. So they said ranchers had to put them in, or stay off that part of the ranch.

So either you're not going to be able to use part of your land, which gives them another reason to tell you, you don't have enough forage to run enough cows, or else you put out all the dollars it takes to fence this.

The ranchers were told they could not use the streambeds because of the loach minnow,

because it'll kick off too much sediment in the creek and kill the little minnows. The amazing part to me is that the little minnows have lived here for years and years with the floods like we've been having, that bring down all the mud. How are a few cows at a time kicking off a little dirt into the creek going to affect the minnows when they live through these floods that are so muddy. . . . (Bunnell 1998)

In a separate interview, Rose Coleman Awtrey, also a major loser in the 1995 NEPA evaluations, concurred with Mona Bunnell.

How the minnow can come back after [those devastating floods] beats me—but it always does. Still, we're not allowed to keep any cattle along the river. In my time, we've never used the river for a grazing pasture, only a holding pasture; we don't want to graze the thing to the ground. . . . When we do use [the river pasture], in May and June, is the driest time of the year, so it might sometimes look like they're being abused. But all it takes in this country is a little rain to come alive. But we're off the Blue River, and in my allotments in the high country, I'm off the streams.

Q: Did you have to put in fences?

When they first decided we had to be off the streams—this was another result of the '95 stuff—they were in such a hurry they put in electric fence. Well, that was a joke. It didn't work a day. The first time elk came down there, it was wiped out. . . .

And they put up these electric fences with no gates in them, so they were keeping everyone out, including people on horses. So people just cut the things. And people also stole the solar panels, and just vandalized them. I really don't know who did that. But I was able to find better pasture to go to anyway, so I haven't used my own high country for three years. (Awtrey 1998)

Note the ranchers' skepticism about the alleged harm their cattle were doing to fish—primarily the loach minnow (*Tiaroga cobitis*). They reason that the Blue, which has been grazed for a hundred years, and much more intensively in the past than recently, still harbors loach minnow while the species has disappeared elsewhere: therefore, how can their cattle be to blame? "We don't have endangered species out here," Barbara Marks told a *Washington Post* journalist, "What we have are abundant numbers of species that are rare in other places" (Kenworthy 1998c).

On the other hand, not just environmental activists but the rank and file of Forest Service and Fish and Wildlife fishery biologists have held as dogma the conviction that cattle degrade minnow habitat and therefore endanger the species. As Bill Wall, Fisheries Biologist for both the Alpine and Clifton Districts, told me, there is "solid evidence that grazing harms minnows" through cows kicking up sediment and changing the vegetation in the riparian areas (Wall 2000). And the *Washington Post* journalist who quoted Barbara Marks above, also presents the conventional wisdom: "The loach minnow [is just one] of the many species that government scientists say are at risk in [the Southwest], and numerous government studies have pointed to cattle grazing as a significant cause of their decline" (Kenworthy 1998c).

These "numerous government studies" constitute the evidence that environmental groups regularly present to the courts, but scientist dissenters exist. The testimony of Mary Darling at the Las Cruces trial was quoted earlier. She had also been scheduled to testify for the cattlegrowers at the Tucson trial. She believes little solid evidence exists of cattle actually harming the fish and that recreationists are more guilty than cattle of disturbing streambeds by crossing them. Also, that "game fish are the biggest threat to the minnows . . . all these fish eat minnows in an instant." The game fish are non-native trout, bass, and catfish introduced by the state for recreational fishermen (Darling 1998).

Another dissenter has been John N. Rinne, a research fisheries biologist at the Southwest Forest Science Center, Rocky Mountain Research Station in Flagstaff, Arizona, which is an independent research arm of the U.S. Forest Service. He was also on hand at Tucson to testify if the Forest Service had decided to contest the environmental groups. As someone who had done considerable research on fish and grazing—including a site in the Apache-Sitgreaves National Forest—he had come to the same conclusion as Darling: there is insubstantial scientific evidence to support the idea that cattle harm fish. In 1999 he published a peer-reviewed article in the journal *Fisheries* (Rinne 1999) entitled "Fishing and Grazing Relationships: The Facts and Some Pleas."

In his article Rinne recognized that since the turn of the twentieth century, due to the introduction of nonnative fish species for sportfishing, and "associated changes in aquatic ecosystems in the Southwest caused by damming, irrigation, and groundwater mining,...all native species have declined greatly in range and numbers."

Agreeing that "scientific consensus...has been that grazing has irrefutably harmed fishes and their habitats in the West and Southwest," he nevertheless finds in review of some 200 papers that this literature on grazing, fish, and riparian relationships fails to document such harm. Most of the studies focus on the impact of livestock grazing on vegetation and streambanks, but not on the fish themselves. "Very little of the literature addresses fish-grazing relationships...a low proportion of the studies document the impact of livestock grazing on fishes." Instead many report on "general, often hypothetical, effects of grazing on fishes." Some of the papers were "opinion, summary or review papers that discussed previous study results, and presented no new data, and primarily promoted the [negative] litany on the effects of grazing on fishes." Most studies were flawed due to lack of controls, replication, quantitative data, pretreatment data, or statistical analysis of data. Moreover, most of the papers analyzed conditions for trout species, rather than nonsalmonids such as *Tiaroga cobitis*, which have radically different environmental needs. Only eight papers were on the Southwest, and only four of these were data based. Finally, eighty percent of the literature addressing fishes and grazing relationships appeared in publications that are not peer-reviewed.

"Because of the lack of peer-reviewed literature containing sound data on grazing-fish relationships," Rinne recommends future studies have more rigorous scientific designs.

Finally, the time has come to remove ourselves from promoting and sustaining the litany about [negative] effects of grazing on fishes and to embrace collection of scientifically sound, defensible information that can be used by land managers. Too often, qualitative, nonscientific data are collected. In retrospect the reliability of these data is low; however, their use and incorporation into management and public opinion have been too common. . . .

. . . Selective rather than objective comprehension by individuals has dictated management alternatives for the past several decades. We as environmental groups, managers, and researchers need to stop expressing opinions, disputing, and constantly litigating or threatening to, and start collecting data from well-designed, defensible research and monitoring activities. . . . As the saying goes, "Without data, one is just another person with an opinion." (Rinne 1999:18)

If a leading expert on Southwestern fisheries could come to this conclusion, may one not forgive the ranchers for their long-held suspicion that in controversies over grazing, "science" has often been simply a mask for prejudice against livestock?

14

Cattle Versus Elk
and Wolves

In late January, Interior Secretary Bruce Babbitt traveled to a remote area on the New Mexico-Arizona border on what he called a mission to "erase the sins of the past." Accompanied by officials of the U.S. Fish and Wildlife Service, Babbitt brought three captive-bred Mexican wolves to a holding facility in the Apache-Sitgreaves National Forest, the advance guard of what biologists hoped would become a thriving wild population of a predator exterminated from this region earlier this century.

TOM KENWORTHY, *Washington Post*, November 17, 1998(b)

IN THE 1990s, the Forest Service justified its fencing of riparian areas, as well as its National Environmental Protection Act (NEPA) reductions in permitted livestock, as necessary steps to end overgrazing, especially along the banks of streams and rivers. But after fencing and livestock reductions, overgrazing has not ended. In an ironic development that Aldo Leopold would certainly appreciate, a new ecological threat on the Blue Range emerged in the 1990s, just when cattle numbers were being drastically reduced: an elk explosion. By the end of the decade, elk would greatly outnumber cattle during some seasons in many if not most mountain pastures.

Hunting and perhaps disease had rendered extinct the native Merriam's elk of the Southwest by the early twentieth century. Another elk subspecies, the Rocky Mountain elk, was introduced from Yellowstone National Park in 1913 for its value to hunters. Over most of the century, elk numbers remained low enough in the region that no problem was perceived, despite the fact that elk and cattle compete for the same forage. But as early as 1989, a complaint from a Blue rancher, Charles Coleman (Rose Coleman's husband at the time), appears in a letter in the Forest Service files.

I have observed pastures of the Lazy YJ, the VM and the WY-Bar ranches. Some have had no cattle for two years, many not for one year, and two private land places which have had no cattle for several years. These places all show extremely heavy use and very little difference in available feed. I see willow stands hedged down less than two feet high. I see alder stands with the bark eaten off of many trees. All of these areas above show 70% to 100% of all available food having been already removed as of May 7. All of this use is by big game species. This has been the pattern of use in the spring, summer and fall for the past several years. The hundreds of thousands of dollars spent by the Forest Service and the permittees on fences, waters and good, sound management practices over the last 30 years is being thrown out the window. We've been producing an adequate and ever increasing amount of forage for both wildlife and livestock until the last 4 or 5 years. The gradual buildup of wildlife and livestock had gone hand in hand. Suddenly, because of a lack of sound management judgment by the Forest Service, a population explosion of certain big game species [elk] was allowed to occur. Now we are approaching a crisis situation. . . . (USFS 1989b)

The same rancher followed with another letter the next year protesting in even stronger language the reduction of cattle numbers as elk populations were allowed to expand.

The drought has very little to do with the lack of forage on our high country. The management practices that were in place would have provided an ample amount of all feed to accommodate livestock and a reasonable number of wildlife through several years of dry weather; in fact, had done so in the 1970s.

The livestock industry made its share of mistakes in early days, and we have never lived it down. We are constantly beat over the head with reminders by the Forest Service and every radical group in the country. We will probably make more mistakes, because we're working people and people who do something sometimes make mistakes. However, this mistake is not ours, and we are not going to take the blame. This mistake clearly belongs squarely upon the shoulders of the Forest Service. Now we will see if the Forest Service will stand up and correct its errors, and admit its errors as the livestock industry had to do.

We at the VM Ranch will voluntarily remove 20% of our cattle from the summer range for the 1990 grazing year. These cattle are being removed because we care about the habitat and are trying to be responsive, not because of the drought but because of the elk. Perhaps the range and the wildlife staffs of the Apache-Sitgreaves [National Forest] should voluntarily forfeit 20% of their gross income into a fund. This fund could either be used for habitat improvement or perhaps further education. (USFS 1990)

Official records from the region indicate a rapid growth of elk populations and increasing livestock-elk conflicts (Hess 1998:1–4). However, the "mistake" that this rancher wants "squarely upon the shoulders of the Forest Service" cannot justly be placed there: that federal agency lacks jurisdiction over wild game species. By law, such power is reserved to the states and their game commissions. In response to cattle growers' complaints, the state of New Mexico passed legislation to compensate affected ranchers with valuable elk-hunting permits that could be sold if the rancher could prove elk "depredation" of his privately owned pastures. But Arizona has no such legislation. One Blue rancher had to build a $50,000 fence eight feet high to protect his eighty-five acres of hay fields from elk (Luce 1998). And in any case, ranchers have no rights of compensation when elk graze their allotment pastures, for these are government-owned lands.

The Forest Service can easily limit and manage grazing by domestic ungulates such as cows by specifying how many livestock are permitted on which pastures during which seasons. It cannot manage grazing by such wild ungulates as elk in this way, since elk cannot be herded and can easily jump or break down fences built for cattle. The only way to control elk overgrazing would be through culling or permitting more elk hunting. But in Arizona only the Arizona Game and Fish Department can issue hunting permits.

Arizona Game and Fish positively advertises the abundance of elk in Blue country.

Elk are widely distributed throughout the northern half of Unit 27 [the Blue watershed and nearby mountain allotments].

The opportunistic elk is thriving in habitats ranging from pin-yon-juniper woodlands in lower elevations to spruce-fir forests at higher elevations. Hunters pursuing elk during September and October should have no problem finding plenty of animals, both bulls and cows, on high elevation summer range located above the Mogollon Rim. Late season hunters. . . will have to brave the rugged, winter range country located below the Mogollon Rim, in the Blue River and Eagle Creek watersheds, if they hope to harvest a mature bull. . . . (AZGFD 2015)

The Department estimated in 2004 that over 2,000 elk roam Unit 27 South, which encompasses the Blue and neighboring areas, for which 1,175 hunting permits were sold in 2002 (AZGFD 2004). Arizona Game and Fish has been resistant to substantial reductions in elk numbers, for the sale of hunting permits generates large amounts of state revenue. Elk also generate revenue indirectly through the elk-hunting industry. Hunters' lobbies have wanted as much elk forage as possible. So have environmental activist groups that in their many lawsuits against the Forest Service usually ask for all of the resource to go to the elk and other wild species, and none to cattle. But a new question arises: what if the elk are now overpopulating, overgrazing, and harming endangered species and the environment?

In the public debate over the Tucson deal that took cattle off the riparian areas of the Southwest, Caren Cowan of the New Mexico Cattle Growers had defended cattle: "I don't think anyone is taking into consideration the damage wildlife do, particularly elk." The Forest Service regional rangeland head, David Steward, refused to address this question; instead he preferred to criticize the ranching industry for denying the problem of overgrazing. And probably most of the public, as well as environmental activists, would resist the idea that a wild species could degrade the environment.

But of course Aldo Leopold knew better, as he had learned from the extirpation of the wolf in the Southwest. The deer then overpopulated, denuded their environment, and starved (Leopold 1949:130). And despite David Steward's evasion, the Forest Service was in fact increasingly concerned with the growth of elk numbers. John Bedell, Supervisor of the Apache-Sitgreaves National Forest, told me:

We've been working with the Game Department for many, many years on reducing the herd size of elk. And until we've taken all the cows off, and there's still over-utilization, we now have come to realize. . . [we] have just as much damage to the riparian habitats on the Apache side as there was when there was a lot more domestic livestock. And the Fish and Wildlife Service is aware of that. And so they're now exerting similar pressure on the Game Department for the same reasons—listed species and utilization standards. Last year one of the reasons no cows went to the mountain [high altitude summer allotments] was the elk never came off of the mountain. They consumed all the forage and there was no forage the cows could use, even as late as July. . . . (Bedell 2001)

According to officials, the strategy of the Forest Service has been to use its cattle reductions to gather data to make the case against elk overgrazing. Part of the strategy also is to persuade the U.S. Fish and Wildlife Service to issue biological opinions that could be used in conjunction with the Endangered Species Act to pressure Arizona Game and Fish into reducing the elk herds. The Alpine District Ranger commented,

[Elk] now can be looked at under the ESA. That's what we'll be looking at. They're destroying the riparian habitat just like livestock are. We've excluded the livestock now; now we're looking at the elk. It's now up to Game and Fish to manage the numbers, give more permits [to allow more hunting] . . .

This is the first time in the history of the Alpine allotment [an allotment on the upper Blue], last year, that we held the permitted livestock off because the elk had used it too much. It's documented. The grazing permittee was upset with me doing it, but I said, "Wait a minute—you need to be thanking me for doing this. I just brought to a head the issue you've been trying to deal with for the last twenty years. Now you can turn around and thank me. . . . Because it's documented: the elk used all the forage up before the livestock. People [ranchers] have been running down the Alpine District for the last couple, three years about what we're doing. Well, I think they're going to find out that they're going to be thanking us here in the very near future for what we've done. (Settles 2001)

One may doubt that ranchers, who lose their livelihoods through the demonstration by default of the effects of elk overgrazing, are really thankful to the Forest Service. In any case, in the new millennium, discussions on reducing the elk population have gone nowhere so far. At present, elk herds are larger than ever, and the deer population has also grown (Dolphin 2015). It is the number of permitted cattle that remains reduced.

"Erasing Past Sins": Wolf Reintroduction

Environmental activists, however, had long been campaigning for what they regard as the perfect solution to the problem of elk overpopulation. They wanted to reintroduce the Mexican gray wolf to the Southwest. Ecological balance would then be restored to the natural systems of the Southwest through a necessary predator. They drew on the writings and the spirit of Aldo Leopold. In his essay "Thinking Like a Mountain," Leopold first raised the notion—revolutionary at the time—that wolves might be desirable to keep down the populations of other species. In the same essay he also relates his famous experience of killing a wolf and "seeing a fierce green fire dying in her eyes." This encounter symbolized the beginning of his evolving ideas about predators, the balance of nature, and wilderness. The experience took place near the Blue (Flader 2012; Leopold 1949:129; chapter 4, note 1).

Therefore it was perhaps fitting—though ironic—that the first Mexican gray wolf pack to be reintroduced to the wild was released on the lower Blue, on the Wildbunch Allotment of the Cathcart family. This occurred in January 1998, overseen by Secretary of the Interior Bruce Babbitt, to "erase the sins of the past" (Kenworthy 1998b). However, it was not Babbitt but ranchers like the Cathcarts who would actually pay for those collective sins of the past: within a year the wolves were attacking and killing their cattle, losses for which they were usually not compensated.

The Mexican wolf (*Canis lupus baileyi*), a subspecies of the North American gray wolf, had been eradicated entirely from the wild in the United States and Mexico during the twentieth century. As early as the late 1970s, the U.S. Fish and Wildlife Service began planning its reintroduction. Five wolves (including one female) captured from the wild in Mexico were established as a breeding population in zoos and wildlife sanctuaries. But from the beginning the plan was controversial, as biological critics considered the breeding population too small and claimed the wolves were actually hybrids whose genes were mixed with those of dogs—charges the agency heatedly denied (McAndlin 2003; USFW 2000; Parker 1997).

Federal agencies designated a "Blue Range Wolf Recovery Area" that covers the Apache-Sitgreaves National Forest in Arizona and the adjacent Gila National Forest in New Mexico. When New Mexico refused to allow the predators loose into the state, the U.S. Fish and Wildlife Service proceeded to introduce wolves in eastern Arizona, confident that the species would eventually migrate across the border. The goal was to establish a wild wolf population of one hundred by 2006.

A few Blue ranchers witnessed the release project unfold. One was Bill Wilson, the manager of the T-Links ranch, whose owner lived in Phoenix. The acclimation pens to hold the wolves were only three and a half miles from his ranch house, "right in the middle of four ranches. They didn't have signs up or nothing." He thinks they chose places to put wolves that they could almost reach with vehicles so they could feed them.

> My theory on these wolves is that if they can get the wolves out here and get them established, they'll get the environmental movement behind them, and say, "Look, the humans living in this country right here are interfering with the repopulation of the Mexican Wolf," and who's going to leave? It's just one more way to get this land. (Wilson 2000)

The releases went disastrously wrong the first year. In March, a post office employee from Tucson, Richard Humphrey, his wife, their two young daughters, and two dogs were camping about a mile from the site of the first release—a place they had often camped before—when they noticed wolves. "I looked around and saw what I thought at first was a dog. It was close, low to the ground and was stalking me. Then I saw it had a collar and a transmitter box. I assumed it was a hybrid wolf. I noticed a second one among the trees. I thought they had been released in a wilderness area far to the north, near Alpine." Humphrey loaded his rifle and yelled, and the wolves backed off. "They acted more like dogs than wildlife unaccustomed to humans.... We didn't break camp and leave, because we thought the wolves were just passing through" (Walley 1998).

The next day, after breakfast, they heard one of Humphrey's dogs shrieking as it was attacked. Humphrey took his rifle and began yelling to run two wolves off. One ran away, but, "All of a sudden, a wolf came around a tree toward us, and not in a walk but in a run. That's when I shot. I was thinking how fast wolves could run and I couldn't let him get any closer." His shots stopped the wolf less than fifty feet from his family.

For this act Mr. Humphrey was thoroughly interrogated by government agencies, who declined to press charges in the midst of what became a media circus. Environmental activists were enraged that the Fish and Wildlife Service did not punish the killing of an endangered species, and they promoted a public campaign to make an example of the wolf killer. "Even if the dog had been attacked," said Peter Galvin for the Southwest Center for Biological Diversity, "it would not legally or morally justify killing a severely endangered species. It is looking more and more like the killing was malicious, not just ignorant" (Walley 1998). The activists refused to give any credence to Humphrey's claim that he was protecting his family from imminent harm—in which case, shooting a wolf is legal.

Through the spring and summer of 1998, other wolf releases occurred, one near Alpine in the upper Blue. Wolves did begin to appear in New Mexico. The whole Blue Range Wolf Recovery Area and communities beyond were convulsed with controversy over the wolf presence. Virtually all ranchers and probably most of the town dwellers in the rural area vehemently opposed the wolf recovery effort, while environmental activists and supporters in their urban redoubts in Tucson, Albuquerque, and Santa Fe kept up a steady drumbeat of support. New Mexico and Arizona media feasted on the story, playing up the conflict.

In fact four wolves were found shot in eastern Arizona during the fall hunting season of 1998, which runs into November. The unsolved wolf killings involved different guns, and occurred in different locations on different dates; no evidence connected them to anyone. Environmental activists saw a rancher plot and alleged that bounties were being offered. Ranchers thought the killings were probably those of gun-happy urban hunters who could not tell a wolf from a coyote. The federal government sent in grim investigators. And people on the Blue kept finding themselves quoted in the big city media (Burchell 1998). With a wealth of colorful detail, the following story from *The Arizona Daily Star* appeared November 15, 1998:

ALPINE—The local blacksmith pauses to spit tobacco from the front porch of the tackle shop.

"If a wolf came on my property and molested any of my animals, I would dispatch it immediately," says David "Dink" Robart, before shouting at the unruly mules he's transporting to pasture. ["Dink" is a goat farmer and brother of Forest Service permittee Tim Robart, a victim of the 1995 NEPA cuts.]

"That's the way most folks are out here. If they get messed with, they'll mess back—but I don't think locals are shooting those wolves. . . ."

Make no mistake. Anti-government sentiment is as common in these remote parts as extended-cab pickup trucks and baseball caps. (Bodfield 1998)

The story accurately noted that most residents around Alpine did not see the wolf project as a "romantic venture to restore Western heritage." They saw it as just one more predator that endangers people and their domestic animals.

The wolves have not killed any livestock, but they have tried. A wolf bit a miniature colt on the neck before its mother chased the wolf off. One rancher's stock dog, Peppy, was killed by a wolf, federal officials have confirmed. The conservation group Defenders of Wildlife paid the rancher $150 for the dog and paid the colt's veterinary bills.

Rancher Bobby Fite has pictures to back up his account of a wolf running among his cattle, testing a calf. He said the wolf also visited his prize sheep barn.

Fite, armed with a rifle and a camera, waited until the wolf was 20 yards from the calf before scaring the wolf off with warning shots. Officials have confirmed the wolf hung around town for three weeks before being caught and returned to captivity.

"If I waited just two more minutes until she bit that calf, I could've killed her and it would have been perfectly legal. I don't think there's a person on this mountain out there deliberately shooting those wolves. If that was the case, that would've happened the first month they were released," Fite said.

Fite was rankled by the sabotage theory: "I think it's very negative for the town. It's very possible people will say this is a backwoodsy hick town."

Alan Armistead, a worker for Animal Damage Control assigned to handle the wolves, said he has been berated for everything from the government's ills to the fancy government truck he drives.

But he sides with the locals on this one: He does not believe the killings are a local sabotage effort. "You're talking about four or five animals wandering a huge area. It would take a tremendous amount of luck and effort for one person to track these animals."

The wolves are especially vulnerable, Armistead said, because their fear of humans has been offset by their dependence on them for food in captivity. "Once we have some wild pups out there, we'll have a more realistic recovery program."

Many local people did not appreciate all the resources being expended on the wolves or that wolves were being released only seven miles from the town. They were convinced that people were being sacrificed for wild animals.

With money scarce, the large expenditures for the wolf program grate on some. Already, the bill is up to $4 million while planes fly overhead twice a week on monitoring flights and more trucks are seen with government emblems.

"It's a waste of taxpayer money. We need some industry in here so people can make a decent living," said carpenter Leonard Rogers, who says his ostrich kicked one of the wolves.

Paul Morey, a Fish and Wildlife biotechnician with the wolf program, said wolves were released closer to town because monitoring and transporting in the more primitive areas would require horses, helicopters or snowshoes.

Morey does not think the wolves' town visits have been all bad. "In a way, it was a good thing for the project because it made people realize the wolves won't be taking children out of their back yards."

And, he said, just as it was with the Yellowstone recovery program, he has met tourists who have come to glimpse the wolves.

As at Yellowstone, however, tourists were unlikely ever to see the elusive creatures.

The Blue ranchers, much more likely to see the wolves, were incorporated into the story. Rose Coleman (remarried, now Rose Awtrey) was interviewed.

> Cattlewoman Rose Coleman-Autrey [*sic*] had a permit in 1995 to graze 230 head of cattle on public land before the Forest Service started trying to protect the endangered loach minnow in the Blue River.
>
> This year, her cattle dropped to 100. Next year, she will be down to 39. She rented private pasture for one month and it cost her $4,500, about half the income the cattle brought in, she said.
>
> Coleman, whose family has lived in the nearby Blue Range area since the 1800s, said lions and bears kill about 10 percent of her calves each year. If the wolf program meets its goal of restoring 100 animals to the area, she predicts, "It will be wipeout city."

Environmentalists had the last word.

> Environmentalists counter that the economic problems are rooted in local practice.
>
> "It's interesting they blame environmentalists for the demise of their communities, when excessive logging and overgrazing have abused the land and led to the demise," said Shane Jimerfield, assistant director of the Southwest Center for Biological Diversity. "Nobody is cramming the wolf program down their throats. The public at large is just saying we want wolves on public lands and this land belongs to all of us."
>
> Secretary Babbitt emphasized Friday that the program is here to stay.
>
> "The future survival of these rare and beautiful creatures must not be jeopardized by bullets and senseless killings," he said. "We want to work with local communities and solve these crimes. We are committed to the recovery of the Mexican wolf and the goals of the Endangered Species Act." (Bodfield 1998)

The program might be "here to stay" but at the end of the first year, the results looked bad. As the Southwest Center for Biological Diversity itself reported on November 25 in its Internet bulletin "alert":

"5TH WOLF CONFIRMED SHOT, no free roaming wolves left. . . . Of the 11 reintroduced wolves, 5 were shot, 3 were removed after leaving the recovery area, 1 is missing. The two remaining males were captured and placed in release pens with two new females. No Mexican gray wolves are in the wild at this time. The four penned wolves will be released soon" (SWCBD 1998).

WOLVES ATTACK COWS AND CALVES

However, the government kept releasing captive wolves, and some were occasionally found shot or dead from other causes. More had to be captured and taken out of the wild for repeatedly attacking livestock. But the wolves did extend their range over the Blue and Gila recovery area and kept controversy raging as they began successfully to prey on livestock. The lower Blue probably suffered more than other areas, as it was not real elk country nor rich in wild game for the wolves. Bill Wilson of the T-Links ranch sums up: "More wolves were introduced [in 1999], and then attacked cattle. We lost one cow, two calves, and had one cow chewed up real bad." But not as bad as other ranchers: the neighboring 6K6 ranch, for example, had eleven wolf attacks (Wilson 2000).

> And Scott [Derringer, a neighboring rancher] had a couple hounds chewed up by the wolves. But according to the wolf people [an environmentalist group that had offered to compensate ranchers for wolf kills], a dog has no material value. It's not livestock. No matter if it's on your private property or nothing. A dog's a dog. But if [wolves are] killing a cow or a horse on private land, then you have the right to shoot 'em. I've been told that even chickens count as private livestock, and if I had the money I could beat the charges if I killed a wolf taking my chickens. But not for a dog. My dogs, they didn't cost anything, they're nothing special except to me and my family. But Scott used special dogs [for hunting]. He would buy them for four or five thousand apiece. But according to the wolf people, that wasn't worth nothing.
>
> I've got one dog over there I've had since he was seven weeks old. He used to ride on the front of the saddle with me when he was a pup. And I know that if it come down to my dog or them wolves, them wolves would die. I wouldn't hesitate to shoot one

of them. I don't know if you have any religious in you or not, but as far as I'm concerned, this whole environmental movement is an Anti-Christ type thing, because they're putting animals, plants, trees above man, which is *not* the way things is supposed to be. For me, that's not right. (Wilson 2000)

Bill Wilson believed the whole wolf-release program has been botched. "The worst thing with the whole wolf program is that they [the Fish and Wildlife personnel] walk right up there and feed the stupid things. It's no different than with a dog." Since the wolves in captivity have been raised and fed by humans, they are not afraid of people: they see them as a source of food. The wolves did not know how to hunt. Some of the wolves were nearly starving to death when they were removed. Therefore, after release, Fish and Wildlife had to keep feeding them what they claimed was roadkill and "zoo logs."

Wilson met many specialists sent in to work with the wolves, and professed little respect for them.

The day that them wolves killed my cow up here, they [the U.S. Fish and Wildlife] was flying in their little airplane monitoring the wolves from the air, by their collars, and they watched the wolves chase that cow, separate the cow and the calf, right here on this flat. From the airplane they radioed it back, saying they had their first confirmed elk kill. . . . The cow had a big yellow ear tag, and was blacker than coal and had a long tail. . . . I was in the bottom of a canyon over here, and looked up and saw both of them sitting in the airplane, that's how low they were to the ground. And they couldn't tell an elk from a cow. And then they went up to my neighbor Scott's, up here, and told him, "Well, you don't have to worry about them wolves. We just saw them kill an elk just east of the corrals."

I think they're just educated idiots.

Then we found the other two kills. They killed a cow and a calf the first day, the second time down they killed a calf, and the third time they came down. . .I was really jumping up and down and screaming. And we had those guys monitoring, we had those guys sitting on the hill in pickups all night long with their receivers waiting for the wolves. (Wilson 2000)

Fish and Game adopted a policy of removing individual wolves from the wild if they attacked cattle three times—"three strikes and you're out."

Neighboring Wilson's ranch is the Cathcart ranch, on the east side of the Blue River. One of the most remote ranches in America, it is accessible only by four-wheel drive, fording the river when it is low enough. It is completely off the grid. Without a telephone line, and with mountains blocking cell phone communication at the ranch house, the Cathcarts must drive up a high hill when they need to telephone someone, including the county sheriff in Clifton to see if he has any messages for them.

The Cathcarts have their own stories about the wolves, originally released on one of their allotments. Martie Cathcart, the ranch wife, has the brown and weathered face of a cowgirl who has spent much of her life on horseback. She related to me how the wolves had constantly attacked their stock over the past few years. "We had three cows killed, that was verified." Other cattle disappeared or died without enough evidence to blame the wolves.

To minimize opposition to wolf restoration, an environmental group, the Defenders of Wildlife, had offered to recompense owners whose livestock were killed by wolves. But the Cathcarts (like many other ranchers) were not recompensed in the end, for various reasons. "One of the reasons we were not paid, is that the Forest Service told the Defenders of Wildlife that we had our cows in the wrong pasture" [i.e., were violating their grazing plan]. But, she claimed, this wasn't true. "The only ones we had out of place was the ones that were being chased. They pick out one and finally get her down." The wolves had driven their prey over a ridge into the off-limit pasture (Cathcart 2000).

The Cathcarts at the time were in constant conflict with their District Ranger in Clifton over proposed NEPA cuts, water rights, and many other issues. The denied compensation fit into their view of Forest Service persecution.

In the first years of wolf release, wildlife specialists were frequently around. Although the specialists and the ranchers disagreed profoundly on the wolf release plan, nevertheless they got along. The ranchers offered hospitality, including meals and a bed when needed. One specialist lived several months with the Cathcarts, "because we were having so much trouble." Martie's eighteen-year-old son, Patrick, was even hired by Fish and Wildlife to work with them for a time. Patrick commented,

We were having so much trouble trying to keep the wolves away, I rode every morning and afternoon on horseback with telemetry equipment to where the wolves were at, I was basically living with them. I didn't do a darn thing with the cows, I just kept track of them wolves. As a matter of fact, I caught the wolves killing the last cow. She was still alive, and they were running around her, trying to figure out how to get past me to the cow. Her insides were laying on the ground, about twenty feet of gut was strung out. (Cathcart 2000)

For Fish and Wildlife, Patrick also hauled five or six loads of meat, about a thousand pounds, to feed the wolves. He was skeptical there could have been that many road kills on the lightly traveled highways around the Blue. Fish and Wildlife said it was roadkill, but Patrick saw few broken bones. His theory was the government were shooting the elk in the mountains, and then hauling the meat to the wolves. This was a common belief among people on the Blue.

The Cathcarts' ranch and the lower Blue in general had no elk: the elevation was too low. Why then did the government want to release wolves there? Bill Wilson had asked the same question. Patrick answered,

Well, they thought the wolves could live off the deer. The wolves could drive all the bears and lion out of the country, the coyotes would leave, and there would be only wolves that wouldn't touch a cow. The only way they would eat a cow if she was sick, in misery or dying.

I guarantee you, the three confirmed kills [of Cathcart stock], even the biologists said . . . were not sick, they were fat cows. What the wolves would do, is get them into a tough spot, like up against a bluff or a fence, even on a steep hill slope. But there were eight of them including five pups, one yearling male and one alpha female and one alpha male. (Cathcart 2000)

Martie added her view of how flawed the release program was.

I talked to their game specialist, Dan Grebner. I said, "You guys have millions of dollars—millions. When you came to my house, I tried to tell you. The best friend you'll ever have is a rancher: that way you'll know what the truth is." He said, "If there had been something for those wolves to eat, we wouldn't have had the problem. I'll tell you, Martie, we made a mistake." And I said, "Dan, there hadn't been anybody here to check the whole deal out." He said, "I think there was one person."

They had a couple biologists go in, and Ellen was one, and she said, 'My God! What's wrong with these people [Fish and Wildlife]? This isn't even habitat!"

So they get a helicopter, and $10,000 later after the chopper arrives, they come over here and set [the wolves] on the other side of the hill. There's no elk! There's no deer. Nothing. So, they come up out of the canyon and they're right in on our cows.

A bad, bad plan. (Cathcart 2000)

With rancher hospitality, the Cathcarts gave food and shelter in their remote homestead not only to the biologists who were importing wolves onto their ranch, but also to students out on an environmental educational camping trip. Martie comments,

You probably heard about Prescott College [in Prescott, Arizona]. A lot of environmentalists go there, it's an environmentalist college. Well, for an initiation, they send these kids up and down this river. And they're like twelve to a group. And they basically make it on their own. They have their soy protein, and this is about what they live off of.

Last year we were having our wolf problems, and Pat ran into them and said, "Look, the wolf biologist is up at our house," and they said, "Well, can we come up and meet him?" And we said, "Sure." And we were with all these kids, their hair was down to their—well, one of these boys was the goldurndest thing I ever saw, anyway.

The river rose and flooded the students' campsite, forcing them to camp at the Cathcarts' ranch.

They camped here [she laughs]. You never seen such sad specimens in your life. They were all wet, they were dirty, they were hungry...ohhh! They were all mad at each other. Some of the kids, their beds had washed away—oh they were a sad sight. But bless their hearts, they finally got on their way.

When we had 'em all up here, and they had a place to stay, and a hot meal, they all go, "We just can't believe you did this for us." I said, "Guys—you get in trouble out here, like you were this time, and there's a ranch anywhere in that area, go there and they'll help you."

They said, "That's not what we've been told." I said, "It's the truth, they'll help you."

They've been told [by environmentalist teachers and activists] that ranchers are horrible! And that cows are the ruination of the world, and that ranchers were as bad as their cows. Gee whiz!

Anyway, there were thirteen of them that got a different side of the educational process. . . . But they got enough trouble on their own, that the College picked them up in a few days. But they were supposed to hike all the way to the highway in New Mexico. . . . But there was no way they could have made it. But there were several groups up here. They'd drop a group off here and there, and sometimes someone off to themselves with no one to talk to. . . . Real kind of a strange thing. And they'd have like these great big plastic bags; if it rained, that's what they slept in under. Quite an experience for them, and a lot of those kids had never been out on the land, didn't have an idea. Oh, they got a crash course [she laughs]. (Cathcart 2000)

Livestock and Wolf "Coexistence"

The Mexican Wolf Recovery Program suffered ups and downs, but made slow progress. From its captive breeding program, the government kept releasing wolves, and eventually wolf cubs were born and raised in the wild. The number of wolf packs grew, and their range soon extended over a large part of the higher mountain country of eastern Arizona and western New Mexico. By the summer of 2015, the official estimate claimed nineteen packs, amounting to 110 wolves in the wild, fifty-five of them with tracking collars (Dolphin 2015; USFW 2015). Three wolf packs—the "Blue Stem," the "Maverick" and the "Elkhorn"—roam allotments where Blue ranchers graze cows and calves, mostly at the higher elevations in the summer pastures.

Wolf predation on cattle and calves continues. The number of domestic animals attacked or killed is not officially recorded, and all kills cannot be verified, especially of calves when they disappear. Blue ranchers have lost cattle occasionally. In March 2015 the Marks' LWJ ranch lost a cow, killed near the Blue post office. Wolves are a constant concern to the ranchers.

To address this concern and reduce the hostility manifest in the rural communities, U.S. Fish and Wildlife and its state partners (such as Arizona Game and Fish) have set up bodies within which they can "work diligently with affected stakeholders to prevent, reduce, and compensate for negative economic impacts felt by affected stakeholders" (USFW 2015). The Mexican Wolf/Livestock Coexistence Council was established in 2011, to bring together "ranchers from Arizona and New Mexico, environmental groups, [the two Apache] tribes, and two county coalitions that represent counties in New Mexico and Arizona" (Mexican Wolf/ Livestock Coexistence Council 2015).

Barbara Marks was appointed one of the members of the Council, along with four other ranchers. Defenders of Wildlife and the Conservation Fund were two environmental groups represented; subsequently also the Mexican Wolf Fund. Naturally, government agencies were greatly involved also—the Forest Service as well as U.S. Fish and Wildlife and the game agencies of Arizona and New Mexico.

The first business of the Council was to develop guidelines for paying "depredation compensation" for cattle verified as killed by wolves. The money comes not from the government but from the environmental organizations participating in the Plan. Furthermore, payments are provided for "wolf presence" that causes hardships for ranchers and to support "conflict avoidance measures" that ranchers volunteer to implement. "Tools and techniques such as increased human presence, timed calving, range riders, turbo fladry (temporary electric fencing with flagging), and use of alternative pastures are just a few of the approaches that have been used successfully to keep both livestock and wolves safe" (Mexican Wolf/Livestock Coexistence Council 2015).

In practice, as described by Barbara Marks, money is received to offset the costs of a "range rider"—the rancher or ranch hand—scouting the countryside, looking for wolves. The range rider is provided with a telemetry unit, loaned by Arizona Game and Fish, which can locate wolf packs via the radio collars on many individual wolves. In this way, cattle and wolves can be managed to keep them apart.

At a hearing on the plan in Glenwood, New Mexico, some environmentalists protested lending the telemetry units to the ranchers: this would make it easier for ranchers to find and shoot the endangered wolf. The U.S. Fish and Wildlife representative at the meeting defended the ranchers, pointing to the record: no rancher in the recovery area has ever been charged for harming a wolf.

The Coexistence Plan states that

> [it is] designed to reduce livestock/wolf conflicts and the need for management removals of depredating or nuisance wolves. In addition, our program will support livestock producers, the values embedded in the western landscapes, and the growth of wild Mexican wolf populations through natural reproduction and recruitment.

The Plan claims to be guided by three interdependent goals: "healthy western landscapes, viable ranching, and self-sustaining wolf populations."

This effort will probably never overcome rancher misgivings about the wolf program. But it certainly represents a contrasting approach to the anti-grazing, litigious, and, in fact, anti-coexistence mindset of the environmental activist groups that previously plagued the Blue. The Coexistence Council represents a collaborative approach to environmental issues and a model for moving forward.

15

Blue Ranchers' Stories

Part I

Previous chapters have covered the history of the Blue and the various environmental and regulatory issues that helped shape this history. The ranchers themselves have been frequently quoted. However, another way of apprehending the history of the Blue is to hear the stories of individual ranchers and rancher families, especially how they adapted to the changes that began late in the twentieth century. Recounting their histories also gives them an opportunity to voice their own opinions of developments on the Blue.

The next two chapters feature the stories from a selection of ranchers, living on the Blue, whom I got to know and interview in depth. Also, I use information from the family histories in *Down on the Blue* (1987). Most of these people have appeared briefly in earlier chapters.

The first three stories are from ranchers who faced the sudden and severe NEPA cuts of 1995 (chapter 10), the full force of the environmentalist reckoning.

ROSE COSPER COLEMAN AWTREY

[S]ome have suggested that tourism is the future [for those in the dying cattle industry].

Rose Coleman-Awtrey, a wiry woman who manages a Blue River ranch single-handedly, responds: "There's no reason I couldn't take trail riders out and things like that, but I guess being a doggone independent rancher you just hate to have to deal with the public if you don't have to."

When the Forest Service cut her grazing allotment this year, however, she came close to giving up. . . ." (Kenworthy 1998c)

Lillian Rose Cosper was born to Dewitt and Katharine Cosper in

1946. Dewitt was a son of Blue pioneer Toles Cosper, whose story is told early in this book. Katharine, who came to the Blue in 1936, was one of the new breed of cow-woman who worked the range on horseback with her husband after they were married in 1945.

> We bought the VM Ranch and all the cattle and the old RNH place, also. Our daughter, Rose, was born in 1946. I continued riding as usual and helped DeWitt work the cattle. We made drives of 15 miles back and forth to our summer range on top of the White Mountains near Hannagan Meadow. We took turns carrying Rose from two months of age, along on a pillow, in front of us in the saddle. Just before she was two years old, she won the prize for being the "youngest cowgirl riding alone" in the Fourth of July parade in Springerville, Arizona. Twenty years later her daughter, Leddy Coleman, age two, won the same prize.
>
> Dewitt and I did well with the cows and were very happy until his death from a heart attack in 1954.
>
> After Rose and I were alone on the ranch awhile, Clell Lee, famed big game hunter from Paradise, Arizona, came to the Blue at the request of ranchers who were losing much stock to predators. He and I were married in 1955.
>
> Clell conducted hunting parties for bear and mountain lions with good success and we continued to operate the ranch. Sometimes when he was busy with hunters Rose and I would work the cattle, pack out salt, gather yearlings, etc. We prospered and later bought the old Balke Place. . . . Most of the time we had no hired help. (*Down on the Blue* 169)

Rose herself remembers riding at a very early age, and having her own horse at two years old.

> My folks never let me slow down their work. I went everywhere and all day long. As a kid, I can remember lots of long hours. When we got ready to drive the cattle to the mountain, we would get up at 2 a.m., leave the house at 4 and hit a long trot up Grant Creek, four miles to the corral, where the cattle were penned from the day before. About dark that night we would have them at the Balke cabin near Hannagan. We would brand the calves and move them on another couple miles the next day, and then the following day ride on back to the Blue.

After completing grade school, I boarded out with friends in Silver City, New Mexico, to go to high school. (*Down on the Blue* 71)

In Silver City, Rose met her future husband, Charles Coleman, also from a ranching background, and when he returned from serving in Vietnam they moved to the Blue in 1965, working on several ranches including her mother's. They had two children who learned to ride early and "consequently, they turned out to be good riders and good hands!" (*Down on the Blue* 71.) The children went to the same grade school on the Blue that Rose had attended and then to high school in Springerville—the roads now being good enough to commute. Later, both of Rose's children would continue in the ranching life in western Arizona.

Meanwhile, Rose and Charles came to manage the Lazy YJ ranch owned by a Phoenix family, the Quinslers, as well as buying her mother's VM Ranch after Rose's stepfather, Clell Lee, died in 1982. Rose's recollections in *Down on the Blue* are full of the details of a hard working ranching family.

We take very little time off but we like to go to the big city occasionally. We like to dance, go to rodeos and fairs, and stock shows. Charles has recently taken up golfing and he enjoys that a lot.

The people here do very little visiting back and forth. There isn't time! We do try to get the community together about once a month for potluck and usually dance to the local Barbwire Boys & Girls. If it is an afternoon event the guys play washoes or horseshoes and the gals gossip! (*Down on the Blue* 72)

Such bucolic order on the Blue was destined to be short lived. The same year the NEPA actions and decisions came down threatening their ranching way of life, 1995, was also the year that Rose and Charles Coleman divorced. A few years later, some ranchers, convinced by then of the malevolence of the Forest Service, would speculate darkly to me that Rose's allotments were chosen for the NEPA cuts precisely *because* she was going through a divorce, and therefore seen as more vulnerable. This allegation seems doubtful, and in any case Rose had bounced back from her double ordeal by the time I first interviewed her in 1998.

A dark-haired, trim and comely woman in her 50s (*The Washington Post* also characterized her as "wiry"), she had remarried. Her new husband, Carl Awtrey, owned a prosperous log-home construction business in Nutrioso, not so far from the Blue. But Rose continued to ranch. "I was born and raised here on a ranch, and have been in that business all my life except for the time I went off to school. After Dad died, I took over this ranch and I still have it—barely," she laughed sardonically. She had testified in the Las Cruces trial the ranchers lost (chapter 12) a few months before we spoke (Awtrey 1998).

> When I read the letters of old-timers, they're often afraid the Forest Service is going to put them out of business. There's always a threat. . . . Mom was always terrified of the Ranger— "Oh, we got to go meet with the Forest Service today"—like he was some high-powered figure. They thought they had it bad, but it's nothing like it is now. Really, up until this 1995 permit renewal, it wasn't that bad. Obviously they had rules and regulations they had to follow, one thing and another, but you could reason with them. When you went in to do your Annual Operating Plan, you just discussed where you would put the cattle, what improvements we need to make this year, and do you think you can supply the labor, and the Forest will supply the materials. . . . It was managing the range. But anymore you go in there and it's, "Who's sued you today?"

Rose blames the Forest Service for being slow to come into compliance with the National Environmental Protection Act then springing it suddenly on the ranchers.

> What really hurt some of us with year-round permits was that they had to get this NEPA study done by '95 in order for us to continue at all. So they just ran out there and came up with all this baloney, cutting you, and you won't be on the forest for a month, and you no longer can graze here, and you have to do this, and you have to do that—and there was no scientific stuff whatsoever, no nothing, you know. Just punched a few keys on the computer, and this is what you're going to do.
>
> My original permit was for 230 for the winter, and 177 in the summer. And the reductions are being implemented over three years. This year I'm allowed 136, and then down to 99, and finally down to 39.

Why were the cuts so deep? What were the reasons for the cuts?

> I do not know where they came up with such radical cuts. I do
> not know. . . . If they had cut us in half, we still could have got by.
> The darned Supervisor [Bedell]. We had an opportunity to visit
> with him, one on one, and try to get into compromise somewhat,
> but he just wouldn't hear nothing of it.
>
> [The reasons for the cuts were] a variety of things. The num-
> ber one reason was endangered species. I can't see it, because I
> don't think they're endangered. But taking us off the river bot-
> toms, the stream bottoms, that would have been bad enough,
> but to take us off the mountains—to make the reductions they
> did. . . .
>
> You might say there are no endangered species there, but
> well, cattle can send sediment down these little tributaries [to
> affect the minnow].
>
> To my knowledge, I've never seen anyone or heard of any-
> one coming down there to see, of anyone actually being there. In
> the Blue area, it's the minnow mainly, and a little bit of it is the
> goshawk, and then in the high country the Apache trout. And
> they've fenced off all streams because of the trout. But our utili-
> zation has gone way down, what we're able to utilize grass-wise,
> due to the owl and the hawk. . . . They say cattle eat the forage,
> and the little critters the owls and hawks prey on can't hide as
> well, and coyotes and other things eat them up, to where [the
> birds] don't have prey base. . . . What amazes me is that for over
> a hundred years they've existed [with cattle] but now suddenly
> they're not going to, because of cattle grazing.
>
> I guess I have every endangered species on the list, except
> the flycatcher.

She doesn't believe the land is overgrazed.

> Oh yeah, they always say that. But if they looked out there, and
> cattle were out there, and you say "look" [the grass looks good],
> they would say, "So what—the soil is only so deep, and the slope
> is more than thirty percent, and there's so much trees. . . ." It
> doesn't matter what it looks like, the soil type and other things
> come into play. . . .

In that Blue River country, one of our main forage bases in the wintertime is the browse—and there's tons of it. And they've never monitored it. They have no way. There's oak brush, mountain mahogany, and quite a variety of little brushy things. There may be grass there too, but cattle desire the brush in the winter. But this doesn't even come into play [in the Forest Service model]. It's *not* that there's not enough forage out there—they're so worried about this darned endangered species stuff that they can't see the forest for the trees.

Like other Blue ranchers, she tries to interpret developments within the Forest Service.

It all boils down to, they want us off. And they're going to do whatever it takes to do that. The bottom line is that they're going to get rid of us, no matter what it takes. There's no rationale.

I think that a particular group of people [in the Forest Service] are anti-ranching, they're anti-grazing, so they're not going to help you, they want you off. . . . I do think there are others who work for the Forest Service who *do* think grazing is part of the multiple use, which it's supposed to be, and are afraid of their superiors.

There's something about this Alpine District. It's run differently than any other in the area. It's like they have an agenda to get rid of us, and they're doing a pretty good job of it.

Some of these Forest people have told us, "Look, you're going to have to sue us to ever get what you want." They give advice on what to sue on! They know it's a bunch of malarkey, and they want us to stay here. . . . I think a good share of them are on our side and want to help. But take John Bedell, for example, I really do think that he's for cattle, he wanted to see grazing, but he knew what he was doing to me and the rest of them, that it could very well put us out of business. By just going along with this, he'd put us out of business. Now, he didn't have to do that. I don't know if he didn't think about it that much, or . . . I don't know.

She plans to adapt to the new situation and keep running her cattle, but she sees the end of the older era.

Obviously, if Carl [Awtrey] and I hadn't got married, I'd have been out of [ranching]. In fact, I had intentions of selling the cattle last fall. But there's no way the ranch could make it—I don't care who you are, how many kids you have to help you, or anything else, these little old ranches cannot make it on their own. You've got to have some supplemental income. And that was *before* the cuts.

Our old Blue River looks like it may be coming to an end. . . . I'm afraid there will come a time when the Robards will have to sell off their private land and go elsewhere, or subdivide it.

It's kind of frustrating and discouraging when over the years you've spent the kind of money he and some of us have in improving this darn Forest permit; we've spent lots of money on corrals and fences.

It seems that people don't have as much time as usual. . . . Two jobs. Meetings: you could go to a meeting every day in the world, if you wanted to. The wolf, there's just something all the time. You can write letters, spend hours every day, writing to your congressman. (Awtrey 1998)

In an interview with *The Washington Post* later the same year (1998), Rose admitted that, given the few cattle allowed her, her VM Ranch just "doesn't pencil," though outside income might keep her on the Blue. "'Depends on how good the log house business is,' she says with a laugh" (Kenworthy 1998c).

Mona and Bill Bunnell

BLUE, ARIZ.—Far down the steep canyon formed by the Blue River, Mona Bunnell and her husband, Bill, climbed into their Dodge pickup on the morning of June 8 [1998] and began a long and somber drive from the MM Ranch to the local U.S. Forest Service office in Alpine, Ariz.

They carried with them a three-paragraph letter from Mona's parents to the Forest Service district ranger, Phil Settles, who is the face of the federal government in this isolated region of eastern Arizona where the jagged beauty of the Blue Range leads up toward the White Mountains and their distant snows.

The letter, signed "Respectfully, Herschel & Ramona Downs," had a formal, deferential tone that masked an ineffable pain: This was a death certificate for the MM. The ranch, nestled under sycamore, cottonwoods and walnut trees where KP Creek flows into the Blue River—a cool oasis in dry country of dramatic cliffs and steep hillsides speckled with pinyon pine and juniper—was going under. Citing the government's recent environmental review of their grazing permit on 45,000 acres of the Apache-Sitgreaves National Forest, and its directive to reduce the size of their herd from 225 cattle to 46, Herschel and Ramona Downs concluded: "We are forced to accept the fact that there is no way to continue to operate this ranch." (Kenworthy 1998c)

So opens a *Washington Post* article, November 29, 1998, by Tom Kenworthy, entitled "Grazing Laws Feed Demise of Ranchers' Way of Life." With elegiac overtones, it summarizes the denouement of the 1995 NEPA cuts.

The Downs's anguished concession concerned only them, but it may also turn out to be a kind of death knell for nearly all ranching on the Blue River. Half a dozen ranches in operation here since the late 1800s are bearing the brunt of a new ethic about public land in America and a litigation war by environmental groups seeking stronger protections for endangered fish and wildlife whose habitat, they maintain, has been degraded by decades of livestock grazing. (Kenworthy 1998c)

The Downs's ranch was homesteaded by the Cospers and named for the MM brand, MM being the initials of Tommy Cosper's wife, Marion McLey. Down the years, the ranch and brand were sold a couple times until in 1945 they ended up in the hands of Herschel Downs, a Kansas rodeo rider. "He liked the country, the people, and the ranch, so he bought it and has been here ever since" (*Down on the Blue* 194). He married Ramona Rehurek in 1954, and they had two daughters, Debra and Mona. Debra married a rancher in the Bloody Basin country of central Arizona, but Mona stayed on with her parents and married a local boy, William Scott Bunnell, who came to help work the MM.

By 1998, Herschel had retired to a care center in Springerville, and his wife had gone to live nearby. (Both would pass away in 2000.) Mona and Bill, with their one daughter, were left on a ranch whose permit had been cut to an unsustainable level. The letter they carried to the Forest Service in November announced their intention to give up their permit and allotments. But they would try to remain on their private land.

I interviewed Mona at the small Blue Post Office halfway down the Blue River Road. She was Postmistress and sole employee. The office was open a few hours, three days a week, but she did rural deliveries to the end of the Upper Blue road, where the Downs's ranch lay. The interview was August 5, 1998. They would sell their cattle on the first of September. Were they going out of business for good?

> I think so. I don't think there's a chance of getting back, personally. When they wanted to base it on the forage and the condition of the range, there was something you could fight. You could go out there and show them that you had the feed for animals. But when they brought in the Endangered Species Act—if it is habitat or potential habitat, they can take you off of it or restrict your use of it or whatever they want to do. In my opinion they could [close down] New York City with potential habitat if they wanted to. So it kind of leaves it up to them to say what they want or don't want, and that means we're going to have trouble fighting it. . . .
>
> The loach minnow, Apache trout, goshawk, and spotted owl—I guess were the ones. Our mountain country was hardest hit. It was a little of this pasture and a little of that pasture, and you either go in and spend thousands of dollars fencing those little areas where your cows can't get to them, or else you don't use them. These are areas where they say the goshawk feed, where the owl feeds, and these are the areas they would require you either to fence off or not use the entire pasture. . . .

(Mona and Rose Awtrey's arguments against the Forest Service fencing off pasture, purportedly to protect the loach minnow, are recounted in chapter 12.)

Mona is convinced the whole NEPA process was unscientific and arbitrary, a façade for a plan to shut down ranching on the Blue and eventually acquire the private property there.

> [Now the Forest Service has] got the precedent set of all of us who've gone under. . . . So in my opinion, they won. And that

means they're going to use that as a device to pressure the next one. I personally feel like they did a tremendous job of studying their people and picking their victims. If you look at the ones up and down this river that were hit first. Miriam Robart, she's in her 70s; she can't get extra finances; she has to pay her son to run the ranch. So you know that one's easy to put in a bind. My folks were the same thing. My Dad is now eighty-five years old, unable to run the ranch on their own anymore, they have to hire help, and even if it's family it means you have to pay them. Rose was at the time unmarried, her husband had just left her, it was a situation of a very depressed, down woman who's not the type to be a liberationist and stand up and holler and make a big a deal of it. So they knew they wasn't going to have to fight a situation like that. And then the Quinslers: he now has Alzheimer's. They have the money, but there's no way they can fight it with him in the condition he's in. To the Quinslers it's a summer place, and they can enjoy it the same with having the private property as they could having the cows. So somebody really used their head, in my opinion, when they picked the first people [to cut using NEPA].

(The NEPA assessment was done for the first time in 1995 on the Apache-Sitgreaves Forest. It was scheduled for people whose permits needed reviewing after ten years. However, there were many more candidates than could be assessed that year, so the Forest Service chose whom to go first. Hence Mona's belief.)

> I think it comes down from Washington. It's Washington's plans that want these lands shut off, they want [the people] out. It's always been a speculative thought, since Mo and Stu Udall [Arizona politicians and environmentalists] wanted it for Wilderness. And they got it put into Primitive, and there was such a big issue about it, and we managed to fight it off from Wilderness for years, and it is now the last and only Primitive Area in the U.S.
>
> They could have Wilderness with a corridor of private lands down the center. . . . It doesn't really suit what they want. They prefer to get ahold of the private. I have no use for Babbitt whatsoever [Secretary of the Interior under Clinton at the time]. The man is from Arizona but that don't make him good. . . . But I feel

it is coming down from Washington. They want these areas, and they'll get them regardless of how they'll get them.

It's frightening to me to think what the poor world's turning into. . . . I don't see the freedom we're supposed to be having. I don't see where it's there any more. Whenever they can dictate what you can do on your private property, you're losing your freedoms. You see more and more of that all the time.

Mona agrees with Blue neighbor, Dr. Luce, who thinks the spirit of community on the Blue has suffered.

Yes. We used to go play volleyball one or two days of the week at the school, just as a community gathering, during the summer. It was nice. People used to have time to get together and have a party and enjoy it. Now we get together and discuss all the bad things that are happening, and everyone goes home depressed, if anything worse than when you arrived!

I guess I spend too much of my time feeling heartbroken and devastated about what's going on. Now I get to watch my own parents, and all the neighbors I've been close to, lived next door to. And it is a very horrible thing just to see people emotionally broken over what's happening. And all they've done is spend their life trying to take care of the land and do what was right for it. Someone who's passing it down from one generation to another is not out to destroy the land. . . . That's not what's in their minds. So they have tried desperately to take care of it and make it a profitable business, and something they can be proud of, and their kids can be proud of, and grandkids and on and on and on.

You hear people say that there are the cattle barons who've destroyed the land, who were around for years, who were selfish and wanted all the cows they could stack on there, and fatten them and sell them and make a fortune—well, the cattle business is not that lucrative to start with. Maybe once there was that kind of business, but there certainly isn't today. Now it's one that people just barely get through. If you got enough cows you can make a little living off of it, but you're never going to be a rich person. And you certainly don't destroy something you're wanting to pass on to your kids. So it is just heartbreaking to watch what [the government is] doing with no real basis. . . .

How will the Bunnells manage after they sell their cattle?

> Well, we're going to rent cabins and have a guest ranch. Something's got to happen, or else we're going to end up having to sell the private property. I've spent my entire life here, and I refuse to believe that's going to have to happen if I can have anything to do with it. . . . And we do hunters in the fall; we do elk hunts and such. We have friends we work with for the hunting. . . . But the cabin rentals is something that's essentially new, we've done a little bit of it before, but only a little bit. (Bunnell 1998)

The Bunnells put these and other plans in motion to adapt and stay afloat. The next two summers I found Bill Bunnell unavailable for an interview, as he was mostly absent from the Blue. I learned he was in Tucson training to be a prison guard. During the Christmas season I received a holiday form letter from the Bunnells that explained what the Downs were doing and included a brochure advertising their ranch: "The Downs' Ranch Hide-Away is Bill and Mona Bunnell's pride and joy, located in scenic Blue, Arizona. In Eastern Arizona, at 5,200 feet, this is the perfect get-away!"

> Dec. 31, 2000
> Dear Friends,
> Another year has come and gone and tomorrow starts 2001—WOW does time ever fly!
> We hope you all had a joyous Christmas and may 2001 be a beautiful, exciting year for you.
> Our lifestyle has seen several changes in the past year. Bill entered the academy for the Arizona Department of Corrections July 3 in Tucson and graduated seven weeks later to immediately begin work at the prison in Winslow. He got special recognition as an expert with a 9mm handgun. We're real proud of him! He was transferred to the Apache Unit, between Springerville and St. Johns, in late October and works graveyard shift, so he has three days a week at home.
> We're still operating the guest ranch with trail rides, Indian ruin sight seeing trips, photography trips, etc. along with Bill

continuing to be a licensed Arizona guide and taking hunters (primarily elk) in the fall. . . .

Mona is still Postmaster at the Blue Post Office (which is only open three days a week), works as a part time caretaker for one of the neighbors and is building a fair clientele for her Deer and Elk antler lamps.

She was President of Blue River Cowbells this past year; is helping plan a Blue School Reunion for summer 2001, and in general stays quite busy; which she must right now as she lost her mom, Ramona Downs, in early November.

Marci Jo is growing so fast, turned 11 in October and now is 4'11¾" tall, only a little over 3 inches to overtake Mom, she can't wait! 2000 was her first year in 4-H, she showed her horse, Snip, in the County show and placed second in Junior Showmanship at Halter, also was in Junior Western Pleasure and the Junior Trail class, AND had so much fun! She qualified to go to state in Halter and showed against 25 or 30 kids there, she and Snip both got real nervous but learned a lot and did good. We're very proud of her.

Her love for riding grows and grows and she is getting to be quite a good helper on the trail rides as well as cleaning cabins, etc. She is still being home taught, continues to love her chickens (tho' varmints have reduced her flock from 65 to 12 in the past eight months), her cats, dogs, and cows, and basically ALL animals.

Best Wishes for 2001! The Bunnell's (Bunnell 2000)

Filled with photographs, the Downs' Ranch Hide-Away brochure offers cottage rates for $60 per night for two people, $250 per week, organized trail rides, corrals for those bringing horses, and other services.

In June 2001, I was able to sit and talk with Bill Bunnell over the MM ranch kitchen table. A tall, strong-looking, laconic man, he seemed formidable enough to cope as a prison guard.

Bill shared his wife's views that their allotment cuts were part of a government plan.

It was already preordained that they were going to cut us. They already knew what they were going to do. They just punched up a computer model; it's what they ended up using. They punched all the stuff they wanted to into the computer, and it spitted out what they wanted it to. There wasn't any scientific data involved in the process.

I'm sure [the orders] came down from Washington. What they wanted to do is use this area, being as they'd had pretty good success with the loggers—getting them out. The federal judges in this district are very environmental friendly. They've passed many decisions down that have hurt a lot of industries in this area. They wanted to use this area as a testing ground. If they'd get it all through, then a precedent would be set in the courts, and they could use it in other areas. In fact, they *are* using it in other areas at this point. . . . The funny thing is at that same time they were doing the Alpine District, they were doing the Clifton District. They were doing the same thing down there, but they didn't cut the allotments hardly at all down in that Clifton District. But they cut the heck out of us up here.

The Forest Service has expressed an interest in their private land.

They want it all, if they could get their hands on it. I think that's one of the reasons they're trying to take the livelihood away from the ranchers in this area, because they do want all the private property.

They want control. And that's one way of getting that control—take the livelihood away from [the people on the land]. You got to do something to make a living, so you go working out.

I think there'll still be people on the river. I can't imagine the Marks' leaving. They've got a construction outfit that keeps them going, plus Bill's the county road person. He's the one that blades the roads and everything in here. Rose—her husband's got a pretty good business out of here, to supplement their income. Stacys—I imagine they'll stay in here. They'll probably keep the private property. I doubt if they'll be in the cattle business for long. I don't think there'll really be any cattle on the river in probably five to ten years; I imagine they'll all be gone. If it keeps going the direction it is now. You can't keep pouring money into anything you're not making anything off of.

[The Forest Service] had an agenda to meet, and I think they've done it, pretty much. I don't see how they can sleep at night, myself. But some of them, I guess, sleep like babies, because that's what they wanted in the first place.

Bill talked about his other occupations.

Renting cabins has only been going on about a year now, a year-and-a-half. We did some guiding before that. We had some friends that had some lion dogs, and we had some lion hunters, and we had some late elk hunting we guided. It supplemented the income some.

I was a licensed guide. I let my license go this year. I don't have time to be guiding anymore.

But he needed to find other work.

I worked a new job prior to applying to the job I'm in now. I worked with Rose's husband up in Nutrioso at the log works there, about a year. Then I decided there wasn't really any future in that, so I went to work for the Department of Corrections of Arizona. I've been working with them for just about a year now.

It's a job. You're not working with the most pleasant people in the world. But one thing about it, it is a steady job.

Now he receives medical and pension benefits that ranchers don't usually have. "Ranchers can't afford to have them. A lot of people figure ranchers are high dollar people making a lot of money, but you're not, especially on one of these allotments. All the maintenance and everything has to come out."

The Bunnells transferred their allotment to Otis Wolkins, a former electronics executive from Phoenix. Wolkins previously had a second home near Alpine but had recently bought the remote ranch of the Robart family, just down the river from the Bunnells. Wolkins's wife Judy was interested in running a few cattle as a hobby, so they obtained the permits for the few cattle still allowed the two ranches.

Yes. We sold the cattle to Otis. And when we sold the cattle, we transferred the permit to him. The permit wasn't worth the paper it was written on. We sold it to him for the price of the cattle. We help him out sometimes with the cattle.

I still got my horses and everything, a couple milk cows here.
We're trying to get this set up as a guest ranch. But we've got to
make ends meet, so I've still got to work out [at the prison].

Sometimes hunters come in season to rent cabins. There are three cabins
plus Mona's parents' house. People might come for other reasons too.

Eventually get the guest business built up. Maybe taking some
rides—if we can. Trying to get in bird-watchers. There's a number of different type birds in this canyon. Try to set up some type
of a little guest ranch type deal—enough to make a living off of.
    Kind of a remote location. That's one of the drawbacks: it's a
long ways in here. An all-dirt road.

They want to hold on to their place not for the money, but for the way
of life.
    Here [on the Blue], ninety percent of them were raised in the
area. They love the country. They want to see it keep producing.
Like Mona, you know, this is the area she grew up in, she never
wanted to leave it. It kind of gets in your blood after a while. I'm
somewhat the same way. I don't want to leave the area. I grew up
just over the hill from here. My roots are here. (Bunnell 2001)

As *The Washington Post* story comments,

Even in the best of times, the cattle outfits on the Blue River are
marginal economic operations and ranchers here typically work
part-time jobs to supplement their income. But facing grazing
cutbacks as high as 85 percent, their very survival is now in question. Their way of life may be the price to pay as the West enters
a new era, but the human cost is high for the people involved—
few in number but rich in western heritage. . . .
    "There are a few of us who were raised here from the time
we were tiny little kids, who tend to make the comments like,
'They'll take our private places from us over our dead bodies,'
Mona Bunnell said, searching for a way to describe what living
on the Blue has meant to her. "We're pretty badly homebodies.
We never really wanted anything else. We've lived by the rancher
motto: 'Mind your own business, leave people alone, let them do

their thing and expect them to do the same to you.' Which really hasn't worked so well." (Kenworthy 1998c)

TIM ROBART

Tim Robart, the Bunnells' neighbor to the south, [is] the last rancher on the upper Blue before the road peters out.... With his bushy black mustache, his easy laugh and his finely tuned ironic humor, he is a rancher straight out of central casting.

He, his wife, Diane, and two young children got by on about $20,000 a year, half from the ranch and half from his part-time work on the county road crew. And yet, with his arm sweeping over the view and his mind wandering over the wholesome upbringing his children are getting, Robart insists he's "the wealthiest man in the world."

Like Bill and Mona Bunnell, however, Robart has had to throw in the towel on the only kind of life he ever wanted to lead. Forced this summer to cut back his cattle from 72 to 16 head, Robart has sold his ranch. (Kenworthy 1998c)

In August 1998, I came to see Tim Robart at his ranch at the end of the Blue Road. Now it is officially the "Elk" ranch (after its brand, a backward "E" with an L and K; but many on the Blue still remember and call it the "Y Bars" (or Y Bar Y) as it was known historically. One of the oldest ranches on the Blue, it was homesteaded by the pioneer Toles Cosper (see chapter 1) at a location on the river that could be irrigated for crops; he named it after the brand he owned. When he quit ranching, he sold the brand to Freddie Fritz, but the ranch retained the Y Bars name as it was sold, and resold, through a series of other ranchers (*Down on the Blue* 216).

Around 1971 the ranch was sold to "Dink" and Marian Robart. Dink was a cotton and alfalfa farmer who also had a cattle feedlot near the Salt River Indian Reservation in the Phoenix valley. For ten years he and Marian would vacation on the Blue in the summer, while letting Clell and Katherine Lee (Rose Awtrey's parents) manage cattle for them on their joint allotments (Fish Creek, Fish Hook/Steeple Mesa, Hannagan). Their son Tim, a Vietnam veteran just out of the Marine Corps in 1971, arrived to help the Lees work their cattle. In 1981, in semiretirement, Dink and Marian moved to the Blue, where Dink could practice a little farming off the river while leaving the cattle ranching to the others. Tim's brother Dave also came to the area, and eventually started a goat ranch near Alpine.

By 1998, Dink had been deceased a number of years, buried near the ranch airstrip, which a previous owner constructed. Marian had her own little house, and Tim had the original Y Bar Y ranch house for his wife, Diane, his two little daughters, and two-year-old son. But Tim and his mother had decided to sell the property.

> The deal is being drawn up as we speak, and there will be certain deed restrictions. My Mom will stay here until she decides otherwise, which I doubt she will, for this is her home, and she'll probably be buried next to my Dad on the airstrip. And the rest of the kids in the family, we were taught that if you want something, you get out and work for it, you obtain it that way. . . .
>
> As far as the livestock industry, I have the intention of staying alive in it, but it won't be in the capacity as I know it here. This was a little old Ma and Pa operation, what we call a "heartbreak outfit." Just enough between this and working the county roads, and the combination of the two of them, I was able to keep my family structure together and keep us off the government rolls the best I could. I could make about ten [thousand] a year off the county, and ten a year off this ranch, which I considered a heck of a nice living, because that was after my overhead. I thought I was a millionaire. This is my back yard, 160 acres of it. . . .
>
> But it's all coming to an end.

Like other Blue ranchers, he consciously identified with his "culture" and "way of life."

> There's a whole lot to say for the culture behind this way of life. I could bring ten men out here with their families, and give them the same job and same opportunities I have, and a year later there wouldn't be one family left in here. It takes a unique individual. This is a hard old country. It's a hard old life. But to me, this was a sanctuary; this was my back yard, as far as I could see. It isn't mine [it belongs to his mother], but it's my feeling which evolved from being right here. Nobody could touch you.

When my Dad got me in here, I was just a kid, fresh out of the
U.S. Marine Corps, twenty years old, hell, and I'd already served
three years in the military, and he says, "You know, you're going
to have to wear coveralls on the job, you're going to have to beat
your brains out here. But you can make a living, and then by
God, you're king of the world, no one can touch you."

The only decent thing about my Dad's demise is that he was
not here to see the crux of what's going on. . . . So I'm angry,
I'm real angry. But there's no way of venting my anger. I can't
do it via attorneys, because I can't afford them. Most of them
don't want to take up the fight. People don't give a damn anyhow.
They're not concerned with what's going on with me and my
family. People are out of touch with my way of life as I understand it. It's not going to be available to me in the future.

To stay in this industry, I'm going to take a few of these old
cows here, because I hate to just send them all to auction. I have
some old cows here who've worked as hard as any of us have to
keep me in business, and done me right every year. I just can't
give them up. That's another thing—being in this business, you
just got to love them old cows. If you think you're here because
of the money, you're all wrong. It's all lifestyle, that's all it is.
(Robart 1998)

He regards the sixteen cows left on his permit by the Forest Service
as a laughable number.

Yeah, I can keep that in my front yard. And among that sixteen, I
got to have one bull, so that's fifteen calves. I've got to have four
new heifers coming on along among that sixteen, so that's now
down to eleven. When you got that few calves, they're going to
run together, stick together, and when they do, the predators are
going to eat on them. I'll be lucky to produce four or five [calves]
in a year. And they [the Forest Service] know it! It's obvious to
them.

Like other ranchers, Tim believes the sharp permit cuts were based
on a political decision at the top, not on any scientific evidence; the numbers were "preconceived." He believes the Forest Service has totally
changed, from supporting local communities to sacrificing them to environmentalism.

We went through an era for half a century, when the FS was behind their communities,...and there was an old guard there that believed in building logging roads, and believed in logging sales, and knew how to take care of the forest, and knew that they needed to be out there to take care of it, and there wasn't such [a clamor] for not having any cattle out here. And you dealt with [the Forest Service], and they made things difficult from time to time, but if you stood your ground and showed them common sense about what was going on in your allotment plan, they could be met at the table, and it wasn't really comfortable and it wasn't terribly uncomfortable. You dealt with them.

But that old guard has long since gone, and the new one that has taken over in the past ten to fifteen years is of another nature. And [the new guard] told [the old guard], "Hey, it's a whole new Forest Service and we're environmentally backed and we're environmentally inclined, and unless you guys come aboard and do it this way—your careers—you're going to have to take a lateral move, you're going to end up somewhere else, doing something you don't want to do."

There are guys up here [in the Forest Service] who know what's going around, and there are guys who were in that office fifteen years ago that would have stood up and said, "Hey, up until this point I was riding for the brand, but you guys are doing to my community what is not healthy for it, and you're putting families out of business on a daily basis—I'm not going to be part of it, guys, I'm taking early retirement, or I'm leaving here, or you better give me a different position, because I'm not going to be part of this." But instead you have guys up there now that run around smirking and clapping their hands. You have range cons [range conservation specialists] whose wives run the White Mountain Nature Conservancy League [an environmental organization, critical of ranching]. It's a total environmental structure.

Tim is planning to sell his property and permit to "a friend of the family who has a lot of money, and will keep the deed restrictions in there that I want for my mother and father."

He's a very dynamic individual, and since my father passed on, the guy's taken me and my family under his wing, and he's a

wealthy man and a generous man, and probably the reason I've
kept my sanity has been because of him. . . . This will enable my
mother, who is seventy-eight, to live her life out the way she
would like to.

This friend is Otis Wolkins, mentioned above in Bill Bunnell's story.
What Tim also likes about him is that Otis shares Tim's view that the
government should never get its hands on the property.

For the present, Tim plans to keep living on the ranch as a caretaker
with his family, but he will go out to run his cattle on other allotments.

Well, my intentions are that there are two or three little outfits around a spot in New Mexico, a friend of mine owns one
over there—little permits, FS permits, but they're not on these
shrines like the Frisco or the Blue or the Gila. [The Forest Service
is] not hitting those people as hard. Right out of Silver [City],
up against those Mogollons that don't reach the Gila. Little old
heartbreak outfits like this, but if I go in and stock two or three
of them over there, I'll do what they call gypsy ranching. I'll
lease these broke-down poor outfits from these old boys and run
cows on them while I can, and harvest my yearlings and calves
off of them. It's nicknamed "gypsy ranching." I'll have to travel
a lot, and I'll be dislocated from my family and whatever, but it's
something I will be able to do to stay in the industry. I'm too old
to retrain. I've got no more business making someone's computer
chips for him down in Tucson than I do flying a B-29 bomber.
Alpine's getting to be too big for me! [Laughs.]

Tim figures he might be able to invest in small pieces of land in
New Mexico, keep on ranching until he's broke—anything to support his
family.

I turn on the television day after day and listen to our President
[Clinton] tell us how important it is to keep your family structure together, and to work for your family. . . . But yet everything he's doing out there is breaking mine into bits and pieces.
Dislocating me. Making me have to spend time away from my
family to support them.

My Mom's health's good right now. I got my little boy, my
daughters, my wife. Five years ago, I had the world. Five years

ago I thought I was the richest man in the world, and my wife was happy, just crazy about this place, kids raising animals, looking forward to going to that little school, and learning things, and learning values I want to see them get. And I'm not going to hide them from that world out there, but when they decide to make a step out into there, they'll at least be prepared, and they'll have a few of the values and morals that I think are important.

And small scale as I am, I was always proud of the livestock industry, or agriculture, because I was a producer. People were consuming my product. I was helping. (Robart 1998)

The following summer of 1999, I find Tim still living with his family on the ranch, but he had given up trying to ranch in New Mexico. "It just wasn't working. It was like trying to be an absentee rancher." The place was too far to take care of and still be with his family. Also NEPA threatened the new areas too. He sold off all his cattle in New Mexico. "So I came out fair."

He has a year or two of work with Mr. Wolkins, building improvements on the ranch. Eventually, he thinks, he will end up driving heavy equipment somewhere for a living. He doesn't want to move his family out of the Blue, but he won't have a choice in a few years. He has taken up smoking again due to stress (Robart 1999; 2001).

By the summer of 2000, however, I discover he has bought one of the two general country stores in Alpine, and he and his wife are running it. In June, 2001, I have a chance to interview him beside the brightly colored flowers he has planted outside the store, on the highway through town. "I didn't want to leave these mountains. I had no place to go. I wouldn't survive in Phoenix, Tucson, Albuquerque. I'm not made that way. I'd go—I was on the edge of going insane, I was so upset, [when] it finally hit home that I had to leave" [the ranch] (Robart 2001).

Before the store, he was in the hospital with a bleeding ulcer. "Man, I was over the edge." If it hadn't been for his family, his wife, and his mother, he didn't know what would have happened.

He thought he would go back to driving tractor-trailer trucks. But he discovered the general store in Alpine was for sale. "Diane and I, when we got it, did everything by ourselves. . . . I start in here at eight o'clock in the morning, and I don't finish sometimes until two or three in the morning. . . ." He's putting improvements into the store himself because he can't afford to hire people. He also has another job in the mornings, pouring concrete.

Otis Wolkins cosigned for the purchase. Tim, as always, has only praise for Wolkins.

> He's a man of his word, he's got integrity, and when he tells you something, you can bank on it. . . . I said to Otis, there doesn't need to be anything written up [when he sold him his ranch], but I would really, really like a handshake, your word, that whatever happens to this ranch, it will never be traded to the government. He knows. He doesn't want the government to get their hands on it.
>
> I wasn't crazy about this store, but if you had to move, it's about as good a move as you can make.

He could be home with his family, his wife Diane could work in the store. She does the books, and they have a home in back. It's a four-acre commercial site, and the property will appreciate. He wanted his mother to live with them in Alpine. But she went to Phoenix to live with his brother and to be closer to good medical care. He says he would never let his mother live in a nursing home.

He'd like to go back to ranching, given a chance. He doesn't like Alpine (year-round population 256): "Too much traffic, cars all night long." Otherwise, it's a good situation.

> I told someone, "At least we don't have to mess with that government any more." Well, hell. If you look at my bulletin board over there, I had to make a trip to every office, pay a $200 fee to every office, liquor license, business license, second-class pharmacy license, there were fifteen other things I had to buy. I don't know why they don't put it all in one little package, and charge you fifty dollars. But no, you have to fill out all these forms and send them to Phoenix.

He was also investigated on suspicions of butchering wild game in the back of his store, which violates some regulation. Undercover agents tried to entrap him into butchering.

He has Forest Service customers, people he knows.

Oh yeah—you'll love this. I had to sign a contract with them, see. You wouldn't believe this contract! There were clauses in there that I was to treat them better price-wise, than my most preferred customer. I told them that every man and every woman that walks in that door is a preferred customer. I'm not going to sign that page. They also wanted "right of acquisition," that if there were an emergency, a big fire, they would have the right to take over my store for the duration. They told me, "It would never happen." I told them, "I was in the ranching business one time, and you told me not too many years ago, 'This would never happen,' and it did." I ended up charging the Forest Service more, not less, for bulk orders, because if they buy me out, regular customers will be disappointed, and I would lose profit on individual item markups, say as on a can of beer.

Former neighbors from the Blue come by.

Most everybody down there has done a considerable amount of business with me. . . . And I've offered them all cost plus ten percent, if they want to come in here when my wife is ordering and order direct from my catalogues, and I'll just tag on ten percent to cost. They were good people, and they saw me through a lot of times.

I'm at peace with myself now. I'm not angry anymore. I try to make it a good situation. I'm extremely happy for my wife and kids. I think I've made a pretty good deal. (Robart 2001)

But things did not go well with Tim. I never had a chance to see him again, because by the next summer, his world had imploded, and he had left the Blue. No one knew the exact story. What was clear was that Tim's marriage had broken down, and his wife had left him. Otis Wolkins, Tim's benefactor, explained in July, 2002,

Tim Robart is in Prescott working in the Sturm Ruger [firearms] factory. His brother Dave is looking out for him. I'm worried about him. He's still distraught over the loss of his wife and family, and now basically he's lost his business. The business is dead. I think the fellow who holds the paper on it is in the process of repossessing it. (Wolkins 2002)

16

Blue Ranchers' Stories

Part II

THREE OTHER STORIES FOLLOW. These ranchers were not victims of the 1995 cuts but suffered from later actions by the Forest Service.

DENNIS AND DOUGLAS STACY

At about the turn of the [twentieth] century Fred Austin Stacy settled in Juan Miller Canyon [on the lower Blue]. The ledge he built for his cabin is still there. . . . He ran cattle there and in order to sell them he drove them to Clifton.

One of the overnight stops he made was at the old H Bar L Ranch, which was owned by David Laney. David had a large family. One of his older daughters was Mary. Mary was her mother's helper. There were five small brothers and sisters to train.

Fred Stacy was so taken with the ladylike decorum of Mary that he waited for her to grow up, then married her. They were married in Clifton on February 14, 1906 by Curry Love, the Nazarene preacher. Mary always said they were married by Love and in love. They immediately went to Fred's ranch, the WJ's. Mary said that there was a dishpan full of doughnuts there when they arrived so her bridal supper was beefsteak and doughnuts. (Martha Stacy, daughter of Fred and Mary, *Down on the Blue* 226)

Fred Stacy came from Kansas and Mary from the Mormon pioneer community in Luna, New Mexico. They eventually bought the LUE Ranch on the lower Blue, where their marriage produced ten children. In the 1990s a branch of the Stacy family still ranched the LUE. But in 1937 one daughter, Fay, and her husband Tulley Moore, bought the Bar 8 Ranch on the upper Blue. After World War II, the ranch's allotment of ninety head of cattle proved too small to support the Moores and their son, forcing them to seek income outside the ranch.

> In 1957 Tulley went to work for the Arizona State Highway Department. We lived first at the Strayhorse camp and were transferred to Grey's Peak where we spent a lot of years. He had to ranch on weekends and whenever Tulley got a vacation, but we managed somehow to do it. We are very fortunate now to have a couple of nephews, Douglas and Dennis Stacy, who have spent a lot of time with us and who love ranching. They have taken over all the ranch work since Tulley is no longer able to do it. Without them we couldn't make it. (Fay Stacy Moore, *Down on the Blue* 112)

Dennis and Doug are broad-shouldered, friendly twin bothers who also think identically. I met with them first in a restaurant in Morenci, Arizona on August 6, 1998, and later interviewed them again at their ranch on June 17, 2000. Growing up, they tell me, their home and school were in Clifton, but they wanted to spend the rest of their time ranching.

> We used to come up here after football games in Clifton or Morenci, we'd get home at one o'clock, two o'clock, get in the pickup and come to the ranch. Get here about five-thirty, six o'clock in the morning. Sometimes after a football game, you're so beat up being a running back you couldn't hardly get home. Sometimes we wouldn't go back to Clifton until early Monday morning. We'd get up about three in the morning, take off, get down there and ready to go to school by eight o'clock in the morning. (Stacy 2000)

The Stacy twins could never have supported their families on their mountain allotments. Their winter Red Hill Allotment lies on the Blue. Their summer Grandfather Allotment lies twenty-five miles west, on the Black River, and is named for their grandfather, who first worked there on coming to Arizona. The permit on the allotments traditionally allowed only ninety cows, plus calves. In good years, the calves can provide supplemental income. But the brothers hold regular jobs at the giant Phelps Dodge copper mine in Morenci. Their ranching is mostly for the passion of it—"hobby" would seem too weak a term. To get to their ranch

on the Blue they must drive eighty-nine miles from their homes in
Morenci up winding, climbing Highway 191. The drive takes two hours
and fifteen minutes, if they push it. They work the ranch on weekends,
vacations, holidays, "every chance we get." No one lives at the ranch year
around.

> If my wife and I can put in a mobile home, we plan when we
> retire to live on the ranch. . . . If my wife would retire today, she
> would move up there and leave me here [in Morenci]. (Laughs.)
> It's been in our family a long time. It's a good place to take kids
> to teach them how to work, ride on a horse, and teach them the
> cow business. I think a lot of the problems that we have come
> from there being so few people in the U.S. now who raise food
> for the majority, that people don't realize how much work it is
> and where that food comes from. Our calves we sell to farmers in
> Kansas and Nebraska and Oklahoma, and this contributes to their
> livelihood. Our calves are born in March, April, May, and we sell
> them about the middle of October. We turn out our mother cows
> and bulls then on our winter country, and they run through the
> winter down there, and the cycle begins again. (Stacy 1998)

Because the Stacys have held regular jobs and depended less on cattle
than some ranchers on the Blue, they were also less economically damaged by permit cuts. Nevertheless, the Stacys react just as strongly to
the Forest Service actions. In 1998, they were going through the NEPA
process for the first time.

> We rode with the Forest Service on our ID [Interdisciplinary]
> Team ride back in 1997; and we did about half-a-day ride on a
> portion of our winter ranch country; and the following day we
> did about half-a-day by automobile; and that was about the
> extent of the analysis. They didn't do any measurements, they
> just looked at the transects [areas for measuring plant growth,
> comparing grazed with ungrazed]. They didn't count them [the
> plants]. June is historically the hottest driest time of the year in
> all of this country, and it was before our cattle were moved back
> to the summer country. And that is what they did to the Markses
> too. One of the worst times: it doesn't give you a good picture.
> The so-called range people say that's not the time you do range
> analysis.

And what's really funny was that in fall of 1996 one of the guys, Steve Herman, who had been doing some range analysis and checking the transects, he came up to us while we were shipping calves in October of '96, and told us how good our range was looking, that everything looked like it was on an upward trend since 1961. . . .

And then when they called us in October of '97 to come up to the Alpine Ranger Office, they had already done a preliminary decision, the numbers they gave me over the phone, there was going to be a shade over an eighty-three percent cut on our total numbers: from ninety head to thirteen head on our winter country. And that makes you just want to throw up. It made me literally sick to my stomach when they told me that. When before they'd been telling you how good the range has been looking. . . .

I just wanted to puke. All this work that you do, and you try to work with the agencies, and then you just get the shaft. It's unreal.

The Stacys kept arguing.

We went up in December, and we met. . . . They're saying, We're only going to allow you thirteen head on your winter country, and we're going to cut your summer numbers from seventy-nine grown stock, mother cows and bulls total, to a forty-three or a forty-five. And I said, "My gosh"—this was just a desperation statement—I said, "Can't we at least carry forty-five head on our winter country, then we won't have to buy more cattle or locate more cattle to put up on our summer country. Let us at least keep forty-five head on our winter country. . . . That was just a desperation statement I made. That's not our preferred.

Thirteen would be putting us out of the cow business. You'd have to have at least a couple bulls. . . you'd have nine mother cows. If you could come out of there in the spring with one or two calves alive, you'd be lucky.

The predators will kill the rest. They'd literally put you out of business.

I think they know that there's people who will give up. I think they want people to give up. They sat in the Alpine ranger office and told us, "Guys, the environmental groups, when they get you guys gone, they want to eliminate the hunting guides and get them out of there too." Sometimes I wonder, with them not stocking rainbow trout, I wonder if they don't want the fishermen out too. (Stacy 1998)

Like many on the Blue, Dennis and Doug believe the ultimate goal of the Forest Service, and the environmentalists behind them, is to turn the Blue into a wilderness area and eliminate human activity, including ranching. Dennis, in particular, has looked into ecological issues and is very critical of how government agencies have mismanaged the land.

Another thing that bothers me, is some of the media. . . . They've portrayed the cattleman as the one that's done all this damage, and that's why the Apache trout disappeared. But it wasn't the cowman in the state of Arizona that did it. We had a lot more cows on the country when I was growing up, and I remember going up to KP Creek near Hannagan meadow, and we'd go on picnics and we'd fish for those little natives. And back in the early '60s, the Arizona Game and Fish Department came in and either shocked the streams or poisoned the streams and got the natives out of them and put in rainbow trout. That's when rainbow trout came into this country, and that's what happened to the Apache trout. They gave fisherman a bigger fish, more sporting fish. . . .

My uncle was real aggravated because those little natives were real good eating, and they were a lot of fun to catch. You had to be really stealthy. . . . It was not the cowman, not like the newspapers portray it [responsible for the decline of the native trout]. It was [Arizona] Game and Fish. . . . (Stacy 1998)

Like the Forest Service, Dennis blames the Arizona Game and Fish Department for the growing elk herds overgrazing the mountains. "They make a lot of money on that huge elk herd [selling licenses], and I think it's another way of putting us off the country, to overgraze it with their huge elk herd. That was the reason we couldn't go on top" (to their summer pastures) the past year. The grass had been grazed by the elk to the extent little was left for the cows (Stacy 2000).

The Stacy brothers also remember there once was a lot more water in the streams and river. "In the spring of the year, a lot of times we couldn't drive across the river, we had to get a horse." They used to go fishing a lot. Now there is lack of run-off. "The piñon-juniper encroachment, the Forest Service will tell you, it sucks the water up." The government policy of fire suppression in the forests has caused the problem. The land could be restored to better condition by allowing more fires. "A lot of fires, or some logging. Let people cut wood. We've offered to go out with a chain saw. We've asked them every time we have our renewal, why can't we cut some of these piñon and these junipers? You don't have any grass growing around these piñons—did you ever notice?" (Stacy 2000)

In 1999, Dennis attended a Forest Health Meeting in Pinetop, Arizona, where a forester named Garrett spoke. He said there were 200–300 pine trees per acre now in parts of the Apache-Sitgreaves Forest, whereas in Presettlement times there were only 10–23 pine trees per acre. The loading of dead, decaying wood on the forest floor chokes out grass; also, the crowd of trees sucks up groundwater. Asked who is mostly to blame, the forester said the past practices of the Forest Service, starting in 1929, stopping all fires, has created this situation. The problem has to be addressed, or there won't be forests in twenty years, because of disease and catastrophic fires.

Restrictions on logging have made the situation worse. Timber could be a valuable commodity, but the environmentalists have opposed any tree cutting. However, if one is concerned with saving old growth and endangered species, one must recognize these will be destroyed by the inevitable fires from the build-up of fuel and timber. The forester said, "You're not really protecting endangered species, you're going to destroy them all." After reporting this talk, Dennis stated, "I would like to have some contract or job helping them to clean it back up. I would like to do that" (Stacy 1999).

Because Forest service regulations make so little sense ecologically, the Stacy brothers can only interpret them as anti-rancher: to force people out of ranching.

> Now it's got to the point they don't want us to cross even one cow through the water at any time during the year. We've got a pasture on both sides of the river, and they're not allowing us to cross even one cow through the water, because it might be the taking of a loach minnow. So they say. And the reason we're not allowed to do that, and elk and deer and bears and whatever can cross, is because we're a permitted use. That's the difference. . . .

When we had our first meeting in Alpine, the people who were up there—and those guys are now gone—they told us they didn't see why we couldn't use the river pasture again, it's supposed to be in one of our rotations. They said it needs to be grazed a little bit. Well yeah, we don't have a problem, let's graze it a little bit. . . . We thought we were going to be allowed to use that pasture a little bit, but then the annual operating plan comes out and they'd have to have a consultation with the US Fish and Wildlife Service prior to any entry. And then the amended plan comes out, and this is when all of this Forest Service settlement agreement [was happening] with the Southwest Center [for Biodiversity] and the Forest Guardians, the two of them, and then all of the sudden in our annual operating plan: absolutely no livestock grazing and no cattle crossing the river on National Forest lands. Not one cow, at any time during the year. And we've been told by the Forest Service, Mike Reising, Phil Settles, Buck McKinney, in a meeting, that the critical time for loach minnows is in April and May when they're spawning and nesting. The rest of the time it doesn't make any difference. But yet we can't use it at all. . . . (Stacy 1998)

In 1999, the Stacy brothers learned the verdict. By 2004, their new grazing permit was going to be cut down to the low levels that had sickened them when they first got word: from ninety cows down to thirty-two on the Grandfather allotment, and only fifteen cows on their Red Hill allotment on the Blue. In other words, the "animal unit months" of their grazing permit had been cut by seventy-five percent (Stacy 1999; USFS 2000c).

ABE MARTINEZ SR. AND DANIEL MARTINEZ

"There is a clear trend occurring on the forest lands from Clifton to Alpine," says [Morenci] rancher Jeff Menges. "Cattle have been removed first from the river areas, now the upland areas; roads are being closed at an alarming rate and the Forest Service is acquiring most of the private land in the area. Years ago environmental groups targeted these lands as an area they would like to use strictly for wildlife, with emphasis on introduction of wolves, grizzly bears, and jaguars into the area. While they cannot accomplish these goals in one swipe, radical environmental groups feel they can methodically accomplish their goal by chipping away and attaining one piece of their ultimate goal at a time. Actions from local Forest Service officials over the past decade indicate a willingness to help the environmental groups attain their objectives." (Pitts 2006:7)

SPRINGERVILLE, AZ. The Forest Supervisor of the Apache-Sitgreaves National Forests has announced that impoundment actions will start soon to remove unauthorized livestock on the Pleasant Valley grazing allotment located northeast of Clifton, Arizona, in Greenlee County. About 250 head of cattle apparently belonging to Mr. Dan Martinez are currently illegally using the allotment without authorization from the Forest Service. All of the allotment is located within the Apache National Forest. . . .

Mr. Martinez' father had a permit to graze the Pleasant Valley Allotment from 1948–2004 but refused to sign a new permit in 2004 and failed to pay any grazing fees. (News Release, July 25, 2005, Apache-Sitgreaves National Forest; USFS 2005)

I first met and interviewed Abelardo "Abe" Martinez Sr. in August 2000, at his ranch near the confluence of the Blue and the San Francisco. Surrounded by dry hills and mountains, the 140 acres of private lands of the ranch are a green oasis, watered by irrigation. It is a scenic ranch, its ambience indicated in the name given its surrounding allotment: "Pleasant Valley." Abe Martinez was eighty-three years old at the time, but active and hearty despite back problems.

Abe's father was a Spaniard from Burgos who immigrated to America in 1912. Hearing of the mines near Clifton and Morenci, he went straight to Arizona and got a job. In 1929, he went into goat raising; he had been a herder in Spain. He was soon running 3,000 head of angora goats. During the same period four or five other families immigrated to the Clifton area from Burgos, Santander, and Asturias—all in northern Spain. They had a lot of sheep and goat experience and went right into the goat business in Arizona. Abe's father married a woman from Burgos, Abe's mother. Her parents came from Santander and were also goat herders (Martinez 2000, 2001).

Mohair was a good price. Angora goats is what we had. At that time, they used mohair a lot for suits, and car seats, and stuff like that. I was raised on [a goat ranch], and I'm eighty-four years old, and I was herding goats when I was ten or twelve.

Why didn't you raise sheep?

For the country we were, goats would do a lot better. A sheep likes more grass. And the goats like brush. In that country where we were at, there's a lot of brush.

I used to like the goats for the money and the business, but you have to be with them every day. Herd them on foot. We didn't have any horses, or money to buy feed for them. (Martinez 2001)

The Forest Service restricted and then eliminated goats from its lands, believing them partly responsible for the overgrazing that led to the bad floods of the early twentieth century (chapter 4). However, on BLM and state lands around Clifton, goat herding continued until the Taylor Grazing Act of 1934 ended the open range by requiring grazing permits similar to the Forest Service. And the BLM did not like goats either.

The last bunch of goats was 1937. That was our bunch. The deeded land held the range. But we didn't have a permit [from the BLM]. When they gave us a number [of goats, it was so small] we couldn't make a living there, so we sold them, and then we ran cattle for years.

The goats were hard on brush, oak, mahogany, all of that. They'd work on them so much they were killing off the plants.

Cattle eat plants too. But not like goats. Goats got a little narrow mouth and nose, and they can reach in there and get all those leaves, and peel those plants down to the wood. The goats didn't care so much for grass. . . . But [the BLM] didn't like the goats. So the last bunch I know of was down there by Winkleman. My father-in-law had a bunch of them down there. In the Black Hills over here, Mr. Zorrilla had four or five thousand. My father-in-law [Gomez] had about three thousand over there on the Turtle Mountains, over there behind Morenci. And the Cuetos, they had about a couple thousand down there in the Black

Hills next to Zorrilla. Then there were some other people there, the Lucios, they had about a thousand.

There was no real conflict between the cowmen and goatmen on the open range. "We'd argue a little bit with the ranchers, but not a lot. We kind of agreed on a border. We'd herd them and go to that border and go back from there." Abe claims that in the country north of Clifton, on the Blue, cattle and goat people got along pretty well. In any case, the goat men became cattlemen after 1937 (Martinez 2001).

In 1947 Abe Martinez struck out on his own, buying an old ranch on the San Francisco near the mouth of the Blue.

> When I first bought the ranch, it was all run down. This [ranch] house was built in 1903. Since then it's had several changes. And when we came here in 1947 there was no improvements on it. We had to clean the field. They had some old-timers working here who couldn't do much.
>
> And the first time we came over when I brought my family up here, Abe [Jr.] was about five, I think, and Danny was three, and Bobby was a year old. And we had to pack in—we had to come in over Sunset—and the two oldest boys, we put them in those kayak boxes that you pack stuff on the donkeys. And Bobby I held him in my arms all day, it took from seven in the morning 'til six in the evening to get here.
>
> In the 1940s we could reach the ranch by road along the [San Francisco] river only in the dry season. In May-June, we'd haul our salt; we'd haul 200 pounds of flour and beans. . . . Then we'd just have to go [to town] for little things. We had our own meat. We had sheep and goats, and we had chickens and eggs. We had all the milk we wanted; we had milk cows. And we'd butcher a big fat cow and put it up. We didn't eat too many groceries. We made cheese and made butter. Milk. Plenty of meat. We had beans. We had potatoes. A hundred-pound bag. Ah, things were different from now. (Martinez 2000)

Today, however, the ranch still has no telephone, and has electricity only from its own generator. When the children needed to go to school in the 1950s, the Martinez family moved to Clifton for most the year. In the 1960s, a new year-round road was put in from Highway 78 to the

South, and the old dirt river road along the San Francisco from Clifton was closed; but it's still a long drive.

Meanwhile, over the years, Abe improved his ranch. He had to develop the waters on his ranch himself. As he explained to a journalist in fall, 2000,

> "I scattered the cattle by developing our water. At one time [ranchers] had a lot of cattle here and it hurt the country because they weren't able to spread the cattle out. I could see that when I came here, so I developed water way up high where there's a lot of grass. I also kept cattle out of the lower country when the grass was growing. . . ."
>
> Over the years, Martinez built 26 water storage tanks in various sections of the ranch, and with that water development, wildlife numbers and diversity have increased dramatically. "That's one thing people don't seem to understand," he said. "We wouldn't have half the wildlife around here without the stock tanks."
>
> It costs between $5,000 and $8,000 to build each of the stock tanks on the ranch, more if a well needs to be drilled. Martinez wonders aloud, "Who will be there to make sure the wildlife has water when the ranchers are pushed off the land?" (Shirra 2000:28)

In anticipation of future disputes, the Martinez Ranch consulted a biologist and began monitoring the range (something the Forest Service had failed to do over the years), using sixty different stations around the allotment.

> Using Forest Service criteria to assess the condition of the range, the data indicates that his 23-square-mile allotment should be able to graze 317 head of cattle. Amazingly, the Forest Service will not accept this data.
>
> "Their own criteria said this country would run 317 head, so I proposed to leave it at the 250 head—what we've been running since we've been here. And that's where it stands. We're still in the [NEPA] process. They're even telling us that because of the pressure [from environmental groups], they need to cut cattle numbers in this country regardless of the scientific data or what they see on the range. . . .

"These people who call themselves environmentalists get together and sue the Forest Service for not doing this and not doing that," [Martinez] said. "It's our tax dollars that reward them for doing it. They don't care if a lawsuit is substantial or not. Why? Because bureaucrats push through regulations that are unrealistic and unworkable in the first place. That's the main thing. Too much regulation from people who really don't know what's going on. . . ." (Shirra 2000:28)

Abe Martinez told me, "For years the Forest Service always said that this was one of the best-improved allotments, and we never had any troubles here until the environmentalists got after them. And now they just want to catch you, that's all, make a show to satisfy the environmentalists" (Martinez 2000).

By 2000, environmental lawsuits had forced Abe not to use his riverside pastures, about a third of his ranch, because the distance is too long to fence. The government claims that loach minnow, spikedace, and Chiricahua leopard frog are being threatened, but Abe claims they are not—he has seen no evidence of them even existing in his section of the San Francisco. But the Martinez allotment was specifically named in the 1998 Tucson lawsuit over fencing off riparian areas from cattle (chapter 13), so Abe ceased running animals on the river areas. However, he believes he has a legal right to do so because he has water rights to the river.

He is certain that the Forest Service wants his family to give up and sell out. "They won't say that they will cancel your permit. But they tell you how to run it so you starve to death and go broke." He thinks he sees the handwriting on the wall from what has happened to other ranchers on the Blue. He's had many offers to sell the land: it would be a scenic place for some developer to build on, or for someone rich who wanted to retire away from the world. Or, someone could buy it to trade to the government for commercially valuable land elsewhere. This has happened to neighboring ranches over the years (Martinez 2000).

[The Martinez Ranch] is the last working ranch on this stretch of the San Francisco River. Their neighbors on the river have long since been forced out of ranching for one reason or another. Ultimately, these lands have made their way off the tax rolls and into the possession of the Forest Service through the federal land exchange process.

Martinez doesn't believe the Forest Service will be able to take care of any of the improvements on the range. "They will all just go away," he said. "It's not just the cattle, but the birds, deer and wildlife that will go away, too. Ranchers are the reason why there's so much wildlife in rural Arizona. These so-called environmentalists think that elimination of the range manager will be a good thing, when in reality it will be quite the opposite. No water for wildlife, no supervision of hunters, hikers, and nobody to take care of the trash urban Arizonans bring into the national forests. Do you think the Forest Service is going to take on that responsibility?" (Shirra 2000:28)

Another problem worrying Abe at the time was the uncertainty whether any of his three sons would want to take over the ranch. His oldest son owned seven McDonald's franchises in the distant Pinetop, Arizona, area. His second son, Daniel, who trained as a pharmacist, was managing apartment buildings in Texas.

When I got in touch with Abe a year later, in August, 2001, the issue was still unresolved, and his health had deteriorated. "The ranch is still there and I'm still here. But barely. I've got a lot of pain. I've got a bad back, worse than last year."

What is going to happen to his ranch?

Well, I'm sure the ranch will stay there. It's what's going to happen to me. [Laughs.]

Several people want to buy [the ranch]. I had it sold, and then the boys didn't want to sell it. I don't know; it's a lot of work for them. They got so much business [with their other jobs] they can't hardly do anything with it.

There's nobody to hire here. You can't find anybody wants to work on a ranch.

Who wants to buy the ranch?

Well, the Arizona Game Department would like to have it. It's a political deal. They have to go through all the channels to get the money. Then there's a fellow from up around Snowflake that wants it, and he's got the cash. He's a real estate man. Then there's a lady in Tucson who sure wants to get a crack at selling it—she says she thinks she can get the money from some rich guy. (Martinez 2001)

At the beginning of 2004, Abe Sr. finally did sell his ranch—to his sons. They had decided to not only to keep the ranch but also to challenge the Forest Service by claiming private rights in their allotment. Son Daniel, acting as the family's lawyer, would contend that ranchers on allotments own their water rights and grazing privileges as vested rights. This contention is based on certain legal theories and legal interpretations recently developed by private property advocates in ranching circles. One of the first legal skirmishes had been in the Gila National Forest of New Mexico where a ranching couple had defied the Forest Service. As described in the *Eastern Arizona Courier* on February 19, 2004:

> The fight between ranchers and the U.S. Forest Service regarding the validity of grazing permits on private property is making its way to Greenlee County as the agency struggles to enforce the debate's precedent-setting decision.
>
> Wray Schildknecht is the legal researcher for New Mexico ranchers Kit and Sherry Laney. He said in an e-mail that Greenlee County rancher Dan Martinez will follow in the footsteps of the Laneys as he contests U.S. Forest Service grazing permits on his ranches. The Laneys are involved in the case between the Diamond Bar Cattle Company and the Forest Service.
>
> "Dan filed a Constructive Notice to the Forest Service, giving them notice that he owned the vested fee interest and that it is private property under the jurisdiction of the State of Arizona, not the federal government," Schildknecht said. . . .
>
> Martinez' claim of ownership of the fee coincides with the enforcement of the Laney case. Kit and Sherry Laney are ranchers in Catron County, N.M., and recently lost the ability to graze on their private property.
>
> Gila National Forest Public Affairs Officer Andrea Martinez said on Feb. 11 that access to the area encompassing the Laney's ranch was closed at 8 a.m. She also said the removal of the Laneys' cattle will begin in mid-February. . . . (Kamin 2004a)

Despite the ominous defeat of the Laneys (Kit Laney would eventually be sent to prison for physically trying to obstruct the confiscation of his cattle), Dan Martinez was undeterred. As the *Eastern Arizona Courier* of March 22, 2004, gives the account ("Rancher requests Greenlee's help"),

> Martinez and Hickey ranches owner Dan Martinez and his legal adviser, Wray Schildnecht [*sic*], asked the Greenlee County Board of Supervisors to help him uphold state law on March 16.
>
> Martinez gave a presentation to explain his position in a debate with the U.S. Forest Service over who really owns portions of the two properties. He owns the Martinez and Hickey ranches and grazes on the allotments. The U.S. Forest Service's grazing allotment fees and reductions in the number of cattle allowed on the allotment are part of the reason for the debate.
>
> "If the Forest Service wants to impound my cattle and charge me with trespassing, they must follow the laws of the state," Martinez said. "They have to go to state court for that."
>
> In February, Schildnecht told the Courier that Martinez "filed a Constructive Notice to the Forest Service, giving them notice that he owned the vested-fee interest and that it is private property under the jurisdiction of the state of Arizona."

The article then recounts the story of the cattle removed from the Laney ranch in the Gila Forest.

> The Laneys lost grazing privileges in federal court last December, but Martinez and other ranching advocates are saying the case could be won in state court.
>
> New Mexico State University Associate Professor Angus McIntosh said, "Most land in the U.S. exists in a split estate." He said laws that separate water rights, easements and mineral rights from the actual property itself are at the heart of this type of legal argument.
>
> McIntosh used the stretch of Highway 70 east of Safford as an example. He pointed out that while the land was federally owned before the highway existed, the federal agency owning the land gave the state of Arizona an easement to build the highway on its land.
>
> "Once Congress granted that easement, that easement became the property of the state," he said. "An easement is pri-

vate property, even though it may cross over land that the federal government owns. . . . The federal district court doesn't have the jurisdiction to rule what is defined as property."

Dan Martinez went back to an 1839 ruling, *Wilcox v. Jackson,*

"[W]hensoever a tract of land shall have been once legally appropriated to any purpose, from that moment, the land thus appropriated becomes severed from the mass of public lands."

Greenlee County owns the rights of several roads that the Forest Service claims jurisdiction over (when they close the roads), he said.

Martinez noted that some of these rights are referred to as Vested Property Rights. These were granted to ranchers by federal adjudicators in the late 1800s and early 1900s to help settle land disputes. This included easements addressing grazing paths, water rights and more.

Schildnecht [*sic*] said the Tenth Circuit Court of Appeals (from the Laney case) never questioned this. Martinez said he has had these easements passed down through his family for several generations.

Forest Service Public Information Officer Andrea Martinez and other officials have told the Courier numerous times that the land in question is still owned and must be regulated by the Forest Service. The federal agency has held strong on its stance that it maintains jurisdiction over the grazing allotments and its right to revoke permits for the allotments or reduce the number of cattle on them. (Kamin 2004b)

A somewhat different account of the legal basis of the struggle emerged later in a report, "Showdown in Greenlee County," appearing in *Paragon*, the magazine of the Paragon Foundation of Alamogordo, New Mexico, an organization dedicated to fighting for the private ownership rights and other interests of ranchers.

Abe had been paying $5,000 per year into a range improvement fund and when he sold the ranch the Forest Service demanded that he sign a "waiver of permit" which the Forest Service said was a mere formality and that the permit would then be transferred to the three brothers. Along with the waiver came a demand that Daniel and his brothers reduce the stocking rate by 25 per cent.... The Forest Service also demanded that they remove cattle from all riparian and river areas. But Daniel then did what most people DO NOT DO when signing a document. He read it. According to the small print if his father signed the waiver of permit he was relinquishing all rights and property to the United States. Daniel urged his father not to sign it and he agreed....

Because Daniel would not sign the waiver the Forest Supervisor for the Apache-Sitgreaves Forest said that Daniel no longer had a grazing permit and on July 25 [2004] the Forest Service sent Daniel a notice of intent to impound unauthorized livestock. (Pitts 2006)

If the legal ins and outs of the case seemed hard to follow, a Morenci rancher tried to explain the essence of the case in a letter to the editor of the *Courier*.

While the Forest Service has rules and regulations to follow, it is nonetheless an unfortunate event any time the heavy hand of the federal government comes down on hard-working, tax-paying citizens. It is particularly troubling when a family that has lived and worked and paid taxes in Greenlee County for generations is the recipient of such negative actions.

The eventual court proceedings that will probably be forthcoming are going to answer some very important questions for ranchers. For example, is it constitutional for the Forest Service to require a rancher to "waive" his permit back to the Forest Service before it reissues it to a new rancher? The Martinezes don't think so, and they believe that when ranchers sign such a waiver, in the process they waive private rights associated with their allotment, some of which predate the existence of the Forest Service.

Can a grazing permit be transferred from one owner to another without a waiver? Where does the legal authority lie for such a requirement? Shouldn't the government be required to, at a minimum, have a court order before confiscating and selling someone's private property (cattle in this instance)?

The courts will eventually answer these questions and more. Similar questions were answered in Nevada in the *Hage v. U.S.*

case. In that case, the rancher prevailed. The Martinez case, while not exactly the same as Hage, will answer many similar questions in Arizona. Regardless of the outcome, all Arizona ranchers should thank the Martinez family for forcing the issue and getting the courts to answer these very important questions. (Jeff Menges, Menges 2005)

Using a new legal approach, the Martinez family was challenging Forest Service practices that had been in place since the first permits were issued. Also, they were trying to enlist county and state governments in limiting federal rights and denying federal court jurisdiction. They planned to fight the federal government as their own lawyer.

Environmentalist groups were not long in demanding a Federal crackdown on the Martinez Ranch. A press release from the Forest Guardians of Santa Fe on May 14, 2005, announced their intention to sue the Forest Service over the issue.

> Coalition sends notice to remove renegade ranchers from National Forest.
>
> A coalition led by Forest Guardians sent a 60-day notice of intent to sue to the Forest Service, U.S. Fish and Wildlife Service, and two Arizona ranchers citing violations of the Endangered Species Act. After more than two years of allowing Abelardo and Dan Martinez to illegally graze cattle on the National Forest, the Forest Service finally cancelled the grazing permit last August and issued a notice to impound their cattle.
>
> However, despite the cancelled permit, Martinez cattle are still grazing on National Forest land, continuing to damage the land and freeloading on the Pleasant Valley and Hickey grazing allotments....
>
> The notice outlines how the Forest Service has taken no action to actually remove the trespassing cattle nor has the agency taken legal action against the renegade ranchers. The U.S. Fish and Wildlife Service was also sent the notice as they failed to take any action against the owners of the livestock despite knowing that the trespass cattle are harming the federally threatened Chiricahua leopard frog, loach minnow, and spikedace. (Forest Guardians 2005a)

On July 26, 2005, the Forest Service announced that it would remove all livestock from the Pleasant Valley and Hickey allotments.

> Members of the Martinez family were issued impoundment notices today and given a last chance to remove their livestock from the National Forest. If the cattle are not promptly removed from National Forest lands, then the Forest Service will contract with a company to gather the cattle into corrals. The State of Arizona Brand Inspector will examine the cattle to determine ownership through brands. After consultation with the State of Arizona, the owner of the livestock may redeem the livestock by submitting proof of ownership and paying for all expenses incurred by the Forest Service in gathering, impounding and feeding the livestock. If the livestock are not redeemed, the Forest Service will sell the livestock at a public livestock auction, and the owner of the livestock will receive any of the value of the cattle once government expenses are recouped. Cattle will be treated humanely throughout the process. (USFS 2005)

Dan Martinez reacted by sending a letter to Arizona Governor Janet Napolitano asking that the state militia or National Guard intervene, as the issue was a state issue. (He received no answer.) The Forest Service avowed that it was proceeding "under federal laws and regulations that allow us to administratively impound anything that's trespassing on the Forest," and that it was not necessary to get a court order. Dan Martinez replied that his constitutional rights were being violated but that he would not resist the impoundment of his cattle (Mares 2005a).

During the summer of 2005, I tried to call Dan Martinez for an interview, but he was out of state and did not want to comment. At the Clifton District office, Forest Service employees would discuss the case off the record. They thought Martinez was following an inexplicable, eccentric, and doomed legal course, but they would not give me access to the records, as the case was potentially headed to litigation. The District Ranger, Frank Hayes, had always claimed that the Forest Service had no intent to put the Martinez Ranch out of business, and that the permit transfer at issue would have been automatic from father to sons.

By September, as the showdown loomed, Dan Martinez said that removal of his cattle would constitute a criminal act by the Forest Service, and although he would not resist physically (like Laney), he would take action afterwards. "I intend to prosecute criminals. There's not even a court order. We haven't seen any legal documents" (Mares 2005b).

On October 22, the Forest Service began removing the cattle. The Paragon foundation, supporting Dan Martinez, issued a press release expressing its view.

Bush Administration Forest Service Raids Ranch Confiscating 300 Cattle

Sheriff Denies Rancher Due Process of Law Protections

GREENLEE CO. AZ—Since Saturday, twenty armed Forest Service employees and rented cowboys including neighboring rancher, Daryl Bingham and sons, have been gathering 300 head of cattle, valued at approximately $250,000, in a para-military raid on the Dan Martinez Ranch in Greenlee County, Arizona.

Greenlee County Sheriff, Steven Tucker, refused to uphold the law by allowing the federal government to seize the cattle without the necessary court order, denying Mr. Martinez his Constitutional procedural due process of law protections.

On October 3, 2005, in an apparent direct violation of both state and federal laws, the State of Arizona Department of Agriculture entered into a Memorandum of Understanding (MOU) with the Forest Service, which by edict removed the Constitutional obstacle requiring the Forest Service to first obtain a court order prior to the seizure of property, in this instance, cattle. The State previously required a court order to impound livestock and this about-face in policy came on direct orders from Governor Napolitano. . . .

Retired Congressman, Helen Chenoweth-Hage (R-ID) and Chairman of the Nevada Livestock Association, which battled and stopped similar cattle seizures in Nevada, pointed out that, "The State of Arizona, under this MOU, is depriving Mr. Martinez of his Constitutionally guaranteed procedural due process of law protections. The State is allowing the federal government to drive away, sell and slaughter his cattle, depriving Mr. Martinez of his livelihood without ever having a day in court. The State is clearly exposing itself to liability for civil rights and Constitutional Fifth Amendment "takings" of property violations." (Paragon Foundation 2005)

The Forest Guardians, of course, saw the matter differently:

"Move 'Em Out!"—Trespassing Cattle Impounded on Arizona National Forest

A year after canceling the grazing permit on the Pleasant Valley Allotment in the Apache-Sitgreaves National Forest, the U.S. Forest Service (USFS) has finally completed the round-up of approximately 300 cattle that have been grazing illegally on public land. In 2002, grazing permit holder Abe Martinez appealed a USFS decision that slightly reduced the number of cattle allowed on the allotment. Despite numerous attempts by the USFS to negotiate with Martinez, he never signed the new permit. In October 2003, USFS reports showed that Martinez told a Rangeland Management Specialist that the "U.S. Forest Service has no jurisdiction over his land and that we need to leave his cattle alone." "His land," ironically, is actually pubic land that is home to the Chiricahua leopard frog, loach minnow, and spikedace—all listed as threatened under the Endangered Species Act. (Forest Guardians 2005b)

The Martinez cattle were removed to Texas and eventually sold. All proceeds were swallowed up by the expenses claimed incurred by the Forest Service and the state of Arizona in the operation ($400,000); the Martinez family received nothing from the sale of their cattle (Mares 2005c).

Dan Martinez, as he warned, brought suit in Arizona courts against the federal government, filing a raft of criminal complaints against Forest Service officers and other individuals who participated in the impoundment of his cattle (Arizona 2006). His suit was eventually moved into federal courts as a matter of jurisdiction. A District Court found against him, and finally the U.S. Court of Appeals for the Ninth Circuit dismissed his case without oral argument (U.S. Court of Appeals for the Ninth Circuit 2009).

Undiscouraged, Dan Martinez in 2010 still had a case pending with the U.S. Court of Federal Claims to validate ownership rights in his ranch allotments (Martinez 2010). He hopes for justice. However, his father, Abe Sr., passed away in 2008.

BILL AND BARBARA MARKS

Bill Marks, the self-proclaimed end of the line of his family ranch, is riding his horse this day through the Blue River, rounding up cattle and calves.

Though there's now phone service for individual homes (they got rid of the party line two years ago) and running water (1957) and electricity (1958) on the Blue, things haven't changed that much from a century ago when his great-grandfather built the family's first cabin.

Marks is chasing after a stubborn cow that won't listen, and the air is filled with sounds of angry mooing, broken by the splish-splash of Marks' horse hoofing through the river and Marks' voice echoing off the bluffs: "Hah! Hah! Get over here, now! Get down from there! Hah! Hah!"

Barbara is riding on the other side of the herd, trying to keep things straight. Today is a day for branding calves and taking care of the other assorted chores.

Bill is 50 years old with an easy smile, gentle lines in his face and mischief in his eyes.

His cows graze mostly on the public lands of the Apache-Sitgreaves National Forests. The WY Bar has the right to graze 112 sections of forest land, or 112 square miles. . . .[T]he Forest Service allows them to graze no more than 110 cattle.

The old ranch house is still there. Bill and Barbara live in it, and just had it remodeled and expanded, but the original timbers from the house still make up the wall. Perhaps the greatest sign of progress in the Marks' lives is that after 110 years, they now have two bathrooms. . . . *(Arizona Republic,* July 15, 2002, Slivka 2002)

The Blue is truly God's Country! No need for a church and its steeple here, for you could not be closer to God than on the Blue. It touches all who visit, beckoning you back, some of us to stay. (Barbara Marks, *Down on the Blue* 128)

Bill Marks's great-grandfather, Henry Jones, and his brother Sam worked cattle out of Texas to Magdalena, New Mexico, in the late 1800s. There, big cow outfits hired them as line riders, gunmen, to fight in the murderous sheep-versus-cattle wars taking place. But the brothers moved on to the Blue in 1890 and homesteaded what is now known as the Marks ranch, or the WY Bar. "My dad told me there were signs of an ancient irrigation system on the place by the early Indians that once lived there six or eight hundred years before," his son Jerry recalled (*Down on the Blue* 119). Henry also ran a small general store and a post office on the Blue (Marks 1998), while Sam drifted on to other places.

In 1895 Henry Jones married a Texas woman named Mary at the forks of the Blue and Dry Blue, on the Arizona and New Mexico line, under a cottonwood called the "marrying tree." This tree became a site of many subsequent marriages, including that of Henry's great-great-granddaughter Ginger Marks in July, 2002. Henry and Mary raised nine children. One of them, Iona, married David "Scott" Marks. As Bill Marks tells it,

> My grandfather came in here from Wyoming and was cowboy-ing for my great-grandfather and met my grandmother. He had taken some college; he was originally from Illinois, I believe. So anyway that was when the Forest Service came in here, and he got a job as one of the first Forest Rangers on the Blue and married my grandmother. And they moved down to Cloverdale, New Mexico and started a family. He got typhoid fever and died. So my grandmother came back here; and she had five kids; and she raised them on this ranch, and bought out her brothers— they got into government tracking or into the mines, whatever old-timers did to make a living. And so she was a real pioneer woman. She had guts. They gardened, and had alfalfa fields, and raised their family here. (Marks 1998)

One of Iona's sons, who stayed to work on the ranch, was William "Bill" Henry Marks. He had met his wife Elaine, originally from Colorado, during World War II. As Elaine told the story,

> A chance came up to move to California with an aunt and uncle. World War II started so I began working in a defense plant. . . . I worked on parts of the B-17 bomber as part of the war effort. I met Doris "Babe" Richardson there, working on the same project. Doris and I became good friends and planned a trip to the Blue to visit her family.

I met Bill on the Blue when Doris and I came to visit the winter of 1943. On November 15, 1944 I met Bill in Phoenix and we were married. . . . (*Down on the Blue* 125)

Iona died in 1980 at the age of 82 and was buried in the Blue Cemetery. But long before then she passed the ranch on to Bill and Elaine, first as operators and then owners. Bill died in 1974, and their two sons, William "Bill" Henry Marks Jr., and Justin took over the WY Bar, which they expanded by buying a permit to another allotment. Justin would eventually marry into another ranch family in Punkin Center, Arizona, and go to live there.

It was in the 1970s that Bill Jr. met Barbara, a city girl who had been born "back East" and who grew up in Flagstaff and Phoenix. As Barbara tells the story,

I first came here on summer vacations following fifth grade. My dad, now retired, was a Postal Inspector. He traveled over much of Arizona checking the Post offices annually to update them on regulations, correct problems, etc. He came home once and said, "I know where we are going for our summer vacation—Blue." And it started our love affair with the Blue. We camped at the Upper Blue Campground and would stay one or two weeks. . . .

I have lived on the Blue since Bill and I have been married. We were married November 25, 1977, on the Blue at the "Wedding Tree" where Bill's great-grandparents, Henry Jones and Mary Keahey, his Uncle Jack and Aunt Lorna Marks, and others were married. Our daughter, Ginger, is the fifth generation on this ranch. In addition to the ranch, Bill also maintains the road here and co-owns a bulldozer with his good friend, Dennis Swapp from Luna, New Mexico.

Some of my favorite activities are doing fun things and going places with my family, Cowbelle potlucks and dances, getting together with family and friends for games and visiting, just being together and enjoying each other's company. We all like to ride, especially Dustin [her son by a previous marriage] and Ginger. I also enjoy being involved in the Cowbelles. There's a lot of satisfaction in going out and spreading the GOOD word about beef and educating school kids about beef by-products. It's very interesting to us too! (*Down on the Blue* 128)

Barbara was a city person, though Bill swears,

> She's a pretty good country gal now. But she's got the where-withal to be around people. . . . She can sit down and talk to people a lot better than I can. And when we go to Phoenix, I get out of the car and turn it over to her, because she can drive in traffic a lot better than I can. (Marks 1998)

Combining a winsome and outgoing personality with organizing skills, Barbara Marks became an articulate spokeswoman for the ranchers' cause. She was active in opposing the 1995 NEPA cuts (chapter 11). She attends many meetings, writes letters, keeps large files of information where she works at home, and is in constant communication with many people on and off the Blue, by telephone, fax, and computer.

The day I first met Bill and Barbara, at the WY Bar in 1998, they were a little flustered: they had just returned from a visit with the Ranger in Alpine. They had brought him a homemade pie. Their permit was up for renewal, and they didn't know the final outcome, but they had seen what the Forest Service did to their neighbors. I asked Bill about their experiences with environmental regulations.

> [These] seem to do less with the environment as [it does with] using this as a tool to try to steal from us. We put this ranch together from the original Cow Flat allotment, which was thirty-six sections, and now we're up to ninety sections. And we've done it the old-fashioned way. We've worked hard, we've borrowed money and paid it off, and that's how we acquired it. So the way I see it is that they're trying to steal a little here, a little there, and make it no longer feasible for us to turn a dollar out of it anymore. And that's why I'm sour on a lot of this environmentalism, because where I want to go is to better all species out here, and the resources—that just makes sense for us. The better we make it out there, the better the cattle are going to do, the better we're going to get along with the governmental agencies and the citizens' groups. But every time we cure one problem, they find five more, and never come up with anything except to say, get all the livestock off, let's get you out. . . . (Marks 1998)

Bill said he leaves all the meetings on environmental issues and endangered species to Barbara: "She's the one in charge of that, because someone has to keep this place operating, and you could go to a meeting every day of the week." He's frustrated at the moment, because the Forest Service has come up with a new management plan in which they want him to keep cattle off his Blue allotments for April, May, June, to the middle of July (when the rains usually have come)—three-and-a-half months when he'd have to move his stock elsewhere. His 240 permitted cows and their calves couldn't be accommodated on his private land for long.

> But Jack, that's when we have our problems here, that's when animal husbandry kicks in on the ranch—during your calving season, that's when you have your retained after-birth, that's when you need to be watching your first-calf heifers that are having problems calving, that's when we do all our vaccinations, branding and ninety percent of our cattle work takes place right then. The rest of the year we spend a lot of time working on our corrals, and water developments, and things like that. But April through July is when we really got to be with our cattle. While Barbara's fixing breakfast, I go to take care of a cow, give it a shot, but under this FS plan, what am I going to do, jump in my pickup and run over to St. Johns or someplace and vaccinate a cow, and drive back here for breakfast, and then go on and do the day's work? It just literally gutted this ranch. We have all our home facilities here, our doctoring pastures and our heifering pastures and our farm and everything that makes that work.
>
> All this ranch would be then would be some winter pastures. And the cruel thing about it is that this is when these cows are calving. These pastures out here are about two fifteen-section pastures, and it takes us about a month just to gather all the cattle out of the rough country out here, and do it right, and be gentle. That's when these cows are heavy with calves, and have these little newborn calves—can you imagine trying to bring these cattle out of these mountains here, load them on trucks, and ship them out to God knows where?

What reasons does the Forest Service give?

Damned if I know. Their rationale in the paperwork was that they think the cool-season grasses are being hit too hard. But it's primarily a browse country out here. . . . They browse the live oak, the mountain mahogany, and several others, plus the gambel oak, which comes out in May. But all of a sudden there is this concern for the cool-season grasses, the blue grasses and the mutton grass—of which I have seen a tremendous increase in that, since we went into a rest-rotation system—since we've had some big fires. This country was overprotected [from fire] for a hundred years, but in the last five years this whole thing has burned, and half of it twice, and it's just made the difference between day and night. (Marks 1998)

The fires have regenerated the land. Bill says he fenced off his riparian areas in the 1970s, he's bought up enough allotments to rotate his pastures so that half his country is rested every year, he thinks his land is in great shape. But the Forest Service gives him no credit for the positive things he's done. Barbara agrees. "Ranchers are trying the best they can to take care of things, because it's in their own best interest. . . . Out on the land you've got to use a gentle hand, otherwise it's not going to take care of you."

Bill thinks the only way he can judge the real value of his permit is in his children's future in ranching.

They have the right to continue on in agriculture. And I tell you this nation needs young people to continue on in agriculture. If this nation can't feed itself, someday it's going to be in a world of hurt, and we'll have to turn to other nations for our food supply. So we've got to keep our young people interested.

Obviously, our land has enormous wealth for its pristine beauty here, and all these endangered species that are rare other places but which we still have in abundant numbers here. So we must be doing something right, I guess. (Marks 1998)

The next year brought bad news. The Markses had bought permits to an additional allotment, and their 240 permitted head should have risen to 380, based on previous numbers. But all their allotments were being cut, down to 110 cattle. The rationale was the same as applied to his neighbors: endangered species on his land, loach minnow, spotted owl, goshawk, Apache trout.

The Marks' were angry with this. The abundance of these species on their property, they believe, shows they were doing well by them, so why punish the rancher? "Why do they want to steal our permits?" (Barbara Marks 1999). Bill was being forced into depending for income more on his road grading and heavy equipment work, which included helping the Forest Service contain the massive forest fires that were now a yearly occurrence in Arizona's unlogged forests.

In January of 2000, Barbara Marks lamented to me, "The face of the Blue River has changed. It's no longer a ranching community, it's a bedroom community." Everyone on the Blue was driving out to work. "It makes you sick to your stomach." (Barbara Marks 2000)

In July of 2001, I discussed the plight of the Blue ranchers with Phil Settles, the Alpine District Ranger, who had signed off on the cuts to the Marks's and others' permits. Settles—like others in the Forest Service at this time—had come under the influence of the "New Ranch" movement (chapter 9). He was advocating new ranching methods that involved "intensive management," constantly moving the cattle to ensure efficient use of available grazing. However, this kind of ranching is labor-intensive, and ranchers have told him they simply don't have enough time or people to do it. He could not cite one rancher in his district ready to use the new approach. Only six ranchers from the whole Apache-Sitgreaves National Forest had come in February to a seminar on the subject. But he thought ranchers were making excuses.

> Oh sure, it can be done. Easy, if you're willing to spend the amount of time. . . . And you've got to get away from making excuses why it won't work—that's the biggest problem in people today. . . . It's more of their human nature to look for an excuse than to look for a way to do something. It takes a person who really wants to make changes to do something. . . . Other folks, they would be more happy to blame the Forest Service. That's a blunt way to put it, but that's what we're getting into.
>
> Our [Forest Service] folks can only make decisions on how management is carried out. We make decisions based on management. If the permittee can't manage at that extent, then we have to go back to the level he can manage at. So what happens

is a never-ending process where they say, "Well, I'm not making enough money so I can't manage to that extent, then you're
going to take more livestock numbers so I've got even less to
manage." So it's just a revolving thing that keeps going down.
What they've got to make a point of is, okay, do I really want to
stay in the ranching business? If I do, then I've really got to make
a commitment to live and meet the standards and guidelines set
for when we do these range studies to meet the laws the Congress has passed.

But what if the commitment requires more hours than they have, and
they can't afford to hire extra people?

They've either got to do it themselves, or they've got to set
another level of management that they can do by themselves. In
other words, you're not going to see in the future a permittee
that ranching is their hobby, a second job. You won't see those.
You'll see people who are totally committed. That's all they're
going to be doing. They're not going to be running here and
working for Safeway during the day, or build homes during the
day. It's going to be those folks that have time to spend twenty-
four hours a day [on the ranch]. That's a commitment they have
to look at. (Settles 2001)

The examples of intensive management Ranger Settles gave were
ranches in the Southwest well publicized by the Quivira Coalition. What
they had in common was scale: large ranches, running many more cattle
than had ever been permitted on the Blue, and enough capital to afford
the hired hands necessary. But Settles insisted it was still a matter of
commitment.

The point I try to get to folks is, hey, tradition is great, but if
you want to continue running livestock on National Forest lands,
it's not going to be traditional. It's not going to be the old cowboy, you put your cows out, you look at them every two or three
weeks, and move them around. That is out. That's not management. We will set stocking levels [low] at that management. People won't like it; they're not liking it right now. . . .

Did he think it possible for someone to make a living using "intensive management" despite the endangered species restrictions?

> They're going to have to, otherwise they won't be in business. I think it's possible. It's a very large commitment. It's not going to be a family—a man and wife working off the ranch—that's not going to do it. It's got to take the family being committed; you have to have the kids involved and everybody else. It's a twenty-four-hour deal, seven days a week, 365 days a year. They've got to be that committed if they want it to work. If it's the lifestyle they like, a lot of people love to do that, that's what they want to do. Other permittees will say, "Heck, no, I ain't going to do that"—they're not going to make it. They're going to have to get out of the ranching business.
>
> It's at the point, where if you want to graze and use permits on the National Forest land, that you can't be a weekend rancher and have the numbers to make it worth their while. We can deal with weekend ranchers—they're not going to be grazing a hundred head of livestock—they're going to be grazing twenty, twenty-five head. . . .
>
> The point is, if you want to get into this, you can't say, I'm going to go to the dance on Saturday night—that's tradition. Go kick up your heels and go to the bar and have a drink and dance with all the ladies and everything else—you ain't going to do that. With intensive management, you can't do it. All your time is going to be spent managing your operation. (Settles 2001)

I wondered whether many Forest Service employees, with their ample government salaries and benefits no rancher enjoys, would be willing to work as hard as Ranger Settles seemed to expect of ranchers. But instead of voicing this view, I asked, what about the Markses, who had been willing to expand their operations before they were cut back so drastically under NEPA?

> I don't know about Billy and Barbara. They'd like to try something. But they feel the commitment they would have to make is not worth going into a system like that. That's the impression I get. That's fine. I'm not saying that's right or wrong. It's an opportunity, an option for people to try. . . . I do think there

have to be changes made. It might not be low stress; it might be something different—whatever they can do. But there's got to be change away from traditional ranching. . . . With all the lawsuits we have to deal with right now, there is no way the traditional ranching is going to survive on the National Forest. (Settles 2001)

A month later, I talked with Bill Marks and told him what the Ranger had said. His response was that the Forest Service was putting up impossible requirements.

I have a track record there, you know, because we went out and bought other allotments and tried to build it into something where we could [ranch full time], and then they just turned around and whacked us like everybody else. You still got to pay the bank, you know. . . .

We had the original ranch my great-granddad had, which was 144 head, and then we bought another allotment, which was 105 head. And then just trying to make it all fit, with the environment, and wildlife, and everything. So that didn't work out, so we went and purchased that other summer allotment over there. And meantime, we were putting in cross-fences and spending a lot of money. And as man-days go, the people I had hired far exceeded having one man around there year around, like Phil is trying to say. And they still cut us, so that's a crock of crap.

Good grief, I had a fence crew hired here practically year around, putting this pasture rotation system in. And of course Ginger and Dusty are here all summer, working these cows, and moving them around. That's the most ridiculous thing I've ever heard of [Phil Settle's statements], because when you add up the man-hours and days, it far exceeds having one person out there [full-time].

What Phil doesn't realize is everything else that goes with making a ranch run. You got to try to farm a little hay, you got to build all the fences and keep your infrastructure up, plus herd the cows around. He's thinking a multimillion type [ranch]. You actually have one person out herding the cattle, day in and day out, and have another crew keeping up the fences and the water.

There would be nothing better than having a crew of five men out there moving the cows around, and watching out for the wolves and the lions, but still you have the basic infrastructure of the ranch to keep up, the fences, the water, and somebody's got to mop the floor and scrub the toilet and do all these other things. . . .

I'm not trying to criticize Phil. But he went to school [university], and probably mom and dad paid for it, and then he got a government job, nine to five, but the real world out here just doesn't work that way.

I can't remember hardly when I had a full day off. I guess if you call going to Ginger's wedding a day off. Those people have this scheme now that you have to have someone out there with the cattle seven days a week, herding them around, but that just shows just how out of touch Phil is with how things are on the ground. Especially on the rougher country down here; it would take one day to get from one cow to the next, let alone the whole herd. (Marks 2001)

Bill has heard of the intensive management model, and other ranching innovations promoted by the Santa Fe–based Quivira Coalition (Quivira Coalition 2004; Sayre 2001). But he doesn't think that model would work in the rugged Blue terrain.

There are certain things that work out here on the land, and it's just been passed down through the ages. I really don't think [the intensive management model is] for our kind of country. That's kind of my feeling. I'm not criticizing it, because they've got some good ideas.

What tickles me is that these little old family ranches involve so much, day in, day out, that Phil doesn't even have a clue. He probably doesn't even know what a busted sickle on a hay-mower is. . . . [Forest Service employees] ought to come work on a ranch for two years, then they'd have a better understanding. On one of these little family ranches, not some big conglomerate deal that's a tax write-off for Ted Turner, but one of these little places, you've been raised on it your whole life, and it's all you know and everything, but you know how to make it happen.

There are days I should be out with the cows, but I have to go cut hay or try to get it in the barn before it rains on it, and so Barbara will have to go and tend the cows and let something else go. But in the meantime [the Federal government] put the wolves in on us, so she can't take the cow dogs, so I'm worried sick she's out there by herself.

One of the biggest rancher concerns about wolves was their tendency to fight with the ranchers' dogs.

Why sure. And running in under her horse, getting her bucked off or something, and hurt her. There's a certain amount of risk out there. . . . And [the government] increases it. . . .

Heck, I don't know. It's just a hard old world out there right now. Like right now, I'm in the shop, working on equipment, trying to patch something up. And you know, [government employees] are home, probably propped up in front of the TV. (Marks 2001)

Bill cites all the vacant allotments in the Alpine District, people running low numbers of stock or none. "The only allotment that I know that is full to what it's permitted, is ours." But he is down to only 110 head, cut from 381 that were permitted only a few years before on the same land—a seventy-one percent cut. Wryly, he remarks,

Yeah, I'd say I've been cut. And a lot of that was me trying to make it work. But to no avail. . . . But Phil doesn't have any cows on his district anymore. He doesn't have anything to worry about. If he had a boarding house, he'd be going broke, because he's got a lot more vacancy than he has numbers out there. (Marks 2001)

The July 15 issue of *The Arizona Republic*—the main Phoenix newspaper—ran a long feature article on the Markses with photographs of Bill at work. The headlines were somber: "Ranchers a dying breed"; "West's once-thriving cattle industry suffering"; "A Changing Arizona"; "Decline of Ranching."

The small cattle rancher in the United States is on a long, slow trip to the slaughterhouse.

In 1970, there were nearly 2 million ranches in the country. There are barely 1 million today, and the trend is a downward spiral. The average ranching family in Arizona earns more than half of its income from off-ranch jobs. . . .

There's no middle in Western ranching anymore. You can ranch 1,000 head and make a living or you can ranch less than 100 and make it a hobby. But in between?

The article went on to discuss in detail, with graphs, the dismal economics of ranching and the burdensome effects of endangered species and other environmental regulations. It cited other ranching examples from around the West, but at the end the article returned to the Marks family: "Bill is outside, . . . getting out of the white pickup with the trailer attached. Tomorrow he'll wake up and drive the 40 miles to the main road, turn toward Springerville and the day job that replaced the ranch job as the primary source of his income."

So, are the Markses dinosaurs?

Barbara, whose movie hero is John Wayne and who has a copy of *Red River* on her video shelf, looks out the window and bites her lip. Then she begins to answer.

"I used to think that," she says. "And then September 11 happened, and I found out there were a lot of dinosaurs out there, who help their neighbors when they need help and do what needs to be done. . . .

"I guess in some ways it's a matter of what makes you happy. Some people are willing to make a little bit less just to live out here and just to say they ranch for a living." (Slivka 2002)

17

Conclusion

For a hundred years we have heard dour forecasts of the demise of ranching and the cowboy in the United States. As a livelihood, as a way of life, as an economic activity, ranching has been written off repeatedly since the late nineteenth century. Yet persist it does.

PAUL F. STARRS, *Let the Cowboy Ride* (1998)

I'm hard-headed, and not going to give up. We love ranching, and we're not going to get out of it. That's the attitude of us old crusty guys.

DENNIS STACY, rancher on the Blue (2015)

TWENTY YEARS AFTER the severe cuts in cow-and-calf herds on the Blue began, the number of cattle ranched there remains at its lowest since their introduction in the 1880s. But ranching persists. And the ranchers endure.

The ranchers endure not just government edicts, but Nature, which continues to play a dominant role on the Blue. It assures variable rainfall with intermittent drought conditions, which requires frequent adjustments of ranching practice.

Nature's major assertion thus far in the twenty-first century, however, has been the Wallow Fire. Originating from an untended campfire on May 29, 2011, in the Bear Wallow Wilderness of the Apache National Forest, just west of the Blue watershed, it became the largest forest fire recorded in Arizona history. It swept over White Mountain communities, threatened many towns including Alpine and Luna, forced the evacuation of nearly 6,000 people, and destroyed dozens of homes and buildings. The fire was finally contained in early July, after burning over 840 square miles.

The July arrival of the rainy season—the "monsoon," as locals call it—brought heavy flooding as water flowed off denuded slopes. Ash and sediment poured into streams and rivers, killing fish. Roads were damaged and closed.

Blue residents were on the front line of the fire and subsequent floods. Many ranchers' summer allotments in the mountains west of the Blue were burned over. The fire nearly reached the Blue River in several places; some people evacuated. Otis Wolkins, living at the end of the Blue road at the homestead pioneered by Toles Cosper, watched with wonder the hundred firefighters "who came from all over" the United States, set up base near his ranch to fight the fire over the next ridge. Bill Marks's construction company set to work with heavy machinery to help contain the blaze, as it had done for previous, more distant Arizona fires.

In the end, the Blue was fortunate. No lost houses, and livestock had been moved out ahead of the fires. Fences burned down on the affected pastures. Given that in recent years the ranchers had been compelled to fence off streambeds to prevent cattle from bothering the minnows and fish with sediment, this theoretical consideration now seemed glaringly insignificant compared to the soil and ash now stirred into the streams. Nevertheless, following the flood, the ranchers needed to restore the fencing and other infrastructure. In allotments within the Primitive Area, as usual, wilderness regulations disallowed the use of machinery of any kind to aid human labor, lest the noise disturb the officially pristine ambience of the recently burned landscape. The Forest Service refused to waive this regulation, which, of course, had been set aside in *fighting* the fire.

The Blue ranchers grumbled about the machinery restrictions. But by now they are inured to living under regulations that seemed to defy common sense.

Some ranchers also had to contend with numbers of wild horses that escaped the Fort Apache Indian Reservation when fences burned. To date, the government has not done much about these horses, which together now with the elk, compete with cattle for available forage.

Ranchers also reflected on the culpability for such a huge fire. In the years leading up to the Wallow Fire, Arizona had suffered a series of abnormally large forest fires. To forestry experts, the underlying cause was the build-up of dense stands of timber, including old and dead trees, creating tinderbox conditions during dry season (Stecker 2013). Many, including some within the Forest Service, had come to understand that the long history of fire suppression, once championed by the agency, had contributed perversely to create such dense conditions. In effect, when fire did come, it would be much stronger and more devastating than the smaller, natural fires of the past.

But ranchers and other critics of forest management saw an additional culprit. The lawsuits of green activists, such as the Center for Biological Diversity, had shut down most logging in the Southwest national forests in the 1990s. Such bans also left trees to grow denser, older, and die, creating great loads of timber waiting for the big fire that would inevitably arrive. In the ranchers' opinion the activists' fundamentalist opposition to logging, as well as ranching, had been neither good for people nor good for nature.

On the other hand, from the tragedy of the Wallow Fire a silver (or green) lining emerged. Despite the ecological and economic damage, and despite all the burned trees, the fire generally improved the grass cover that regenerated in the burned areas. Ranchers and Forest Service agree on this point. Ranchers were forced for a period to remove their stock from the burned pastures and find alternative feed, which was costly for them. But the grass came back more verdant than ever, with less shade and with the old biomass converted into fertilizing ash.

The More Things Change . . .

Or, *the more things change, the more (some) things don't change.* Despite reduced herds, and despite the catastrophic fire, Blue ranching continues. The ranchers' nemesis also continues: the passel of threatened and endangered species, and the lawsuits and grazing restrictions they bring.

As of 2015, new species of concern on the Blue were the New Mexico meadow jumping mouse, the western yellow-billed cuckoo, the narrow-headed garter snake, the Chiricahua leopard frog, and the narrow-headed garter snake. Due to limited resources, U.S. Fish and Wildlife studies and consultations with the Forest Service tend to drag on, and so does the settlement of litigation brought by activist groups. And wolves continue to roam the Blue and occasionally present a problem.

A proposal to designate the Blue a "Wild and Scenic River" under the 1968 Act of the same name was floated by the Forest Service, arousing the same opposition among the ranchers as the perennial proposal to designate the Blue Primitive Area an official wilderness. Regulation was the main apprehension. In Judy Wolkins's words, "It would take more of our freedoms away, and we don't want it." On the other hand, Ryan Domsalla, who works on recreation issues for the Forest Service, has told me the agency study was not going to recommend the listing—"though it *does* have the characteristics" that would merit such a designation.

Another recent commotion was caused by the U.S. Postal Service's proposal to close the Blue post office (along with many other small post offices). Community meetings were held; protests were lodged. As a result, the Blue post office went from being open three days a week to being open five!

The other symbol of upper Blue community life, the Blue School, also thrives, with fifteen students—up from the past. It now includes high school students.

The postmistress estimates about fifty-two people now live on the upper Blue; another thirty-three reside seasonally. Most nowadays are not ranchers. Some are retired. Some maintain second homes. Some are professional people. In the past, at hearings on the Blue on the wolf issue, non-ranching people have shown solidarity with the ranchers.

Who is ranching, and who is not, has changed some since the 1995 cuts. The Bunnels, forced out of ranching, still run their guest "hide-away" in the Primitive Area, while Mona still works as postmistress of the Blue. Her husband Bill now works now for the town of Alpine (see their story in chapter 15).

Former businessman Otis Wolkins (mentioned also in chapter 15) and his wife Judy continue to live at the end of the Blue Road, on the land once homesteaded by Toles Cosper. They are retired, but are keeping thirty cows and their calves on their allotment.

Tim Robart once lived and ranched at the Wolkins place. Like the Bunnels, he was forced out of ranching by the 1995 NEPA cuts (chapters 10 and 15). After family and legal vicissitudes, he eventually returned to Alpine and was working in construction when he had a heart attack and died. He was buried in a family plot near what was once his family's ranch on the Blue.

Doug and Dennis Stacy (chapter 16) continue to run cattle on their Red Hill and Grandfather allotments as a sideline because "we love doing it." Recently the Forest Service allowed them to expand their herd to forty-five head in a three-year trial.

Dan Heap, of St. Johns, who testified at the Las Cruces trial, still runs his 190 head on his summer pastures of the Upper Campbell Blue.

Dr. Luce, with health problems, still keeps a small herd on his private land on the Campbell Blue.

The Quinslers gave up cattle after 1995. After that year Rose Awtrey kept running the small number of cattle still allowed her but recently decided to transfer her allotment. "I only have *five* cows!! Just keep them on private land (which isn't much!). Yes, the allotment went to the Marks' kids, but I *had* to keep a few to play with!! They are total pets!!" (Awtrey, e-mail communication, June 11, 2015).

Significantly, a new generation has entered ranching on the Blue, as Rose indicates. Bill and Barbara Marks's two children, Ginger and Dustin, and their spouses have formed the LWJ Ranch, named after a brand their ancestors brought from Texas. They now ranch some of the former Quinsler and Awtrey allotments and run over ninety cows plus calves. Bill and Barbara themselves retain their original allotments, running 110 cows plus calves in the winter and 126 in the summer. The numbers are not nearly enough to support these families economically, but as in the past the Markses have their construction company, which employs their son-in-law, while their son has a job for the County maintaining roads. Ginger teaches school in Springerville. Overall, the Marks family constitutes a going business.

Four allotments on the upper Blue (the Alpine district) are currently not being grazed. An environmental assessment of the Lower Campbell Blue years ago led the Forest Service to reduce livestock numbers so low that the rancher then "waived back" his permit to the Forest Service, which put the allotment in "non-use." According to the Alpine range specialist, "There has been some interest expressed by a few folks to obtain the permit for the allotment, but the Forest Service will have to go through some level of analyses and just don't have the time to make that happen very fast right now."

The Hannagan, Fish Creek, and KP allotments were also "waived back" by permittees "due to several endangered species mitigations" that required fencing and made them seem "not feasible" from an economic point of view. However, for the Hannagan allotment, the range specialist says several "livestock producers have expressed interest in obtaining the permit and we are in the slow process of evaluating the current environmental analyses to see if we can grant the allotment/permit back out to someone" (Mortensen 2015). Presumably all these allotments will be ranched again in the future.

The lower Blue in the Clifton Ranger District never suffered the drastic NEPA cattle cuts that occurred in the Alpine District. Nevertheless, it has seen a decline of livestock numbers for various reasons. The large Sandrock allotment in the Primitive Area remains vacant of cattle (as told in chapter 8). When asked if it will ever be open to grazing, the range specialist at Clifton told me it would need another NEPA assessment to determine this question.

The Pleasant Valley allotment, taken from the Martinez family (chapter 16) is still vacant and still in litigation, though the brothers may still keep some cattle or sheep on their private land as before. Their relative, Bobby Gomez, is not using his permit on the Sardine allotment.

Other allotments on the lower Blue being grazed by various ranchers include the Blackjack (325 cow/calf units permitted), the Copperas (135), the Granville (fewer than 200), the Hickey (combined with another ranch out of the Blue), the Mesa (162), and the Strayhorse (a varying seasonal number). All these allotments belong to owners living outside the Blue, who combine them with other ranching and business operations in Arizona and New Mexico.

A special case is the 2011 entry of the Spur Ranch Cattle Company on both the upper and the lower Blue. Based on the Spur Ranch near Luna, New Mexico, this company holds the Coyote-Widmer and Turkey Creek allotments in the upper Blue, authorized presently to run 245 cattle in the summer. Spur Ranch also holds the large Alma Mesa allotment in Clifton District, permitted for 615 cows year around. This is in addition to the cattle it runs in New Mexico. Owner Thomas Paterson comes from a farming and ranching background, having grown up in Morenci, Clifton, and Silver City. He further secured a law degree and advanced degrees in agricultural economics. Today he is a partner in a big law firm in Houston and also practices natural resource law in New Mexico. His Spur Ranch employs four people. The Forest Service range specialist in Clifton praised Paterson's operation for its good management and its willingness to invest in keeping up the ranches so they can make a profit. Paterson has said he does not believe in "lifestyle" ranching; he believes ranching should be commercially successful.

With so much ranching on the lower Blue now carried on from outside the watershed and the Forest, little in the way of Blue "community" can be said to exist there, unlike the community on the upper Blue. The 1940s closing of the county road that ran all the way down the river disconnected the northern and southern parts of Blue country (chapter 8). The retirement of the Sandrock allotment and the end of the XXX Ranch in the 1980s (chapter 8) added to the isolation of the Primitive Area, and the disappearance of ranching families actually living in the Blue watershed. Modern transportation has allowed ranching on the Blue from home ranches around the Forest, rather than from within.

Today on the lower Blue, by my count, only three operations belong to owner-operator families actually living on home ranches there within the Forest boundaries. One is the old T-Links Ranch with the Pigeon allotment (499 cow/calf units); new owners now live there, renaming it the Turkey Creek Ranch. Also recently, the 6K6 Ranch with its AD Bar/ Hogtrail allotment was purchased by a young rancher who plans to live there and raise livestock. And finally, the Cathcarts (chapter 14) remain on their Wildbunch allotment (permitted 311 cow/calf units). The family has a history of differences with the Clifton Ranger District, whose agents have been unhappy about many aspects of their operation. The Cathcarts' allotment is subject in 2015 to the NEPA process, and the word in the Forest Service office is that "there will be restrictions."

Ranching on the Blue: Prospects

In the new millennium, there has been a significant mood shift among Blue ranchers. The frustration, antagonism, and pessimism provoked by the early NEPA livestock cuts beginning in the mid-1990s seem to have dissipated somewhat. Blue ranchers will probably always feel somewhat insecure, wary of a government agency on which they must depend for their livelihood. But today at least, they do not speak of the Forest Service conspiring to remove them from the land.

On the contrary, Blue ranchers agree that recent Forest Service personnel who have replaced the old are generally more sympathetic. "The Forest Service guys are better now. They listen more, they're more flexible than in the past—better to work with." "The new Ranger and range people are friendlier to grazing. The anti-grazing people are gone." These were typical comments in 2015. Thomas Paterson, the new and ambitious rancher on the Blue, sums up his recent experiences: "The Forest Service people I've found to be good, in general. There can be those with a bad attitude who use the rules as an excuse not to do something, but there are others with the attitude, 'Let's make it happen.'"

More surprising, perhaps, is the opinion of a young Arizona Game and Fish agency employee, deployed to serve on the Mexican Wolf reintroduction team in the Alpine area. He believes a "wrong demographic" had been employed in the past. "Leftist, environmentalist officials often don't do a good job relating to people." From a small Western town himself, he claims to be more sympathetic to the ranchers' point of view—though he works for a program virtually all ranchers deplore!

Yet, although the cloud of crisis and distrust seems to have lifted off the Blue for the time being, the forces that gave rise to it still exist. Radical, misanthropic environmentalism may have lost some of its allure, but organizations and individuals often continue to operate under its ideological assumptions. Also, the legal and institutional framework within which the Forest Service operates remains the same. Outside critics of government land management have described the agency as suffering from "gridlock" under a mandate of "multiple-use" that encourages single-interest groups to compete politically to restrict each other and to eschew compromise (Sheridan 2001:147). The gridlock is compounded by the success of activist litigation using the Endangered Species and National Environmental Policy acts, requiring biological assessments not just by the Forest Service but also by the U.S. Fish and Wildlife. Such processes can take years, as both agencies are understaffed for the task. Even then, sometimes

> the scientific evidence is so limited, ambiguous, or poorly interpreted that it would never pass muster if subjected to the common standards of scientific peer review. Nonetheless, ranchers may have their allotments cut, their incomes reduced, and their livelihoods jeopardized, even though they have little say in the decision-making process itself. (Sheridan 2001:147)

This predicament, played out on the Blue, has been analyzed in detail in these pages. But how to get beyond it? The Forest Service on its own is unlikely to escape gridlock. New laws, and a new framework for managing public lands, are unlikely to emerge soon from Washington.

The most promising answer, I believe, lies in grassroots movements to bring together all parties interested in the health of the land: ranchers, environmentalists, public land managers, range scientists, and biologists. The purpose is collaboration to preserve "working landscapes" and to use ranching to achieve ecological goals while ranches simultaneously serve as barriers to real estate development that would permanently impair natural values.

These movements already exist, and are already achieving results. I described this phenomenon in chapter 9. It has been called the "New Ranch" movement and an attempt to create a "radical center." Perhaps a better name might be "common ground environmentalism." The thinking and practice of this new movement are elucidated in two articles by Thomas E. Sheridan (2001, 2007); in the many publications of the Quivira Coalition; in *Revolution on the Range* by Courtney White (2008); and in two recent collections, *Ranching West of the 100th Meridian* (Knight et al. 2002) and *Stitching the West Back Together* (Charnley et al. 2014).

In an overwhelmingly urban America—Arizona itself is more than ninety percent urban (Sheridan 1995)—ranchers must adapt to urban interests. Politically they must seek urban allies. Perforce, these allies must come from the educated "new upper class," and new upper middle class, that have risen to dominate American culture. As analyzed in recent sociological literature, such as *Coming Apart* (Murray 2012) and *Bobos in Paradise* (Brooks 2000), this ascendant information-age elite emerged from our universities, sharing a distinctive subculture heavily influenced by the countercultural values of the 1960s and '70s. These values include the concerns of the new "environmental" movement that arose at that time. Eventually the extremist wing of the movement would attack ranching, trying to expel it from public lands. On the other hand, scenic and wild places possess an allure for the new elite who see a new threat: private ranch lands being bought for real estate development and subdivision into "ranchettes."

It was in this context that the collaborative, common ground environmental movement arose, to appeal to the mainstream, common-sense "center" of the educated class. While committed to the goals of biodiversity and ecological health, this new class also respects tradition and culture that is rooted in the land. Precisely because rural life is so different from the urban, the new educated class can be attracted to its virtues. (See Brooks's discussion of the "Montana Soul Rush" (2000:218–23). The "center" can see the potential for ecological stewardship in the rural people who make their living off the land, people who in their own way cherish the natural world they inhabit. The "center" wants to reconcile the rancher "producers" with the "urban consumers of Western landscapes"—the "environmentalists, hunters, back-packers, birders, equestrians, tourists, and off-road-vehicle users" (and, one might add, those with an academic interest in the West). Common-ground environmentalism wants to overcome the cultural and class divide between urban and rural. "Somehow we need to break down the artificial dichotomy between wilderness and working landscapes, recognize our place in nature, and take responsibility for it, regardless of where we live in the New West" (Sheridan 2007:133–34).

This vision will take years of work to accomplish. But it is beginning to happen, including in small ways on the Blue. In disagreements with the Forest Service over range conditions, Blue ranchers soon found it advantageous to turn for help to academic range experts. Some of these specialists testified for the ranchers in the disputes over the NEPA cuts of the 1990s, including the Las Cruces court case. Biologists and economists also were enlisted. Though the skills of ranching can only be acquired through raw experience, no reason exists why they cannot be combined with university-based expertise or knowledge from the business world. An interesting example, and perhaps a harbinger, is the highly educated Tom Paterson and his Spur Ranch, described above. Another example on the Blue is Otis Wolkins, the retired electronics and banking executive who grew up on a farm. He preserved the old Cosper ranch and helped neighboring ranchers too.

No subdivisions or condos have yet appeared on the Blue. The sheer distance of the Blue from Phoenix, Tucson, and Albuquerque—each about five hours drive—has perhaps spared it from development. The main threat to preserving a truly "working" landscape with ranches has instead been the gradual acquisition of private property by the Forest Service in order to return it to "wilderness." However, one cannot rule out the future possibility of commercial real estate development. Representatives from the Nature Conservancy visited the Blue several years ago, meeting with property owners to explain the utility of conservation easements, but it seems no one has yet taken this option.

A "New Ranch" experiment began in 2004 on Upper Eagle Creek, in the Clifton Ranger District, whose watershed borders the Blue on the west. Ranger Frank Hayes encouraged the formation of the Upper Eagle Creek Watershed Association to bring together ranchers, government agencies, and wildlife and conservation groups to "improve and preserve the watershed," to enhance "habitat for wildlife as well as domestic animals," and "to find a sustainable method of economic survival for the community" (White 2008:73–80). This effort involved one Blue rancher whose allotment extends into the Eagle Creek watershed. Other Blue ranchers have been informed of the project. No similar "association" has yet emerged on their watershed, but the Markses and others have learned how to apply for state conservation grants to help them manage their allotments for environmental benefits.

Another example of collaborative, common ground environmentalism that has included the Blue, is the Mexican Wolf/Livestock Coexistence Council described in chapter 14. Government agencies and ranchers work together to manage wolves and cattle to keep both safe—a true reconciliation of opposites. And environmental groups provide funding to support the enterprise.

Primarily it has been the Marks family involved in the Coexistence Council, but other Blue ranchers have participated in a less formal effort to augment a wild species. The Merriam's wild turkey is not endangered, but it is a desirable "big game" species, as Arizona Game and Fish designates it, and the agency wants to ensure its widespread availability. The Blue contains thriving populations of the turkey, which the ranching people have helped the agency round up to transport elsewhere.

Blue ranchers I have spoken with are more than willing to cooperate with government agencies and conservation groups to protect and enhance wild species as well as the ecological health of the land. They see themselves as stewards. All they ask in return is respect for their attempt to pursue their calling on the same land.

Making a living by ranching has never been easy on the Blue. As described in earlier chapters, the twentieth century saw a steady reduction in the number of cattle being raised, along with a decline in the ranch population raising them. Forest Service policies were only one factor behind this trend (chapters 5 and 6). The economics of ranching have also played an important part. In the western United States, cattle ranching is simply not very profitable (Starrs 1998:71). An investment in cattle ranching on average brings less return (one to two percent) than in any other field (Holechek et al 2011:363; Starrs 1998:71). The larger the ranch, however, the better the return. Benefits ensue from capturing economies of scale (Field 2002).

One result over time has been consolidation. Larger areas are ranched by fewer operations. Allotments are combined. In the most recent example, after the NEPA reductions of the 1990s, the Marks family took over various allotments of other permittees forced to quit ranching. Also, larger operations outside the Blue have taken up some allotments within the watershed.

But consolidation is limited. Most ranching on the Blue is carried on by small- and medium-sized operations that do not provide full-time sustenance for their owners. They combine the sale of cattle with other sources of income. Again, the Marks family is an example. In some cases, ranching clearly serves as a secondary form of livelihood, as with the Stacy brothers, now allowed to run only forty-five cows with calves. Part-time ranching is common on the Blue today, in one form or another. But it is not a new phenomenon: Blue ranchers have always sought to augment their incomes in other ways. They have catered to hunters and tourists since the early twentieth century. They have worked for the Forest Service. They have taken all sorts of off-ranch employment. Nor is this circumstance unique to the Blue. Much of the livestock production in the West comes from part-time operators (Brunson and Wallace 2002:102; Starrs 1998:72, 232). Small ranches abound.

Small-scale and part-time ranching is often termed "hobby ranching" or "lifestyle ranching." In some contexts these expressions may seem dismissive, or condescending. But in most cases, the income from part-time ranching is needed. It helps to provide a family's livelihood and is more serious than the word "hobby" connotes.

But, what I have learned from my experience with Blue ranchers is that their passion for ranching cannot be explained by money. They must make a living, but ranching to them is a way of life, *their* way of life. Their dedication is cultural, not economic. They consciously identify with as ranching as a culture. When I interviewed Tim Robart in 1998 (chapter 15), he was on the verge of being driven off his land. Yet he was still sacrificing himself to "stay alive in the livestock industry" because

> there's a whole lot to say of the culture behind this way of life. . . .
> This is a hard old country. It's a hard, old life. But to me, this
> was a sanctuary, this was my back yard, as far as I could see. . . .
> But you can make a living, and then by God, you're king of the
> world. . . . (Robart 1998).

Paul F. Starrs and others have put forth the concept of "ranch fundamentalism" to explain the attraction of livestock ranching in the western outdoors (Starrs 1998:76–79). Ranchers choose the life because they love it, because they find pride in it, not because they make money at it. They regard it as a better way of life than any alternatives. They appreciate their relationship with the land, with animals, with the open spaces—a way of living close to the natural world, commingled with personal experience, history, tradition, family. They aspire to leave this way of life to their children.

Tim Robart had never heard of the concept "ranch fundamentalism," but he could express all of its tenets. "Being in this business, you just got to love them old cows. If you think you're here because of the money, you're all wrong. It's all lifestyle, that's all it is." "I thought I was the richest man in the world, and my wife was happy, just crazy about this place, kids raising animals, looking forward to going to that little school" on the Blue. "And small-scale as I am, I was always proud of the livestock industry, because I was a producer. People were consuming my product. I was helping" (Robart 1998).

I have heard many other Blue ranchers articulate similar beliefs and sentiments. They will carry on their culture, adapt, and persist, as long as our nation allows.

References

Abbey, Edward

1986   Even the Bad Guys Wear White Hats. *Harper's Magazine*, January 1986.

Abruzzi, William S.

1995   The Social and Ecological Consequences of Early Cattle Ranching in the Little Colorado River Basin. *Human Ecology* 23(1):75–98.

Albuquerque Journal

1998a   "Forest Agency Must Ride Herd on Grazing." Editorial, April 22, 1998.

1998b   "Fenced Out: Ranching in National Forests." May 31, 1998.

AZGFD (Arizona Game and Fish Department)

2004   "Elk Management Summary" of Unit 27.

2015   Website of Arizona Game and Fish Department, www.gf.state.az.us.

Arizona, State of

2006   Verified Criminal Complaint by Daniel Gabino Martinez before the Superior Court of the State of Arizona in and for the county of Greenlee, Case No. CV–2005–030

Arizona State Parks

1990   Letter to John Bedell, Forest Supervisor, Apache-Sitgreaves National Forest, August 31, 1990; personal files of Sewall Goodwin.

Awtrey, Rose Coleman

1998.   Interview with the author, August 4, 1998.

Baeza, Joan

1987   *Down on the Blue. Arizona Highways*, October 1987:36–41.

Bahre, Conrad J.

1991   A Legacy of Change: Historic Human Impact on Vegetation in the Arizona Borderlands. Tucson: University of Arizona Press.

Bahre, Conrad J., and Marlyn L. Shelton

1996   Rangeland Destruction: Cattle and Drought in Southeastern Arizona at the Turn of the Century. *Journal of the Southwest* 38(1):1–22.

Barnes, Will C.

1960   *Arizona Place Names*. Tucson: University of Arizona Press.

1979   *Western Grazing Grounds and Forest Ranges.* New York: Arno Press.
            Reprint of 1913 edition published by the Breeder's Gazette, Chicago.
1982   *Apaches and Longhorns.* Tucson: University of Arizona Press. Reprint of
            1941 edition published by Ward Ritchie, Los Angeles.
Bean-Dochnahl, Janet
2000   Letter to the editor, *High Country News* (Paonia, Colorado), May 22,
            2000, p. 16.
Becker, Virgina J.
2000   Personal communication with author.
Bedell, John
2001   Interview with author, June 20, 2001.
2005   E-mail to author, July 26, 2005.
Belsky, A.J., A. Matzke, and S. Uselman
1999   Survey of Livestock Influences on Stream and Riparian Ecosystems
            in the Western United States. *Journal of Soil and Water Conservation*
            54:419–431.
Bentley, H.L.
1898   *Cattle Ranges of the Southwest: A History of the Exhaustion of the
            Pasturage and Suggestions for its Restoration.* Farmers' Bulletin No.
            72. U.S. Department of Agriculture. Washington: Government Printing
            Office.
Best, Roxanne
2003   E-mail communication with the author by Roxanne Best, Research
            and Statistical Assistant for the Arizona State Department of Economic
            Security analyzing 2000 census data.
Blow, Rita
1998   Economic Loss Analysis of the Marian Robart Forest Service Grazing
            Permit. Final Report submitted to the New Mexico District Court on
            March 10, 1998, in the case Federal Lands Legal Consortium et al.,
            Plaintiffs, v. United States of America et al., Defendants.
Bodfield, Rhonda
1998   Wolf Killings Upset U.S., but Alpine Growls Back. *Arizona Daily Star*,
            November 15, 1998.
Bradford, Dave, and Steve Allen
1999   Herding: How It Works on the West Elks. *Quivira Coalition Newsletter*,
            March 1999:1, 15–18.
Bratton, Howard C., Judge
1998   Memorandum Opinion and Order, in Federal Lands Legal Consortium
            v. United States of America, U.S. District Court of New Mexico, June 15,
            1998.

Brooks, David
2000   *Bobos in Paradise: The New Upper Class and How They Got There.* New York: Simon and Schuster.
Brown, John
1999   Welcome to the New Ranch. *American Cowboy*, Nov./Dec. 1999:47–49.
Brown, Patricia Leigh
2001   Developers at the Door, Ranchers Round Up Support. *New York Times*, Nov. 15, 2001:D1, 6.
Brunson, Mark, and George Wallace
2002   Perceptions of Ranching: Public Views, Personal Reflections. In Knight et al., *Ranching West of the 100th Meridian: Culture, Ecology, and Economics.* Washington, DC: Island Press.
Budd, Bob
2002   Shades of Gray. In Knight et al., *Ranching West of the 100th Meridian: Culture, Ecology, and Economics.* Washington, DC: Island Press.
Bunnell, Bill
2001   Interview with author, June 19, 2001
Bunnell, Bill and Mona
2000   Christmas family newsletter sent to friends and acquaintances.
Bunnell, Mona
1998   Interview with author, August 5, 1998.
Burchell, Joe
1998   Various guns used in killing of four wolves. *Arizona Daily Star*, December 4, 1998.
Butler, Larry D.
2002   Economic Survival of Western Ranching: Searching for Answers. In Knight et al., *Ranching West of the 100th Meridian: Culture, Ecology, and Economics.* Washington, DC: Island Press.
Cameron, Dick
1995   Letter to Ranger, Alpine Ranger District, May 11, 1995. In Range NEPA files, Alpine District.
Cathcart, Martie and Patrick
2000   Interview with author at their ranch on the lower Blue, June 18, 2000.
Charnley, Susan, Thomas E. Sheridan, and Gary P. Nabhan, editors
2014   *Stitching the West Back Together.* Chicago: University of Chicago Press.
Clifford, Frank
1998   "Finding Middle Ground." *Albuquerque Journal*, August 30, 1998:B1, 2, 12. Republished from the *Los Angeles Times*.
Coleman, Rose (subsequently Rose Awtrey)
1995   Letter to Ranger Charles Denton of Alpine Ranger District, May 12, 1995. In Range NEPA files, Alpine Ranger District, Alpine, AZ.

Collingwood, George Harris

n.d.   Sincerely Yours, Harris: Being the Selected Letters of George Harris
              Collingwood to Miss Jean Cummings written by the Young Ranger in
              1914 and 1915 while stationed at the Apache National Forest in Arizona.
              Edited by Joseph A. Miller and Judith C. Rudnicki. Unpublished Forest
              Service document. Files of Clifton Ranger District, Clifton, AZ.

Coor, Cleo Cosper

1984   Claire Vance and Celia Elizabeth Burke Peery, Blue, Arizona. *Arizona
              National Ranch Histories of Living Pioneer Stockman* [sic], Betty
              Accomazzo, ed. Vol. 6, pp. 18–39.

Coppelman, Peter

1998   Testimony of the Deputy Assistant Attorney General, Environment and
              Natural Resources Division, U.S. Department of Justice, before the U.S.
              House of Representatives Committee on Resources, Washington, D.C.,
              July 15, 1998.

Cosgrove, Catherine R.

1998   Economic Impacts of Apache-Sitgreaves National Forests Public Land
              Ranching. Research funded by the Apache County Economic Security
              Corporation, Greenlee County Board of Supervisors, Navajo County
              Board of Supervisors, with support from the Apache-Sitgreaves National
              Forest.

Cosper, Toles

ca. 1940   Y Bar Y Ranch (Toles Cosper). Oral history transcribed by Kathlyn M.
              Lathrop, manuscript form, in "Biographies/Pioneer Interviews" of the
              Arizona State Library, Arizona History and Archives Division, Phoenix.

Cosper

1982   Highlights of the Cosper Family Migration to Arizona. Written by
              an unidentified daughter of Toles Cosper; includes an interview with
              Toles's son James. Arizona National Ranch Histories of Living Pioneer
              Stockman [sic], Betty Accomazzo, ed. Vol. 4, pp. 132–141. Interview
              reprinted in *Down on the Blue* (1987:209–210).

Dagget, Dan

1995   *Beyond the Rangeland Conflict: Towards a West That Works.* Layton,
              Utah: Gibbs Smith; and Flagstaff, Arizona: Grand Canyon Trust.

2005a   Ending the Free Ride for the Get'emoff Gang. *Range*, Winter 2005:22–
              24.

2005b   A Friend of Fish and Cow. *Range*, Spring 2005:68–69

Darling, Mary

1998   Interview with author, July 13, 1998.

Davis, Tony

1994   "Don't Bother Them with Facts." *High Country News* (Paonia, CO),
         May 2, 1994.

Debo, Angie

1976   *Geronimo: The Man, His Time, His Place*. Norman: University of
         Oklahoma Press.

DeBuys, William

1999   Talk before a Quivira Coalition workshop, Albuquerque, August 7, 1999.

Dedera, Don

1967   The Cattleman and the Wilderness. *Arizona Magazine*, December 17,
         1967.

Devall, Bill & George Sessions

1985   *Deep Ecology: Living as if Nature Mattered*. Layton, UT: Gibbs Smith.

Dobie, J. Frank

1981   *The Ben Lilly Legend*. Austin: University of Texas Press.

Dobyns, Henry F.

1978   Who Killed the Gila? *Journal of Arizona History* 19:17–30.

Dolphin, Jeff

2015   Interviews in March 2014 and June 2015. Dolphin, an employee of the
         Arizona Game and Fish Department, serves on the Interagency Field
         Team coordinating the Mexican Wolf Recovery Program in Alpine,
         Arizona.

Domrzalski, Dennis

1999   "Ranching the Right Way: Environmental Grazing." In *Weekly Alibi*
         (Albuquerque), August 5–11, 1999:32–34.

Donahue, Debra L.

1999   *The Western Range Revisited: Removing Livestock from Public Lands to
         Conserve Native Biodiversity*. Norman: University of Oklahoma Press.

Down on the Blue: Blue River 1878–1986

1987   Collection of articles, reminiscences, documents, and oral histories of
         a large number of Blue community residents and former residents.
         Commissioned by the Blue River Cowbelles. Cleo Cosper Coor, editor.
         Goodyear, Arizona: Out West Printing.

DuHamel, Jonathan

2002   Karl vs. Cows. *People for the West—Tucson Newsletter*, June 2002.

Erman, Rick

1995   Letter representing Arizona Wildlife Federation, to Alpine District
         Ranger, May 16, 1995. Range NEPA files Alpine District, Alpine, AZ.

Federal Lands

1998   Federal Lands Legal Consortium et al., Plaintiffs, v. United States of
         America et al., Defendants. Hearing on Preliminary Injunctions before

Hon. Howard C. Bratton, Las Cruces, New Mexico, May 20–21, 1998, District Court of New Mexico (D.C. *No.* 97–1126 HB/JG).

Field, Tom

2002   Making a Living in the Age of Wal-Mart. In Knight et al., *Ranching West of the 100th Meridian: Culture, Ecology, and Economics.* Washington, DC: Island Press.

Flader, Susan L.

1974   *Thinking Like a Mountain: Aldo Leopold and the Evolution of an Ecological Attitude toward Deer, Wolves, and Forests.* Madison: University of Wisconsin Press.

2012   Searching for Aldo Leopold's Green Fire. *Forest History Today,* Fall 2012:28–34.

Fleischner, Thomas L.

1994   Ecological Costs of Livestock Grazing in Western North America. *Conservation Biology* 8 (3):629–644.

Forest Guardians

2005a   "Coalition sends notice to remove renegade rancher from National Forest." Frontline Newsletter #152, May 14, 2005. E-mail.

2005b   "'Move 'Em Out—Trespassing Cattle Impounded on Arizona National Forest." Frontline Newsletter #157, November 22, 2005. E-mail.

Fox, Stephen

1981   *The American Conservation Movement: John Muir and His Legacy.* Madison: University of Wisconsin Press.

Freilich, Jerome E. et al.

2003   Ecological Effects of Ranching: A Six-Point Critique. *Bioscience* 53 (8) August 2003.

Fritz, Fred J., Jr.

1978   Untitled memoir. *Arizona National Ranch Histories of Living Pioneer Stockman* [sic], Betty Accomazzo, ed. Vol. 1, pp. 65–102.

1982   Note to Lois and Sewall Goodwin, March 8, 1982. Personal files of Sewall Goodwin.

Fritz, Katy

1985   Triple X Ranch (as told to Kathlyn M. Lathrop). *Arizona National Ranch Histories of Living Pioneer Stockman* [sic], Betty Accomazzo, ed. Vol. 7, pp. iii–vix. Also in manuscript form, transcribed by Kathlyn M. Lathrop ca. 1940, in the collection "Biographies/Pioneer Interviews," Arizona State Library, Arizona History and Archives Division, Phoenix.

Goldberg, Julia

1998   Hope on the Range? *Santa Fe Reporter,* Dec. 16–21, 1998:13.

Goodwin, Sewall

2000   Interview with author, April 1, 2000.

Graham, Mattie Jane Johnson

1953   My Life Story. *Arizona Cattlelog*, September 1953:25–32.

Greenlee County (Arizona)

1912   General County Register, Official Register of Electors for Blue Precinct. Manuscript.

1914   General County Register, Official Register of Electors for Blue Precinct. Manuscript.

1916   General County Register, Official Register of Electors for Blue Precinct. Manuscript.

1920   General County Register, Official Register of Electors for Blue Precinct. Manuscript.

1926   General County Register, Official Register of Electors for Blue Precinct. Manuscript.

1994   Comments from Greenlee County Prepared for the White Mountain Forum, December 14, 1994. Manuscript in USFS records.

2000   Greenlee County Voting Results by Precinct. Manuscript available at County Courthouse, County Clerk's Office.

Hanrahan, Miles P.

1972   Some Notes on Grazing History on the Apache National Forest, 1972. Report sent to the Forest Supervisor by the Acting Forest Supervisor. Manuscript in Forest Service files, Clifton Ranger District.

Hardin, Garrett

1968   The Tragedy of the Commons. *Science* 162:1243–1248.

Haskett, Bert

1935   Early History of the Cattle Industry in Arizona. *Arizona Historical Review* 6:3–42.

Herbel, C.H.

1986   Vegetation Changes on Arid Rangelands of the Southwestern United States. In *Rangelands: A Resource Under Siege. Proceedings of the Second International Rangelands Congress*, pp. 8–10. Cambridge: Cambridge University Press.

Hess, Karl, Jr.

1992   *Visions upon the Land: Man and Nature on the Western Range.* Washington, DC: Island Press.

1998   *Incentive-Based Conservation for the Sky Island Complex*: A Draft Report to the Wildlands Project on Livestock, Elk and Wolves. Unpublished paper in the files of Gila National Forest, Silver City, NM.

Hirt, Paul

1989   The Transformation of a Landscape: Culture and Ecology in Southeastern Arizona. *Environmental Review*, 13 (3–4):167–189.

Hoffman, Don

2002   Interview with the author, August 9, 2002.

Hogan, David

1995   Letter on behalf of the Southwest Center for Biological Diversity, to
            the District Ranger of the Alpine District, May 17, 1995. District Range
            NEPA files.

Holechek, Jerry L., Terrell T. Baker and Jon C. Boren

2004   *Impacts of Controlled Grazing Versus Grazing Exclusion on Rangeland
            Ecosystems: What We Have Learned.* Range Improvement Task Force
            Report No. 57. Las Cruces: New Mexico State University.

Holechek, Jerry L., Rex D. Pieper, and Carlton H. Herbel

2011   *Range Management: Principles and Practices*, 6th ed. Upper Saddle River,
            NJ: Prentice Hall.

Holloway, William J.

1999   *Federal Lands Legal Consortium Robart Estate YJ v. United States*, 195
            F.3d 1190 (10th Cir. 1999) (No. 98–2211) October 28, 1999. Before
            Baldock, Holloway, and Henry, Circuit Judges.

Hunt, W.W.R.

1905   Clifton Addition to Black Mesa Forest Reserve of Arizona. Report by
            Forest Agent W.W.R. Hunt, document in Clifton Ranger District files.
            (Quite likely the same document cited in some sources [i.e. Flader
            1974:41n] under a similar title, but with W.H. Kent as the author, ca.
            1906, National Archives, Record Group 95. Often more than one Forest
            Service official would sign a report as it passed up the hierarchy.) Found
            in the same file is a copy of the cattlemen's petition to Washington.

Huntsinger, Lynn

2002   End of the Trail: Ranching Transformation on the Pacific Slope. In
            Richard L. Knight et al., *Ranching West of the 100th Meridian: Culture,
            Ecology, and Economics.* Washington, DC: Island Press.

Ingold, Tim

1980   *Hunters, Pastoralists, and Ranchers: Reindeer Economies and Their
            Transformations.* Cambridge Studies in Social Anthropology No. 28.
            Cambridge: Cambridge University Press.

Jacobs, Lynn

1992   *Waste of the West: Public Lands Ranching.* Tucson: Lynn Jacobs.

Johnson, Rex R., Jr.

1995   Letter to Alpine Ranger District, on behalf of Southwest Trout, May 12,
            1995. Range NEPA files, Alpine Ranger District, Alpine, AZ.

1999   *Arizona Trout: A Fly Fishing Guide.* Portland, OR: Frank Amato
            Publications.

Jordan, Terry G.

1975   Texan Influence in Nineteenth-Century Arizona Cattle Ranching. *Journal of the West* 14:15–17.

1993   *North American Cattle-Ranching Frontiers: Origins, Diffusion, and Differentiation.* Albuquerque: University of New Mexico Press.

Kamin, John

2004a   "Grazing permit debate finds its way to Greenlee." *Eastern Arizona Courier* (Safford), February 19, 2004.

2004b   "Rancher requests Greenlee's help." *Eastern Arizona Courier* (Safford), March 22, 2004.

Kaufman, Wallace

1994   *No Turning Back: Dismantling the Fantasies of Environmental Thinking.* New York: Basic Books.

Kenworthy, Tom

1998a   "Species Act Endangers a Way of Life." *Washington Post*, Feb. 1, 1998.

1998b   "Released Wolves Struggle to Survive Their Usual Predator: Man." *Washington Post*, Nov. 17, 1998.

1998c   "Grazing Laws Feed Demise of Ranchers' Way of Life." *Washington Post*, Nov. 29, 1998.

Kiefer, Michael

2000   "Ranch Wars: Tolerance of Ranching Puts the Nature Conservancy at Odds with the Environmental Community." *Phoenix New Times*, April 20, 2000.

Knight, Richard L.

2002   The Ecology of Ranching. In Knight et al., *Ranching West of the 100th Meridian: Culture, Ecology, and Economics.* Washington, DC: Island Press.

Knight, Richard L., Wendell C. Gilgert, and Ed Marston, eds.

2002   *Ranching West of the 100th Meridian: Culture, Ecology, and Economics.* Washington, DC: Island Press.

Knize, Perri

1999   Winning the War for the West. *Atlantic Monthly*, July 1999:54–62.

Lee, Clell and Katharine

1983   History of the VM Ranch. *Arizona National Ranch Histories of Living Pioneer Stockman* [*sic*], Betty Accomazzo, ed. Vol. 5, pp. 68–77.

Leopold, Aldo

1921a   A Plea for Recognition of Artificial Works in Forest Erosion Control Policy. *Journal of Forestry* 19 (3):267–273.

1921b   The Wilderness and Its Place in Forest Recreation Policy. *Journal of Forestry* 19 (7):718–721.

1924   Grass, Brush, Timber, and Fire in Southern Arizona. *Journal of Forestry*
          22 (6):1–10.

1946   Erosion as a Menace to the Social and Economic Future of the
          Southwest. Paper read at a meeting of the New Mexico Association for
          Science, 1922, at which time the author was a member of the U.S. Forest
          Service. Published in 1946. *Journal of Forestry* 44:627–633.

1949   *A Sand County Almanac, and Sketches Here and There.* New York:
          Oxford University Press.

1979   Some Fundamentals of Conservation in the Southwest. *Environmental
          Ethics* 1 (2):131–141. Previously unpublished manuscript, written in the
          early 1920s.

Locke, John

1993   "Of Property." Second Treatise of Government, in *Two Treatises of
          Government,* Mark Goldie, ed. London: Everyman.

Luce, Sam

1998   Interview with author, July 21, 1998.

Mann, Charles C., and Mark L. Plummer

1995   *Noah's Choice: The Future of Endangered Species.* New York: Alfred A.
          Knopf.

Mares, Walter

2005a   "USFS, Martinezes clash on grazing permit issue." *Eastern Arizona
          Courier* (Safford), August 3, 2005.

2005b   "USFS delays road closure for cattle removal." *Eastern Arizona Courier*
          (Safford), September 7, 2005.

2005c   "Martinez cattle are sold by USFS in Texas." *Eastern Arizona Courier*
          (Safford), December 21, 2005.

Marks, Barbara

1999   Conversation with author, July 22, 1999.

2000   Conversation with author, January 30, 2000.

Marks, Bill

2001   Interview with author, August 22, 2001.

Marks, Bill and Barbara

1995   Letter to Steve Herndon, Alpine Ranger District, May 13, 1995. In
          Range NEPA files, Alpine Ranger District, Alpine, AZ.

1998   Interview with author at WY Bar Ranch, June 25, 1998.

Marston, Ed

2002   "Cow-free Crowd Ignores Science, Sprawl." *High Country News* (Paonia,
          CO), Dec. 9, 2002.

Martinez, Abe

2000   Interview with author at Martinez Ranch, August 17, 2000.

2001   Interview with author, August 22, 2001.

Martinez, Dan

2010   Conversation with author, August 30, 2010.

Matsumoto, Kimi A.

1995   Letter on behalf of the National Wildlife Federation to the Ranger, Alpine District, May 15, 1995. Range NEPA files, Alpine Ranger District, Alpine, AZ.

McAlindin, Sean

2003   "The Center for Biological Diversity Speaks Up for Wolves." *University of Colorado Campus Press (Boulder)*, November 2003.

McCarty, Glen

1995   Letter To District Ranger, Alpine District, May 11, 1995. Range NEPA files, Alpine Ranger District, Alpine, AZ.

McDonald, William

2001   The Malpai Borderlands Group: Building the Radical Center. *Quivira Coalition Newsletter*, July 2001:1, 18–22.

McKeen, Hugh Bronson, and Mae Balke McKeen

1982   Hugh Bronson McKeen: His Family History. *Arizona National Ranch Histories of Living Pioneer Stockman* [sic], Betty Accomazzo, ed. Vol. 4, pp. 162–166. Hugh Bronson McKeen wrote the first part of this history about his father, Hugh McKeen. The second part is a first-person account by Hugh's wife (Hugh Bronson's mother), Mae Balke McKeen, in 1956, and is found also in *Down on the Blue* 1987:217–218, entitled "Hugh McKeen's Blue River Adventures."

Meine, Curt

1988   *Aldo Leopold: His Life and Work*. Madison: University of Wisconsin Press.

Menges, Jeff

2005   Letter to the Editor, *Eastern Arizona Courier* (Safford), October 31, 2005.

Merrill, Karen R.

2002   *Public Lands and Political Meaning: Ranchers, the Government, and the Property between Them*. Berkeley: University of California Press.

Mexican Wolf/Livestock Coexistence Council

2015   Website: http://www.coexistencecouncil.org/

Moore, Fay Stacy

1982   Fred Austin Stacy, Clifton, Arizona. *Arizona National Ranch Histories of Living Pioneer Stockman* [sic], Betty Accomazzo, ed. Vol. 4, p. 92.

Morrisey, Richard J.

1950   The Early Range Cattle Industry in Arizona. *Agricultural History* 24:151–156.

Mortensen, Ron

2015   E-mail communication, June 16, 2015.

Murray, Charles

2012   *Coming Apart: the State of White America, 1960–2010.* New York:
            Crown Forum (Random House).

Nash, Roderick Frazier

1990   *American Environmentalism: Readings in Conservation History,* 3rd ed.
            New York: McGraw Hill.

National Research Council

1994   *Rangeland Heath: New Methods to Classify, Inventory, and Monitor
            Rangelands.* Washington, DC: National Academy Press.

National Riparian Service Team (NRST)

2001   Blue River Watershed Trip Report. Document submitted to Apache-
            Sitgreaves National Forest.

Nelson, Robert H.

1995   *Public Lands and Private Rights.* Lanham, MD: Rowman and Littlefield.

Ogilvie, David

1998   The Southwestern Willow Flycatcher and Me. *Quivira Coalition
            Newsletter,* September 1998.

Oppenheimer, Todd

1996   The Rancher Subsidy. *Atlantic Monthly,* January 1996.

Paragon Foundation

2005   Bush Administration Forest Service Raids Ranch Confiscating 300
            Cattle. Press Release, October 25, 2005.

Parker, Dennis

1997   Interview with author, August 12, 1997, Patagonia, Arizona.

Pattie, James O.

1831   *The Personal Narrative of James O. Pattie of Kentucky.* Originally
            published by John H. Wood, Cincinnati. Reprint 1930. Chicago: Lakeside
            Press.

Patton, James M.

1977   History of Clifton. Greenlee, AZ: Greenlee County Chamber of
            Commerce.

Pendley, William Perry

1995   *War on the West: Government Tyranny on America's Great Frontier.*
            Washington, D.C.: Regnery Publishing.

People for the USA

1996   Website www.pfw.org.

Pioneer Meeting

n.d.   "History of the Blue River, Rough Draft of the Pioneer Meeting." No
            author or date. Document in Forest Service Files, Clifton Ranger District,
            Clifton, AZ, appears to be an effort by someone working for the Forest

Service sometime after 1950 to collect oral histories of "pioneers" on the Blue.

Pitts, Kathy

1996 Oral History of the Double Circle Ranch, manuscript. Commissioned for the U.S. Forest Service, Apache-Sitgreaves National Forest, Springerville, Arizona, July 1996.

Pitts, Lee

2006 Showdown in Greenlee County. *Paragon,* magazine of the Paragon Foundation, Winter 2006:6–9.

Public Lands Council

1999 Personal communication from Jason Campbell of the Public Lands Council.

Quivira Coalition

2003 2003 Calendar. Santa Fe, NM.

2004 *Forging a West that Works: An Invitation to the Radical Center: Essays on Ranching, Conservation, and Science.* Barbara H. Johnson, ed. Santa Fe, NM: Quivira Coalition.

Resource Roundup

2004 Caution: Open Range! Cattle grazing on the Black Hills National Forest helps people, the land, and wildlife. In *Resource Roundup,* Spearfish, South Dakota.

Reynolds, Ralph

1991 *Growing Up Cowboy.* Golden, CO: Fulcrum Publishers.

Rich, Steven H.

2004 Special Report: Refuting the Myths. Insert, *Range,* Fall 2004.

2005a Where Have All the Flowers Gone? *Range,* Winter 2005:40–43.

2005b "Pristine" Nature: The Founding Falsehood. *Range,* Spring 2005:72–79.

2005c The Naked Truth: How Resting Rangeland Strips Away Biodiversity. *Range,* Summer 2005:84–87.

Rinne, John N.

1999 Fish and Grazing Relationships: The Facts and Some Pleas. *Fisheries* 24 (8):12–21. August 1999.

Robart, Tim

1998 Interview with author, August 4, 1998.

1999 Interview with author, June 4, 1999.

2001 Interview with author, June 19, 2001

Roberts, David

1994 *Once They Moved Like the Wind: Cochise, Geronimo, and the Apache Wars.* New York: Simon and Schuster.

Robinson, Sherry

2002 "Finding Common Ground." *Albuquerque Journal,* January 28, 2002.

Rowley, William D.

1985   *U.S. Forest Service Grazing and Rangelands: A History*. College Station:
            Texas A&M University.

Savory, Allan

2002   Re-Creating the West. . .One Decision at a Time. In Knight et al.,
            Ranching West of the 100th Meridian: Culture, Ecology, and Economics.
            Washington, DC: Island Press.

Sayre, Nathan F.

1999   The Cattle Boom in Southern Arizona: Towards a Critical Political
            Ecology. *Journal of the Southwest* 41 (2):239–271.

2001   *The New Ranch Handbook: A Guide to Restoring Western Rangelands*.
            Santa Fe, NM: The Quivira Coalition.

2002   *Ranching, Endangered Species, and Urbanization in the Southwest*.
            Tucson: University of Arizona Press.

Settles, Phil

1999   Interview with author, July 6, 1999

2001   Interview with author, July 20, 2001.

Shabecoff, Philip

1993   *A Fierce Green Fire: The American Environmental Movement*. New York:
            Hill and Wang.

Sheridan, Thomas E.

1995   *Arizona: A History*. Tucson: University of Arizona Press.

2001   Cows, Condos, and the Contested Commons: The Political Ecology of
            Ranching on the Arizona-Sonora Borderlands. *Human Organization* 60
            (2):141–152.

2007   Embattled Ranchers, Endangered Species, and Urban Sprawl: The
            Political Ecology of the New American West. *Annual Review of
            Anthropology* 36:121–138.

Shirra, Mike

2000   Scattered Cattle, Grass and Good Water. *Range*, Fall 2000:28–29.

Slatta, Richard W.

1990   *Cowboys of the Americas*. New Haven: Yale University Press.

Slivka, Judd

2002   "Ranchers a dying breed." *Arizona Republic*, July 15, 2002.

Southwest Center for Biological Diversity (SWCBD)

1998   *Southwest Biodiversity Alert* 162, November 25, 1998.

Stacy, Dennis

1999   Interview with author, July 22, 1999.

Stacy, Dennis and Douglas

1998   Interview with author, August 6, 1998.

2000   Interview with author, January 30, 2000.

Starrs, Paul F.

1998   *Let the Cowboy Ride: Cattle Ranching in the American West*. Baltimore:
        Johns Hopkins University Press.

2002   Ranching: An Old Way of Life in the New West. In Knight et al.,
        Ranching West of the 100th Meridian: Culture, Ecology, and Economics.
        Washington, DC: Island Press.

Stauder, Jack

2009   Aldo Leopold and the Blue River: An Ironic Legacy. *Journal of the
        Southwest* 51 (3) Autumn 2009.

Stecker, Tiffany

2013   U.S. Starts Massive Forest-Thinning Project. *Scientific American* website,
        http://www.scientificamerican.com/article/us-starts-massive-forest-
        thinning-project/. March 22, 2013.

Sullins, Martha J., David T. Theobald, Jeff. R. Jones, and Leah M. Burgess

2002   Lay of the Land: Ranch Land and Ranching. In Richard L. Knight et al.,
        Ranching West of the 100th Meridian: *Culture, Ecology, and Economics*.
        Washington, DC: Island Press.

Taylor, Eleanor P., John M. Fowler, and Angus P. McIntosh

n.d.   *Grazing Trends in the Gila National Forest: 1906–1998*. Range
        Improvement Task Force, Report No. 49. Las Cruces: New Mexico State
        University

Thrapp, Dan L.

1967   *The Conquest of Apacheria*. Norman: University of Oklahoma Press.

Turner, Frederick J.

1962   *The Frontier in American History*. New York: Holt, Rinehart and
        Winston.

U.S. Census Bureau

1900   Twelfth Census of the United States, manuscript population schedules.
        Territory of Arizona, Graham County, Enumeration District 19, Precinct
        No. 15. (Microfilm, Arizona State Library, Arizona History and Archives
        Division, Phoenix.)

1910   Thirteenth Census of the United States, manuscript population
        schedules. Arizona, Graham County, Enumeration District No. 40,
        Sheets 5–7. (Microfilm, Arizona State Library, Arizona History and
        Archives Division, Phoenix.)

1920   Fourteenth Census of the United States, manuscript population
        schedules. Arizona, Greenlee County, Supervisor's District No. 2,
        Enumeration District No. 66, Sheets 1–3. (Microfilm, Arizona State
        Library, Arizona History and Archives Division, Phoenix.)

1930   Fifteenth Census of the United States, manuscript population schedules.
        Arizona, Greenlee County, Supervisor's District No. 3, Enumeration

District No. 6–9, Sheets 1–2. (Microfilm, Arizona State Library, Arizona History and Archives Division, Phoenix.)

U.S. Congress

1964   The Wilderness Act, Pub. L. 88–577, 78 Stat. 890, "Definition of Wilderness" at 1014.

1970   The National Environmental Policy Act of 1969, Title I, "Congressional Declaration of National Environmental Policy, Sec. 101 [42 USC # 4331].

U.S. Court of Appeals for the Ninth Circuit

2009   Daniel Gabino Martinez, Petitioner—Appellant, v. United States of America; et al., Respondents—Appellees. No. 08–15948. 2009 U.S. App. LEXIS 27336,*; 356 F.App'x. 979 (9th Cir. 2009), submitted November 17, 2009.

U.S. Court of Federal Claims

2009   *Estate of Hage v. United States,* 90 Fed.Cl. 388 (2009) (Hage VI). Also, cases 35 Fed.Cl. 147 (1996) (Hage I); 35 Fed.Cl. 737 (1996)(Hage II); 42 Fed.Cl. 249 (1998)(Hage III); 51 Fed.Cl. 570 (2002)(Hage IV); and 82 Fed. Cl. 202 (2008)(Hage V).

U.S. Department of Agriculture (USDA)

2004   "Meat Animals Production, Disposition, and Income, 2003 Summary." Website of U. S. Department of Agriculture, National Agricultural Statistics Service, http://usda.mannlib.cornell.edu/reports/nassr/ livestock/zma-bb/meat0404.txt (site discontinued).

U.S. Fish and Wildlife Service (USFW)

2000   Mexican Gray Wolf: Challenge in the Southwest. Brochure for public distribution.

2015   U.S. Fish and Wildlife Service website on the Mexican Wolf Recovery Program, http://www.fws.gov/southwest/es/mexicanwolf/chronology. cfm.

U.S. Forest Service (USFS)

1905   Protest Letter [from 16 cattlemen] supporting the Clifton Addition to Black Mesa Forest Reserve Arizona. Archival History 1680–81. Files of Clifton Ranger District, Clifton, AZ.

1939a   Erosion Problem Area Report, Report 14 on Campbell Blue. Files of Alpine Ranger District, Alpine, AZ.

1939b   Erosion Problem Area Report, Report 16 on Turkey Creek. Files of Alpine Ranger District, Alpine, AZ.

1942   Watersheds of the Apache National Forest, October 1942. Typed report by W.G. Koogler, Senior Range Examiner. Files of Apache National Forest, Springerville, AZ.

1964   Sandrock Allotment Analysis. January 10, 1964. Files of Clifton Ranger District, Clifton, AZ.

1967   Hannagan Allotment Analysis of 1967, by R.B. Solether, including
            memo by H.L. Cox, Apache National Forest Supervisor. Files of Alpine
            Ranger District, Alpine, AZ.

1968a   KP Allotment Analysis of 1968. Files of Alpine Ranger District, Alpine,
            AZ.

1968b   Sandrock, the Allotment Analysis. William Pint, Marty Morrison, and
            Ronald Raspberry. Files of Clifton Ranger Station, Clifton, AZ.

1969a   Letters of January 10, 1969, and January 21, 1969, from Assistant
            Regional Forester John T. Koen to Keith R. Artz of the Nature
            Conservancy. Copies from private files of Sewall Goodwin.

1969b   Fish Hook Allotment Analysis. Introduction by Larry Allen, Ranger.
            Files of Alpine Ranger District, Alpine, AZ.

ca. 1969   Proposal for a Blue Ridge Wilderness in the Apache National Forest.
            Wilderness files of Alpine Ranger District, Alpine, AZ.

1970   Petition of Greenlee County Board of Supervisors to William D. Hurst,
            Southwest Regional Forester, July 24, 1970. Wilderness files of Alpine
            Ranger District, Alpine, AZ.

1971   Proposed Blue Range Wilderness, Arizona–New Mexico. Wilderness files
            of Alpine Ranger District, Alpine, AZ.

1972a   Letter of District Ranger Jerry A. Deiter to Fred J. Fritz, November 22,
            1972. Files of Clifton Ranger Station, Clifton, AZ.

1972b   Letter of Forest Supervisor Hallie L. Cox to Fred Fritz, December
            14, 1972. Files of Apache-Sitgreaves National Forest Headquarters,
            Springerville, AZ.

1973   Letter of District Ranger Jerry A. Dieter to Fred J. Fritz, December 12,
            1973. Files of Clifton Ranger District, Clifton, AZ.

1974   Letter of District Ranger Jerry A. Deiter to Fred J. Fritz, November 25,
            1974. Files of Clifton Ranger District, Clifton, AZ.

1975   Letter of W. R. Fallis, Director, Range Management of Region 3 of the
            National Forest Service, to Fred Fritz, March 17, 1975. Files of Apache-
            Sitgreaves National Forest Headquarters, Springerville, AZ.

1976   Letter of Forest Supervisor James L. Kimball, to Robert Sewall Goodwin,
            June 24, 1976. Reply letter of Sewall Goodwin, July 19, 1976. Files of
            Apache-Sitgreaves National Forest Headquarters, Springerville, AZ.

1977   Memo from Gary A. Davis, Wildlife Biologist, to Clifton District Ranger,
            Nov. 15, 1977, "Subject: Sandrock Grazing Allotment." Files of Clifton
            Ranger District, Clifton, AZ.

1979   Wildlife Habitat Analysis, AD Bar Allotment. By Gary A. Davis, Wildlife
            Biologist, Apache-Sitgreaves National Forest. Reviewed by James L.
            Kimball, Forest Supervisor. October 11, 1979. Files of Apache-Sitgreaves
            National Forest Headquarters, Springerville, AZ.

ca. 1980.   "Guidelines for Classification Plan," copy of a segment of a Forest
             Service document, personal files of Sewall Goodwin, permittee.

1981   Alma Mesa Allotment Analysis. Files of Clifton Ranger District
             (McKeen allotment), Clifton, AZ.

1982a   Letter from Glen E. Hetzel for R. Max Peterson, Chief of U.S. Forest
             Service, to Eldon Rudd, U.S. House of Representatives, February
             16,1982. Files of Apache-Sitgreaves National Forest headquarters,
             Springerville, AZ.

1982b   Letter from Nick W. McDonough, Forest Supervisor, to Sewall
             Goodwin, October 15, 1982. Files of Apache-Sitgreaves National Forest
             headquarters, Springerville, AZ.

1983a   Letter from Greg L. Gray, Range Conservationist, to R. Sewall Goodwin,
             January 7, 1983. Personal files of Sewall Goodwin.

1983b   Sandrock and AD Bar Allotment Fact Sheet, May 16, 1983, by Nick
             W. McDonough, Forest Supervisor, Apache-Sitgreaves National Forest,
             together with "Resumé of Special Country Supervisors Meeting, May 6,
             1983." Files of Clifton Ranger District, Clifton, AZ.

1987   Apache-Sitgreaves National Forest Plan. Files of Apache-Sitgreaves
             National Forest headquarters, Springerville, AZ.

1988   Timeless Heritage: A History of the Forest Service in the Southwest,
             by Robert D. Baker, Robert S. Maxwell, Victor H. Treat, and Henry C.
             Dethloff. College Station, Texas: Intaglio, Inc.

1989a   Clifton Field Trip Report, November 2–4, 1988. Prepared by Reggie
             Fletcher, Regional Ecologist, and sent by W.R. Snyder, Director of Range
             Management, Southwest Region of U.S. Forest Service, Albuquerque
             office, to Clifton Ranger District. Stray Horse Allotment. Files of Clifton
             Ranger District, Clifton, AZ.

1989b   Letter from Charles Coleman, May 8, 1989, in permittee file of Rose
             Coleman Awtrey. Files of Alpine Ranger District, Alpine, AZ.

1990   Letter from Charles and Rose Coleman, April 12, 1990, in permittee file
             of Rose Coleman Awtrey. Files of Alpine Ranger District, Alpine, AZ.

1995a   Scoping Report. Grazing Permits [NEPA analysis]. Accompanying letter
             from Charles W. Denton, District Ranger of Alpine Ranger District,
             April 28, 1995. Files of Alpine Ranger District, Alpine, AZ.

1995b   Screening of issues from scoping input. June 20, 1995. Files of Alpine
             Ranger District, Alpine, AZ.

1995c   Allotment Broad Scale Production/Capacity Determinations,
             Springerville Ranger District and Alpine Ranger District. Files of Alpine
             Ranger District, Alpine, AZ.

1995d   Information Provided to Permittees at September 8, 1995, Meeting in Alpine, Arizona. KP and Raspberry. Summary and Explanation. Files of Alpine Ranger District, Alpine, AZ.

1995e   K.P. Allotment #212. Summary of Acres. Date Prepared: 7/6/95. Files of Alpine Ranger District, Alpine, AZ.

1995f   Final Environmental Assessment for the KP and Raspberry Allotments Grazing Permit, H. Downs, Permittee. Files of Alpine Ranger District, Alpine, AZ.

1995g   Information Provided to Permittees at September 8, 1995, Meeting in Alpine, Arizona. Fishook-Steeple Mesa and Fish Creek and Hannagan (Coleman and Robart). Summary and Explanation. Files of Alpine Ranger District, Alpine, AZ.

1995h   Fish Hook Allotment #206. Summary of Acres. Date Prepared: 7/03/95. Files of Alpine Ranger District, Alpine, AZ.

1995i   Steeple Mesa Allotment #216. Summary of Acres. Date Prepared: 6/26/95. Files of Alpine Ranger District, Alpine, AZ.

1995j   Information Provided to Permittees at September 8, 1995, Meeting in Alpine, Arizona. Beaver Creek and Bobcat-Johnson (Lazy YJ Ranch). Summary and Explanation. Files of Alpine Ranger District, Alpine, AZ.

1995k   Bobcat-Johnson Allotment #211. Summary of Acres. Date Prepared: 6/2/95. Files of Alpine Ranger District, Alpine, AZ.

1995m   File of 1995 NEPA Environmental Assessment, in Apache-Sitgreaves National Forest headquarters, Springerville, AZ.

1995n   List of Draft EA Comments and Commentators. November 22, 1995. Files of Apache-Sitgreaves National Forest headquarters, Springerville, AZ.

1995p   Draft Environmental Assessments for the Issuance of a Grazing Permit [to various permittees] on the Alpine District, September 1955. Files of Apache-Sitgreaves National Forest headquarters, Springerville, AZ.

1995q   Final Environmental Assessments for the [various] Allotment Grazing Permits, Alpine Ranger District, December 1995. Files of Apache-Sitgreaves National Forest headquarters, Springerville, AZ.

1995r   Decision Notices and Findings of No Significant Impact [on various allotments] of the Alpine Ranger District, December 1995. Files of Apache-Sitgreaves National Forest headquarters, Springerville, AZ.

1996a   Letter to Bill and Barbara Marks, regarding Grazing Allotment Appeal #96–03–00–0139-A215, from John R. Kirkpatrick, Deputy Regional Forester, Southwestern Region, U.S. Forest Service. Files of Apache-Sitgreaves National Forest headquarters, Springerville, AZ.

1996b   Letter to Landi Fernley, Southwest Center for Biological Diversity,
            regarding Grazing Permit Appeals #96–03–00–0143-A215 through #96–
            03–00–151-A215, from John R. Kirkpatrick, Deputy Regional Forester,
            Southwestern Region, U.S. Forest Service. Files of Apache-Sitgreaves
            National Forest headquarters, Springerville, AZ.

1997   Letter to Budd-Falen Law Offices, regarding Grazing Permit Appeal #96–
            03–00–0130-A251, from John R. Kirkpatrick, Deputy Regional Forester,
            Southwestern Region, U.S. Forest Service. Files of Apache-Sitgreaves
            National Forest headquarters, Springerville, AZ.

2000a   Website of Apache-Sitgreaves National Forests, Wilderness and
            Primitive Areas, www.fs.fed.us/r3/asnf/resources/wilderness.htm (site
            discontinued).

2000b   Letter to author from John C. Bedell, Forest Supervisor, Apache-
            Sitgreaves National Forests, March 20, 2000.

2000c   Red Hill Allotment file. Files of Alpine Ranger District, Alpine, AZ.

2005   News Release, Apache-Sitgreaves National Forests, July 25, 2005.

Voigt, William, Jr.

1976   *Public Grazing Lands: Use and Misuse by Industry and Government.*
            New Brunswick, NJ: Rutgers University.

Wagoner, J.J.

1952   *History of the Cattle Industry in Southern Arizona,* 1540–1940. Social
            Science Bulletin No. 20. Tucson: University of Arizona.

Wall, Bill

2000   Interview with author, Summer 2000.

Walley, J. Zane

1998   Caught Twixt Beasts and Bureaucrats. *Range,* Fall 1998:18–21.

1999   Saint Kieran? Getting to know the Southwest Center for Biological
            Diversity. On Internet journal www.eco.freedom.org/el/19990501/
            suckling.html, May 1, 1999 (site discontinued).

Webb, Walter Prescott

1931   *The Great Plains.* Waltham, MA: Blaisdell Publishing Co.

Weisz, Michael G.

1996   "Reply to the Agency Responsive Statements" on behalf of the Appeals
            of thirteen allotment permittees against decisions of the 1995 NEPA
            process," by Michael G. Weisz, Budd-Falen Law Offices, Cheyenne,
            Wyoming. Files of Apache-Sitgreaves National Forest headquarters,
            Springerville, AZ.

White, Courtney

2004   The Far Horizon. *Quivira Coalition Newsletter,* June 2004, Santa Fe,
            NM.

2008   *Revolution on the Range: The Rise of a New Ranch in the American West.* Washington, DC: Island Press.

White, Courtney, and Jim Winder

1999   The Quivira Coalition and the New Ranch. *Range,* Winter 1999:13–15

White, Mitchel

2004   Interview with author, August 14, 2004.

White Mountain Independent, Springerville, AZ.

1995a   "Grazing permits may be cut back, ranchers meet to discuss situation." News article by Tom Schultes, September 26, 1995.

1995b   "'We're going to stick together,' rancher says." News article by Tom Schultes, September 29, 1995.

Wilkinson, Charles F.

1992   *Crossing the Next Meridian: Land, Water, and the Future of the West.* Washington, DC: Island Press.

Wilson, Bill

2000   Interview with author at T-Links ranch. June 18, 2000

Wilson, James A.

1967–68   West Texas Influence on the Early Cattle Industry of Arizona. *Southwestern Historical Quarterly* 71:26–36.

Wolkins, Otis

2002   Interview with author, July 3, 2002

Wood, M. Karl

1988   Watershed and Erosion Control. In *Rangelands,* Bruce A. Buchanan, ed., pp. 25–41. Albuquerque: University of New Mexico Press.

Wolff, Patricia

1999   The Taxpayer's Guide to Subsidized Ranching in the Southwest. Produced for the Center for Biological Diversity and New West Research, http://www.biologicaldiversity.org/swcbd/PROGRAMS/grazing/TAX.PDF.

Wuerthner, George, and Mollie Matteson

2002   *Welfare Ranching: The Subsidized Destruction of the American West.* Washington, DC: Island Press.

Zaslowsky, Dyan, and T.H. Watkins

1994   These American Lands: Parks, Wilderness, and the Public Lands. Washington, DC: Island Press.

About the Author

Jack Stauder grew up in the small town of Fowler in southern Colorado, spending summers on his family's ranch. He went to high school in Las Cruces, New Mexico. As an undergraduate at Harvard College, he became interested in cultural anthropology, which he subsequently studied at Cambridge University in England, earning a PhD. He is author of *The Majangir: Ecology and Society of a Southwest Ethiopian People* (Cambridge University Press, 1971). Research and travel have taken him to more than 115 countries. He has taught for many years at the University of Massachusetts Dartmouth.

Index